THEATRE FESTIVALS OF THE MEDICI

1539–1637

PRIMO INTERMEDIO DELLA VEGLIA DELLA LIBERATIONE DI TIRRENO FATTA NELLA SALA DELLE COM:
DIE DEL SER.^{mo} GRAN DVCA DI TOSCANA IL CARNOVALE DEL 1616. DOVE SI RAP.^o IL MONTE D'ISCHIA CON IL GIGANTE
TIFEO. SOTTO.

The auditorium and stage of Bernardo Buontalenti's Uffizi Theatre. On the stage a décor by Giulio
Parigi for the first intermezzo of *La Liberazione di Tirreno e d'Arnea* (1617). Etching by Jacques
Callot.

THEATRE FESTIVALS OF THE MEDICI

1539–1637

by A. M. NAGLER

New Haven and London

YALE UNIVERSITY PRESS

1964

This book was originally written
in German and was translated by
GEORGE HICKENLOOPER

TO MY WIFE

"Such was the exquisit performance, as (beside the pompe, splendor, or what we may call apparelling of such Presentments) that alone (had all else beene absent) was of power to surprize with delight, and steale away the spectators from themselues. Nor was there wanting whatsoeuer might giue to the furniture, or complement; eyther in riches, or strangenesse of the habites, delicacie of daunces, magnificence of the scene, or diuine rapture of musique. Onely the enuie was, that it lasted not still, or (now it is past) cannot by imagination, much lesse description, be recouered to a part of that spirit it had in the gliding by."

BEN JONSON, *Hymenaei* (1606)

Acknowledgments

Certain sections of this book appeared first, in German, in volumes 4, 6, and 8 of the Austrian quarterly, *Maske und Kothurn;* the chapter on the wedding festivities of 1628 was first published in No. 19 of the *Schriften der Gesellschaft für Theatergeschichte* (Berlin); chapter XII appeared in volume 3 (1961) of *Theatre Research.* The author wishes to express his obligation to the editors of these periodicals.

Permission to publish pictorial material in their possession was generously granted by the Gabinetto Disegni e Stampe of the Uffizi, the Biblioteca Nazionale Centrale in Florence, the Biblioteca Palatina, the Archivio di Stato in Parma, and the Victoria and Albert Museum in London. Dr. Günter Schöne, Director of the Theatre Museum in Munich, Dr. Franz Hadamowsky, Director of the Theatersammlung of the Austrian National Library in Vienna, and Professor Dr. Ulrich Middeldorf, Director of the Kunsthistorisches Institut in Florence assisted me in my search for pictorial documents. The Director of the Herzog August Bibliothek in Wolfenbüttel obliged me by letting me study the von Gadenstedt diary entrances on the 1589 festival.

I gratefully acknowledge the financial assistance granted to me, in the final phase of my research, from the James Morris Whiton Fund of the Yale Graduate School.

New Haven, Connecticut
Easter 1964

A. M. N.

Contents

List of Illustrations

The auditorium and stage of Bernardo Buontalenti's Uffizi Theatre. On the stage a décor by Giulio Parigi for the first intermezzo of *La Liberazione di Tirreno e d'Arnea* (1617). Etching by Jacques Callot. *Frontispiece*

Ignazio Danti's periaktoi set, from his edition of Vignola's *Le due regoli della prospettiva pratica* (1583). 45

8. Giorgio Vasari, original design for the chariot of Uranus (1566). Biblioteca Nazionale, Florence.

9. Copy of Giorgio Vasari's original design for the float of Demogorgone (1566). Gabinetto Disegni e Stampe degli Uffizi, Florence.

10. Giorgio Vasari, sketch for the costume of Hymenaeus (1566). Biblioteca Nazionale, Florence.

11. Giorgio Vasari, sketch for the costume of Aesculapius (1566). Biblioteca Nazionale, Florence.

12. Giorgio Vasari, sketch for the costume of a Muse (1566). Biblioteca Nazionale, Florence.

13. Giorgio Vasari, sketch for the costume of Castor (or Pollux) (1566). Biblioteca Nazionale, Florence.

14. Giorgio Vasari, sketch for the costume of Harmonia, wife of Cadmus (1566). Biblioteca Nazionale, Florence.

15. Giorgio Vasari, sketch for the costume of Circe (1566). Biblioteca Nazionale, Florence.

16. Giorgio Vasari, sketch for the costume of Epaphus (Apis) (1566). Biblioteca Nazionale, Florence.

17. Giorgio Vasari, sketch for the costume for the Hyades (1566). Biblioteca Nazionale, Florence.

18. Giorgio Vasari, sketch for the costume for the Pleiades (1566). Biblioteca Nazionale, Florence.

19. Copy of the costume designed by Giorgio Vasari for Erichthonius (1566). Gabinetto Disegni e Stampe degli Uffizi, Florence.

20. Giorgio Vasari, sketch for the costume of Sarpedon (1566). Biblioteca Nazionale, Florence.

21. Giorgio Vasari, sketch for the costume of the allegorical figure of Memory (1566). Biblioteca Nazionale, Florence.

22. Giorgio Vasari, sketch for the costume of the allegorical figure of Modesty (1566). Biblioteca Nazionale, Florence.

23. Copy of the costume designed by Giorgio Vasari for the allegorical figure of Hunger (1566). Gabinetto Disegni e Stampe degli Uffizi, Florence.

24. Giorgio Vasari, sketch for the costume of the allegory of Justice (1566). Biblioteca Nazionale, Florence.

25. Copy of the costume designed by Giorgio Vasari for the allegorical figure of Thought (1566). Gabinetto Disegni e Stampe degli Uffizi, Florence.

87. The barge of Glaucus with musicians, designed by Giulio Parigi (1608). Engraving by Remigio Cantagallina.

88. Tuscan river gods on the Arno River (1608). Designed by Giulio Parigi.

89. The *Mostra* which opened the tournament *Guerra d'Amore* on the Piazza Santa Croce in Florence (1616). Etching by Jacques Callot.

90. Chariots, horsemen, and supernumeraries who participated in *Guerra d'Amore* (1616). Etchings by Jacques Callot.

91. Giulio Parigi's sketch for the costume of Aurora in *Guerra d'Amore* (1616). Biblioteca Nazionale, Florence.

92. A battle scene from *Guerra d'Amore* (1616). Etching by Jacques Callot.

93. A scene from *Guerra di Bellezza* on the Piazza Santa Croce (1616). Designed by Giulio Parigi, etching by Jacques Callot.

94. Mount Parnassus, a float designed by Giulio Parigi for *Guerra di Bellezza* (1616). Etching by Jacques Callot.

95. Giulio Parigi's sketch for Lady Fame in *Guerra di Bellezza* (1616). Biblioteca Nazionale, Florence.

96. The float of the Sun God, designed by Giulio Parigi for *Guerra di Bellezza* (1616). Etching by Jacques Callot.

97. The chariot of Thetis, designed by Giulio Parigi for *Guerra di Bellezza* (1616). Etching by Jacques Callot.

98. A cloud machine for Amor and the Three Graces, designed by Giulio Parigi for *Guerra di Bellezza* (1616). Etching by Jacques Callot.

99. The Inferno for the *veglia La Liberazione di Tirreno e d'Arnea* (1617). Décor by Giulio Parigi. Etching by Jacques Callot.

100. Courtyard for the Reign of Love designed by Giulio Parigi for the final scene of *La Liberazione di Tirreno e d'Arnea* (1617). Etching by Jacques Callot.

101. Joseph Furttenbach's vague impression of the stage of the Uffizi Theatre. From Furttenbach's *Newes Itinerarium Italiae* (Ulm, 1628).

102. Hell scene from *Regina Sant'Orsola,* designed by Giulio (Alfonso?) Parigi (1624).

103. The Huns attacking Cologne, designed by Giulio (Alfonso?) Parigi for *Regina Sant'Orsola* (1624).

104. St. Michael frightens the devils in *Regina Sant'Orsola* (1624), designed by Alfonso (Giulio?) Parigi.

105. Ireo kneeling before the King of the Huns in *Regina Sant'Orsola* (1624), designed by Giulio (Alfonso?) Parigi.

106. A thunderbolt strikes the pagan temple in *Regina Sant'Orsola* (1624). Designed by Giulio (Alfonso?) Parigi.

Introduction: Princely Toys

When we speak of the Theatre of the Medici we refer to the theatrical entertainments given in Florence between the years 1539 and 1637 by the Grand Dukes of Tuscany, who constituted the younger line of the Medici family. These rulers were: Cosimo I (1519–74), Francesco I (1541–87), Ferdinando I (1549–1609), Cosimo II (1590–1621), and Ferdinando II (1610–70).

Such courtly revels were most frequently associated with weddings. From 1539 to 1637, the following marriages were celebrated: Cosimo I and Eleonora of Toledo (1539); Cosimo's son, Francesco, and Joanna of Austria (1565); Francesco I and the Venetian commoner Bianca Cappello (1579); the Duke of Modena, Cesare d'Este, and Virginia de' Medici (1586); Ferdinando I and Christine of Lorraine (1589); Maria de' Medici and the French King Henri IV (1600); Cosimo II and Maria Magdalena (1608); the Duke of Mantua and Caterina de' Medici (1617); Ferdinando II and Vittoria della Rovere (1637); and the Duke of Parma and Margherita de' Medici (1628), whose nuptials were in part celebrated in Florence, though the major fêtes took place in Parma. Other occasions for Florentine revels were state visits by such dignitaries as the Archdukes Karl (1569) and Leopold (1618), the Duke of Mantua (1618), and the Prince of Poland, Ladislaus Sigismund (1625).

Forgotten today are the names of the court poets who were called upon to find a "hinge" upon which "the whole invention moved," though we still remember Ottavio Rinuccini as the librettist of the earliest operas, *Dafne* and *Euridice*. The composers' names are known only to musicologists: Cristofano Malvezzi, Alessandro Striggio, and Francesco Corteccia, composers of the Florentine madrigals; Giulio Caccini, Jacopo Peri, and Marco da Gagliano, closely connected with the beginnings of opera. Best known among the artists working in the Medici Theatre

1

are the set designers: minor ones such as Bastiano da San Gallo, known as Aristotile (1481–1551), and Baldassare Lanci (1510–71); and the major figures such as Giorgio Vasari (1511–74), Bernardo Buontalenti (1536–1608), Giulio Parigi (c. 1570–1635), and his son Alfonso (d. 1656).

What sort of theatrical entertainment was offered in Florence during this century? In the beginning there were straight plays, with musical interludes, or intermezzi, serving as intermission features. We find this theatrical form being used in 1539, 1565, 1586, and as late as 1589. In 1600 (if we disregard the shadowy stage life of Peri's *Dafne*) the operatic form began to take shape on the Florentine court stage, with Peri's *Euridice* and Caccini's *Il Rapimento di Cefalo*. In 1608 the older form, a play interspersed with intermezzi, made a brief return, but from then on, the pure operatic genre held the stage, with *Regina Sant'Orsola* in 1624, *La Flora* in 1628, and *Le Nozze degli dei* in 1637.

Other types of entertainment were related to the court ballet and the tournament. These had such slender operatic action and so little dramatic force that they could be stopped at any moment for a ballet or a stylized combat, calling for active participation on the part of the courtiers. An example of this pseudodramatic form was the *Veglia*, or vigil, typified by *La Notte d'amore* of 1608 and *La Liberazione di Tirreno e d'Arnea* of 1617. In these the ballet that began on stage overflowed the ramps into the auditorium, where a space on the floor was kept open for the development of a figured ballroom dance.

Yet another form of entertainment was the pageant-joust, within an elaborate framework of chivalric or oriental allegorical fantasy. Such was the *Sbarra* (combat at the Barriers) of 1579 and the equestrian ballet of 1637, as well as the horse ballets on the Piazza Santa Croce, *Guerra d'amore* and *Guerra di bellezza*, both given in 1616. Even the Arno was frequently turned into a theatre, traditionally so every year on July 25th, and the *Argonautica* of 1608 may be considered the greatest naval show ever staged on that river.

The very streets of Florence assumed a theatrical aspect whenever a noble bride made her *ingresso* into the city under triumphal arches, most of them groaning with a heavy load of symbolic significance. During the Carnival season certain streets, preferably the Via Larga and the Via Maggio, became the scenes of traditional races. Other forms of Florentine street revels were the *Bufolate* and *Mascherate*. The greatest and most sumptuous of these was the *Mascherata della geneologia degli dei*, a succession of twenty-one pageant floats on which, in 1566, the pagan divinities displayed some four hundred costumes designed by Giorgio Vasari.

Gardens and courtyards were sometimes pressed into theatrical service, for example, the Boboli Garden in 1637 and the second *cortile* of the old Medici Palace (in the Via Larga) in 1539 for the performance of *Il Commodo;* later, the courtyard of the Palazzo Pitti saw courtly entertainments on at least three occasions: for the Sbarra of 1579, for the mock battles and the naumachia in 1589, and for the production of the opera *Le Nozze degli dei* in 1637.

In the Pitti Palace itself a large hall was dedicated to theatrical performances, a hall variously described as "salone di sopra," "sala grande de' forestieri," "stanze del sig. Don Antonio Medici," or simply "sala delle Commedie." Here Jacopo Peri's *Euridice* was performed in 1600 and *La Notte d'amore* in 1608. Whether the hall (or perhaps halls) in the Pitti Palace was permanently fitted up as a playhouse, we do not know.

Unquestionably temporary was the theatre in the Palazzo Vecchio, placed in the largest hall, the renowned Salone dei Cinquecento, which was converted into a playhouse on three important occasions: once by Vasari in 1565 for the performance of *La Cofanaria,* with attendant intermezzi in celebration of Francesco's first marriage; and twice by Baldassare Lanci, in 1568, when *I Fabii* was performed, and again in 1569 for *La Vedova.* After each production, the stage, at the southern end of the hall, and the "degrees," forming the auditorium, were dismantled.

In 1586 the Medici obtained a permanent theatre, which is occasionally called the Teatro Medici, although, to avoid confusion, it might be referred to as the Uffizi Theatre, for it was set up in the Uffizi building and has been termed the "gran sala sopra gli edifizi de' magistrati." A Callot etching (see Frontispiece) still gives us an idea of the grandeur of the auditorium as it appeared in 1617. Designed by Bernardo Buontalenti, the hall had a capacity of between three and four thousand people. The Grand Duke and his honored guests sat on a dais in the center, the ladies were seated on degrees along the side walls, the men took their places on the raked floor, while persons who preferred to remain incognito watched the spectacle through the windows of the *Galleria,* which housed the Grand Duke's art treasures. This playhouse was inaugurated in 1586 with *L'Amico fido,* and was used again in 1589 for *La Pellegrina,* in 1600 for *Il Rapimento di Cefalo,* in 1608 for *Il Giudizio di Paride,* in 1613 for the great *Barriera,* in 1617 for *La Liberazione di Tirreno,* in 1624 for *Regina Sant'Orsola,* and in 1628 for *La Flora.*

Great sums of money were lavished on these shows, since they were often prompted by the desire to outshine competitive courts and to impress the guests with the riches of the Medici. The other motive for such courtly revels was the element of flattery, which was always in the foreground as each court poet strove to devise elaborate compliments for the ruling house and for the bride and groom. D'Avenant, when summing up the impressions left by his *Britannia Triumphans* upon a Stuart masque audience in 1638, hinted at still another function of these entertainments: "Princes of sweet and humane nature," he wrote, "have ever . . . presented spectacles and personal representations, to recreate their spirits wasted in grave affairs of State and for the entertainment of their nobility, ladies, and courts." These princely "toys," as Francis Bacon called them, were an escape from the pressing realities of political life—a flight into the most fanciful unrealities of the baroque theatre.

1. The Nuptials of Cosimo I

1539

When Cosimo I, barely eighteen years old, was unexpectedly chosen to become Lord of Florence, he hoped, by marrying Alessandro's widow, to acquire the fortune of the older Medici line. But Charles V had other plans for his natural daughter Margaret, and urged Cosimo to seek his bride at the court of the Viceroy of Naples. The imperial wish was fulfilled with the marriage of Cosimo to Eleonora of Toledo in July 1539. The calendar of events[1] provided for a processional entrance of the bride into Florence, a banquet with an allegoric *Trionfo* in the second courtyard of the old Medici palace on the Via Larga, and in the same *cortile* the performance of a comedy with intermezzi.

Eleonora landed on the twenty-second of June, with seven galleys, at Livorno. As she set foot on Tuscan soil, she was greeted by the Archbishop of Pisa by mandate of the Duke. On her journey from there to Pisa, the Duke himself came to meet her halfway with his household. Through Pisa, decked out with triumphal arches, they progressed past lanes of thronging inhabitants, and went on, via Empoli, to Poggio a Caiano for a few days of rest. On the twenty-ninth of June the cortege entered Florence through the Porta al Prato, where Niccolò Tribolo had

1. Primary source: [Pier Francesco Giambullari] Apparato et feste / nelle noze del Illv / strissimo Signor Duca di Firenze, et del / la Duchessa sua consorte, con le sue / Stanze, Madriali, Comedia, / et Intermedij, in / quelle reci / tati. / M.D.XXXIX. Important information is found in *Le Opere di Giorgio Vasari*, ed. Gaetano Milanesi, *6* (Florence, 1881), 55–99 (life of Niccolò detto il Tribolo) and 433–56 (life of Bastiano detto Aristotile da San Gallo).

erected an imposing triumphal arch.[2] The main figure portrayed Fertility, who stood with her five children between Security and Eternity. When the bride reached the arch, a chorus of twenty-four voices sang a madrigal.[3] The procession then moved on to the cathedral. After reception by the Archbishop, it proceeded to the Piazza San Marco, where Tribolo had erected an equestrian statue of Giovanni de' Medici, a portrayal of the fiery Medici mowing down his enemies from his fourteen-*braccia*-high charger.[4] Next, the cavalcade headed for the Palazzo de' Medici in the Via Larga. Here we shall ignore Tribolo's ornamental façade and pass directly into the second cortile, the stage for the allegoric Trionfo and the performance of the comedy *Il Commodo* by Antonio Landi.

Many artists had contributed to the decoration of the courtyard, which was roofed over with an artificial sky of bright blue baize ("Cielo di Cilestri rouesci").[5] Under the sky hung an ornamental armorial frieze painted by Bastiano da San Gallo, called Aristotile.[6] The stage proper was set up on the north side. At the south end stood the table for the bridal couple and guests of honor, against a background of crimson satin with gold fringe. Paintings had been mounted between the side loggias and the stage, with six on each side. On the east wall were the following scenes:[7] the return of Cosimo the Great from exile and Lorenzo's visitation in Naples (both painted by Bacchiacca), the state visit of Leo X in Florence and the taking of Abbiategrasso by Giovanni delle Bande Nere (both by Pier Francesco di Jacopo di Sandro), the coronation of Charles V in Bologna by Clement VII (a mediocre effort by Domenico Conti) and Duke Alessandro in Naples (by Angelo Bronzino), in Vasari's judgment the most beautiful canvas in the series. On the west side facing Cosimo's return an unnamed artist had painted the birth of Cosimo I. The following paintings adjoined it: the conferral of ducal rank on Cosimo (by Carlo Portelli, after a sketch by Francesco Salviati), a scene from Book XX of Livy (artist unknown), the taking of Monte Murlo (by Antonio di Donnino), a portrait of Cosimo I with all the insignia of his rank (by the Venetian Battista Franco), and finally, the ducal nuptials in Naples (by Bronzino), again the most stunning painting in this series.

2. For a detailed description, see Giambullari, pp. 6–15.
3. See Federico Ghisi, *Feste musicali della Firenze Medicea* (Florence, 1939), p. xix.
4. The Florentine ell (*braccio*) is equal to 23 inches.
5. Giambullari, p. 22.
6. Vasari, 6, 443. Bastiano da San Gallo had served the Medici before. His scenic work had pleased Cosimo's predecessor, Duke Alessandro, who had commissioned the artist to design the décor for Lorenzino's *Aridosia* when the comedy was performed in 1536 during the festivities celebrating Alessandro's marriage to Margaret of Austria.
7. Cf. Giambullari, pp. 25–29, and Vasari, 6, 443–45.

Tuscan Revue

In this festively decorated courtyard the performance of the allegoric Trionfo, a kind of Tuscan revue, took place on the sixth of July, following a banquet. Tribolo had designed all of the costumes for it, based on ideas by Giovambattista Strozzi the Elder.[8]

To begin with, Apollo appeared before the tables of the guests, escorted by the Muses.[9] He wore a costume of crimson taffeta and sendal interwoven with gold; his waistband was rainbow-colored and a laurel wreath sat on his golden hair. From his shoulders hung a bow, and at his side was a quiver. He held a viola harp in his left hand, and in his right, the bow.

Thalia came in a costume of bright blue silk with a girdle of olive branches. Thyme blossoms and scattered ornamental bees were fastened to her curly hair. Her headpiece was likewise of yellow silk, antique in cut, and embellished with beryls, crystals, and a garland of verbena; a chameleon formed the upper tip. A string of pearls hung from the Muse's neck, with a scarab for a pendant. Across her breast she wore a panther skin. Her footgear was cut from catskin, each foot ornamented by a crab. In her right hand she held a trumpet, and in her left, an escutcheon: THALIA in gold letters on a bright blue ground.

The other Muses were arrayed as follows:

Euterpe: yellow-green dress girded with a snake, a hyena skin across the breast; marjoram blossoms in her long hair; a winged hat with agates, topazes, a chaplet of pimpernels, and on top a parrot; yellow-green neck pearls; shoes of monkey skin; and several monkey's heads immediately below the knees. The Muse of music carried a dolcian (dolzaina) in her right hand, and in her left, an escutcheon with cornel leaves, a goldfinch, and a nightingale, tokens of the Muse of lyric song.

Erato (more voluptuously dressed than her predecessors and heavily perfumed): a silk dress of undefined color; adornments of sendal fluttering about her body; the white skin of a billy goat over her breasts; the girdle of Venus; myrtle blossoms fastened in her golden hair; an antique headpiece of tawny satin, adorned with gold, emeralds, and roses, and on the tip a red coral branch; footgear of rabbit skin. In her right hand the Muse of love poetry carried a violone, and in her left, an escutcheon with swallows, wagtails, pomegranate blossoms, and roses.

Melpomene: costume of gold fabric and crimson silk, sashed with fresh heliotrope blossoms intertwined with semiprecious stones; diagonally across the breast the skin of a young lion; on the lower edge of her robe a gold border with em-

8. Vasari, 6, 89.
9. See Giambullari, pp. 31–64.

7

broidered musical instruments; jasmine blossoms and a cedar garland in her hair; as a headpiece, five rows of organ pipes which came together in a helmet-like structure; shoes of lynx skin; on each foot a scarab cameo. In her right hand she carried a fife (*piffero*). On her escutcheon the Muse of tragic poetry bore peonies, verbena, and two baboons.

Clio: a dark red satin costume with embellishments of red sendal; a girdle of monkshood blossoms and scammonies; across her breast a leopard skin; dark red hair beneath a kind of morion of red satin; as a headpiece, diamonds and amethysts crowned by a woodpecker; shoes of wolfskin, on each a small wolf's head. Her instrument was the flute, and the armorial emblem of the Muse of history, a prickly butcher's broom.

Terpsichore: in yellow silk with Moorish knots of silver sendal, sashed with grapevine; a deerskin across the shoulders; an antique helmet of yellow silk adorned with sapphires and hyacinths, wound about with oak leaves and crowned by an eagle; shoes of snow-white lambskin. Her instrument was the lute, and the escutcheon emblem of the Muse of the dance, two partridges in a garland of ears of corn.

Polyhymnia: in a gold brocade interwoven with black silk, giving the overall effect of a glowing lead color with jaspers spangled across; diagonally across the breast a fowling bag of hareskin; a pyramid-shaped headpiece of three rows of winged angels' heads, in each row small mirrors, Moorish knots, and tiny gold tassels. In her left hand the Muse of sacred poetry carried a serpent (*storta*), and in her right, the escutcheon, decorated with pine boughs.

Urania: in blue sendal taffeta, spangled with gold stars and constellations; diagonally across the breast, the zodiac; bright blue hair beneath a blue beret; as headpiece, a blindfolded Cupid. The Muse of astronomy held a cornet.

Calliope: in a white linen robe with appliquéd cabalistic signs; over this a cloak of the finest silver sendal; white hair adorned with the symbols of the fixed stars; a white ibex as helmet decoration; legs clothed in white with black ornaments. As an instrument, the Muse of epic poetry carried a small rebec (*ribechino*).

Apollo opened the concert with an invitation to the Muses to celebrate the nuptials of Cosimo. The Muses hearkened, singing a madrigal composed by Francesco Corteccia: "Sacro e Santo Hymeneo."[10] Instead of Hymen, however, appeared Flora, encircled by five nymphs (two of whom represented the streams Elsa and Sieva) and the two rivers Arno and Mugnone. Flora's array[11] consisted of a

10. Giovambattista Gelli provided the text.
11. Giambullari, pp. 41–42.

8

dress of heavy brocade with a band beneath her sash on which various implements of the liberal and manual arts were appliquéd. Her golden cape was adorned with red balls. She had a lion's head on each shoulder, and from each of the lions' maws protruded a silver veil. Her long hair, interwoven with flowers, fell upon her shoulders and was coiffed by a ducal beret set with jewels. The imperial eagle formed the tip, lowering his wings protectingly over the *palle* of the Medici. Appearing to pay homage to Cosimo and Eleonora, the patron goddess stepped before the Duke and sang a *canzone* composed by Constantio Festa. She then drew herself up sideways to permit the appearance of Pisa, who, escorted by three nymphs and a grotesque Triton, now drew attention to herself. The nymphs brought the bridal couple products of their respective regions modeled in colored sugar. After Pisa's canzonet (music by Matteo Rampollini) followed the appearance of Volterra with five nymphs, whose costumes and kettle-shaped headpieces pointed to the Tuscan mining industry. Volterra expressed her joy in a song composed by Giampiero Masacone. Then followed Arezzo, Cortona, Pistoia, the Tiber, and even Lady Rome. Apollo had the last word with a bit of flattery for Cosimo and Eleonora. Finally the participants withdrew, and the guests retired to dance in the first courtyard.

The Intermezzi

Three days later, on the ninth of July, came the performance of Antonio Landi's comedy *Il Commodo,* with interludes by Giovambattista Strozzi the Elder, who also took charge of production.[12] After a banquet in the first cortile, the guests removed to the second, where, as previously mentioned, the stage had been set up at the north end. The cortile was illuminated by torches held by *amoretti* suspended from the blue baize sky.[13] A curtain seems not to have been used, since the spectators, immediately upon entering, uttered their amazement at the stage picture (*prospettiva*). Vasari informs us[14] that Tribolo had furnished the instructions which Aristotile followed in creating the setting. The stage picture gave a view of Pisa with bizarre and capricious palace façades, which combined with the appropriate street vistas to form that unity guaranteed by the rules of perspective scenepainting.[15] The slanting campanile and the cupola of the baptistry towered above

12. Vasari, *6,* 442.
13. Giambullari, pp. 64–65.
14. Vasari, *6,* 88–89.
15. Ibid., p. 441: "non e possible mettere insieme mai nè la più variata sorte di finestre e porte, nè facciate di palazzi più bizarre e capricciose, nè strade o lontani che meglio sfuggano e facciano tutto quello che l'ordine vuole della prospettiva."

9

the other buildings. A painted staircase appeared to connect the stage with the courtyard.

The performance began with a sunrise. Here Vasari gives us[16] a few trade secrets. Aristotile had constructed a wooden lantern, which was mounted on an arc behind the houses. A crystal sphere twenty-three inches in diameter was filled with distilled water and placed in front of the lantern, in which two torches were burning. An aureole surrounded the source of light. By means of a winch (*arganetto*), the sun was slowly drawn upward on the arc until it reached the zenith; then it gradually glided down on the other side of the arc until, at the end of the comedy, it sank away. The position of the sun was coordinated with the fictional time (*finto giorno*) of the play.

The prologue was sung by Aurora, who appeared in the eastern part of the heavens in a transparent and luminous costume of red flowered silk with gold and silver stripes. Her wings shimmered in all colors of the rainbow. Instead of shoes she wore roses. She ran an ivory comb through her long golden hair while singing her canzone.[17] Slowly the sun rose behind her shoulders, and the first act of Landi's comedy began.

A pastoral scene was inserted between the first and second acts. Six pairs of shepherds stepped onto the stage and sang a canzonet, a kind of hymn to the sun. Closeness to nature was stressed in their rustic costumes: two shepherds wore costumes of bark, another pair appeared in red goatskins, and a third wore a bird's costume—that is, real birds sewn onto a white ground, their wings having been painted in various colors. Finally, two shepherds appeared in straw. Every alternate shepherd carried a musical instrument, also fitted out in rustic disguise: a cornet was concealed behind a pair of deer's antlers, and serpents (*storte*) were hidden behind chestnut boughs or reeds; a small serpent had been turned in very skillful fashion into a Pan's flute with seven pipes.

A spacious canal had been laid out in front of the stage, painted inside and out to resemble the Arno ("uno assai spatioso canale, dipinto dentro et dintorno in tal modo che pareua l'Arno"). In the second intermezzo three naked sirens emerged from this canal, each with two silver-scaled tails. Shells and red, white, and black corals formed the headpieces. Also in the company of the sirens were three nymphs enveloped in transparent green veils. They accompanied the sirens' song on lutes

16. Ibid., p. 442.

17. The text was by Strozzi. Francesco Corteccia composed all the intermezzi. Aurora was accompanied by the following instruments: "graue cembolo a duoi registri, sottoui Organo, Flauto, Arpe, et uoci di uccegli, et con un Violone" (Giambullari, p. 65).

concealed in shells. Three other musicians joined them, sea monsters covered with algae and women's hair, and sporting beards of moss. Each one played on a transverse flute (*trauersa*), which was camouflaged: one resembled a fish backbone, another a coiled sea shell, and the third a reed.

At the end of the third act of the comedy the sun stood at its zenith. In order to bring the idea of the noon hour into play in the ensuing intermezzo as well, Strozzi introduced a scene from Virgil's sixth *Eclogue*. Mnasyllus and Chromis, escorting the naiad Aegle, come and rouse Silenus, who is sleeping out a fit of drunken stupor in a grotto. They ask him to sing, and he complies with their desire by singing a canzonet about the Golden Age. Silenus himself provides the musical accompaniment on a violone disguised as a sea turtle, stroking it with a serpent-bow "(con uno Archetto à modo d'uno Aspido secco")".

Aurora appeared over Pisa, and the nymphs and sirens shuffled in the ditch in front of the stage. For the scene with Silenus, sylvan décor should have been used, but as this is not mentioned in our source, we may assume that a grotto set piece, a kind of bower containing the sleeping Silenus, was simply rolled into the Pisa décor, so that this intermezzo was still played within and before a medieval mansion-type set piece.

Meanwhile, in the play, evening had arrived, and was suggested—even in the intermezzo—by the appearance of eight nymphs returning from the chase. Evidently they simply stepped into the city of Pisa, since Giambullari mentions "passarono su per la Scena."[18] The nymphs—blondes, with red or green berries and garlands of flowers in their hair—were dressed in silver sendal, and carried bows and quivers. After their canzonet, the last act of the comedy began, followed by an afterpiece.

Night then appeared with black silk veils floating about her. Her long, dark chestnut-color hair was coiffed with a sky-blue headpiece spangled with stars. She wore black velvet stockings and the wings of an owl. To the accompaniment of four trombones, she sang her lay. That the listeners might be lulled to sleep by this sweet song was a danger, hence the sudden appearance of ten bacchantes and ten satyrs. Apart from their hairy breech-clouts, the goat-footed fellows were naked. The female bacchantes wore short robes of extremely thin sendal. Four couples wielding burning torches performed a Dionysian dance and sang: "Bacco! Bacco! Evoe!" Four other couples provided musical accompaniment on instruments adapted to their natures: the drum was disguised as a wineskin; a shawm (*zufolo*)

18. P. 143.

was concealed in a human thighbone; a small rebec was hidden behind a deer's head; a goat horn served as a cornet, and a crane-bone as a serpent; a *tromba torta* resembled a grapevine; and a barrel hoop with rushes became a harp.

The gentle weariness, *la dolce fatica,* of the spectators was banished with sweets and wine. The Duke then dismissed his guests.

Vasari reports[19] that Cosimo was extremely satisfied with the achievements of Aristotile and that the artist was obliged from then on each year to prepare the stage decoration for the carnival comedies. He had entertained the idea of composing a treatise on scene-painting, but found the task too difficult and shelved it. It seems that new men took over the responsibility of arranging the ducal festivities, men who felt that they could dispense with Aristotile's services. Angelo Bronzino and Francesco Salviati may have been engaged as set designers, with Aristotile himself reduced to inactivity.

19. *6,* 445.

2. Giorgio Vasari and his Assistants

1565–66

The wedding of Francesco de' Medici to Joanna of Austria, the seventeen-year-old sister of Emperor Maximilian II, took place during the Christmas season of 1565. This union of the hereditary prince of Florence and Siena and a member of the House of Hapsburg was a political event of far-reaching consequences for the Tuscan state. To impress the "Signori Alemanni," whose attendance at the ceremonies was anticipated, Duke Cosimo arranged for a series of sumptuous festivities,[1] charging Giovanni Caccini with the responsibility of "Proveditore generale." Don Vincenzio Borghini, prior of the hospital of the Innocenti,[2] provided ideas for

1. Primary sources: Domenico Mellini, Descrizione dell' / Entrata / Della sereniss. Reina Giouanna d'Austria / Et dell' Apparato, fatto in Firenze nelle ve- / nuta, & per le felicissime nozze di / S. Altezza / Et dell' Illustrissimo, & Eccellentiss. S. Don / Francesco de Medici, / Prencipe di Fiorenza, & / di Siena. / Scritta da Domenico Mellini / Ristampata & Riueduta dal proprio Autore. / In Fiorenza appresso i Giunti MDLXVI.

[Domenico Mellini], Descrizione / Dell' Apparato / Della Comedia / Et Intermedii / D'essa / Recitata in Firenze il giorno di S. Stefano l'anno 1565, / nella gran Sala del palazzo di sua Ecc. Illust. / Nelle reali nozze. / Dell' Illustriss. & Eccel. S. il S. Don Francesco Medici Principe di / Fiorenza, & di Siena, & della Regina Giouanna / d'Austria sua consorte. / Ristampata, con nuoua aggiunta. / In Fiorenza appresso i Giunti MDLXVI.

[Giovanni Battista Cini], Descrizione dell'apparato fatto in Firenze per le nozze dell'illustrissimo ed eccellentissimo Don Francesco de' Medici principe di Firenze e di Siena e della serenissima regina Giovanna d'Austria, reprinted in Vasari, *8,* 517–617. References to this account read Cini-Vasari, *8.*

2. On Caccini and Borghini, cf. Hermann Walther Frey, *Neue Briefe von Giorgio Vasari* (Burg b.M., 1940).

13

planning the pageants ("inuentione delle storie"). Execution of the artistic tasks lay in the hands of Giorgio Vasari and his staff of assistants.[3]

CALENDAR OF EVENTS

December 16: Formal entrance of the bride into Florence.[4] The cortege proceeded from the Porta al Prato, through a city decked out with triumphal arches, to the Palazzo Vecchio, where Francesco and Joanna were to live. (Cosimo I had already moved to the Pitti Palace in 1553; Vasari's *passaggio* provided the connection between the two palaces.)

December 18: Solemn nuptial ceremonies in the cathedral.

December 25: Performance of the comedy *La Cofanaria* by Francesco d'Ambra in the Salone dei Cinquecento of the Palazzo Vecchio. The actors were members of the Confraternità di S. Bernardino e S. Caterina.[5] Giovanni Battista Cini composed the interludes, for which Apuleius' fable of Cupid and Psyche furnished the subject matter. Giorgio Vasari and Bernardo Timante were in charge of the scenic décor.

February 2: Allegoric cavalcade, the *Trionfo de' Sogni.*[6]

February 17: Siege of a fortress erected in the Piazza Santa Maria Novella which was defended by three hundred knights and assaulted by eight hundred others.[7]

February 21: On the last Thursday of the carnival the procession of the *Geneologia degli dei,* with twenty-one floats and three hundred and ninety-two mythological or allegorical figures.[8]

February 26: Ten *Mascherate delle Bufole.*[9]

3. Cf. also Piero Ginori Conti, *L'Apparato per le nozze di Francesco de' Medici e di Giovanna d'Austria nelle narrazioni del tempo e da lettere inedite di Vincenzio Borghini e di Giorgio Vasari* (Florence, 1936).

4. Cf. Agostino Lapini, *Diario fiorentino,* ed. G. O. Corazzini (Florence, 1900), pp. 148–50.

5. Cf. Ubaldo Angeli, *Notizie per la storia del teatro a Firenze nel secolo XVI specialmente circa gli intermezzi* (Modena, 1891), p. 16.

6. [Anon.], Descrizione / del canto de / Sogni. / Mandato dall' Illustrissimo, & Eccellentissimo / S. Principe di Fiorenza, & di / Siena. / Il secondo giorno di Febbraio. 1565 / in Fiorenza. / In Fiorenza appresso i Giunti. MDLXVI. Cf. also Cini-Vasari, *8,* 580–86.

7. Cini-Vasari, *8,* 586–87; Lapini, p. 151.

8. [Baccio Baldini], Discorso sopra / La Mascherata / della Geneologia / degl'Iddei de' / Gentili. / Mandata fuori dall' Illustrissimo, & Ec- / cellentiss. S. Duca di Firenze, / & Siena / Il giorno 21. di Febbraio / MDLXV. / In Firenze Appresso i Giunti / MDLXV. Cf. also, Cini-Vasari, *8,* 587–614.

9. [Anon.], Le dieci / Mascherate / delle Bvfole / Mandate / in Firenze il giorno di Carnouvale / L'anno 1565. / Con la descrittione di tutta la pompa delle / Maschere, e loro inuentioni. / Con Licentia, e Privilegio. / In Fiorenza appresso i Giunti. / MDLXVI. Cf. also Cini-Vasari, *8,* 614–16.

March 10: A musical-theatrical representation of the Annunciation scene in the church of Santo Spirito.[10]

Spectacle in the Hall of the Five Hundred

The *Descrizione* of Domenico Mellini gives us details of the furnishings of the auditorium, the "Sala vecchia del Consiglio" in the Palazzo Vecchio.[11] Seating accommodations for approximately three hundred and sixty ladies were built along the length of the hall, "a vso di Teatro antico."[12] Ramps led up to a railed terrace situated four *braccia* above floor level. Six rows of *gradi* ascended from this terrace, all of them laid with carpets. In the middle of the hall stood a dais or *rialto;* three steps round about led up to it. Guests from Austria, who comprised the Duchess' retinue, envoys, and persons of princely rank took their places on gilded chairs. Those courtiers who were not guests of honor had to content themselves with benches on the floor of the auditorium ("per tutto il vano della sala"). Twelve light sources in the shape of crowns hung from the ceiling,[13] which Vasari had freshly painted, after raising it by some twelve braccia. Three of these chandeliers resembled papal crowns, in allusion to the three Medici popes, Leo X, Clement VII, and Pius IV. They were suspended at the north end of the auditorium—that is, over the so-called *Udienza*. Three imperial chandeliers hung close to the stage—one for Charles V, another for Ferdinand I, father of the bride, and the third for Maximilian II, Joanna's Emperor-brother. A royal crown glowed for Catherine de' Medici, and next to it hung a "royal-bridal" crown ("vna corona reale, e nuziale") for the newlyweds. Both were suspended in the middle of the hall and flanked by four ducal coronets. The chandeliers were of cut glass and crystal, and were decorated with precious stones; the lights inside were intensified by distilled water with the refracting function of a lens. Additional sources of illumination were provided by ten silvered female figures supporting crystal bowls. These statues were mounted at various points throughout the auditorium between paintings which showed *vedute* of cities in the duchy. Each bowl was filled with colored water and lighted from behind.

Set up at the south end of the hall opposite the Udienza was the stage. It was raised four braccia above the floor, hence at the same height as the terrace from which the female spectators reached their gradi. The trap room was screened off

10. Cini-Vasari, *8*, 616–17.

11. Mellini gives the following dimensions for the great hall: a length of 100 braccia, a width of 40, and an elevation of 36.

12. *Apparato,* p. 4.

13. Ibid., p. 7.

by a parapet thirty-eight braccia in width. In the middle of this screen was painted a staircase, which appeared to be three-dimensional ("che parea di rilieuo"). Mellini characterized its manneristic jumble of styles as "inuentione bizzara & cappricciosa."[14] To the right and left were painted straight staircases in profile. On each side of the stage rose a Corinthian column to a height of thirteen braccia, closing off the sides of the stage and connected by an architrave with frieze and cornice forty braccia long and three and a half braccia high, which ran above the stage opening. The ducal escutcheon was supported in the middle by putti.

The stage was closed off by a house curtain which, according to Mellini,[15] was twenty-three braccia broad and fifteen braccia high. (Cini gives the dimensions as twenty-two by sixteen.)[16] On it was a hunting scene painted by Federigo Zuccari: a large number of hunters on horseback and on foot with their hounds and falcons in a landscape to delight the eye (Figure 1). After the manner of the ancients, the curtain dropped as soon as the guests of honor had taken their places on the rialto.[17]

A Florentine street scene[18] furnished the setting for D'Ambra's comedy: the Santa Trinità quarter with the Arno bridge as it was before 1557, when it was destroyed by a flood. The wondering eye was led in this perspective along the Via Maggio as far as the Church of San Felice.[19] In the foreground stood the houses which bordered the right bank of the Arno.[20] The scene painters had added a triumphal arch symbolically depicting the Arno and Danube Rivers, an allusion to the occasion to be celebrated. Eight suspended putti[21] carried torches, which augmented the stage lighting.

Mellini called Giorgio Vasari the "autore di tutti questi ornamenti." Settimani does not mention Vasari in his *Diario,* but writes instead: "The scenes were painted by Bernardo Timante, the capricious artist, best liked by the bridegroom, Duke

14. Ibid., p. 5.

15. Ibid., p. 6.

16. Cini-Vasari, *8,* 621.

17. "Fu subitamente fatta cadere la tenda" (Mellini, *Apparato,* p. 10); "al cascar della prescritta tela" (Cini-Vasari, *8,* 572).

18. For a description of the setting, see Mellini, *Apparato,* p. 9, and Cini-Vasari, *8,* 572.

19. "Nella qual prospettiua sfondando molto ingegnosamente con la parte più lontana per la dirittura del ponte, e terminando nel fine della strada che Via Maggio si chiama" (Cini-Vasari, *8,* 572).

20. "Et i casamenti della prospettiua, che erano innanzi, con variati modi per dar più bellezza, e con grandissima diligenza lauorati, che faceua con i lumi scoperta insieme con tutto l'ornamento vna vista molto magnifica & gratiosa" (Mellini, *Apparato,* p. 9).

21. "Angeli . . . a vso di Amori" (ibid.).

Francesco de' Medici."[22] Nor does Vasari's name appear in Grazzini's description of the intermezzi; Il Lasca speaks only of the "Pittor capriccioso"—Bernardo Timante, called Delle Girandole—as the artist responsible under Cini's direction for "the opening of the heavens and the traps in the stage floor."[23] Mellini, who gives us a long list of Vasari's assistants, does not mention Timante in relation to the scene design, but maintains that Prospero Fontana was in charge of carrying out Vasari's designs into paintings: "The work on stage and the perspective scene, designed and invented by Messer Giorgio, was carried out to perfection by Prospero Fontana of Bologna, a painter of fine judgment and a master of his craft."[24]

Closer scrutiny of these assertions yields no contradiction. We need only make an advance distinction between the *prospettiva* for the comedy and the surprise effects of the intermezzi. Vasari designed the setting for *La Cofanaria,* which Fontana then painted. No actual settings were needed for the intermezzi. The scenic requirements for the interludes that featured Cupid and Psyche consisted, as we shall see, of cloud machines and trap effects. Bernardo Timante was responsible for these "tirari del cielo, e l'uscite di sotto 'l palco." When Settimani speaks of the "pitture" which were the work of the capricious Timante, he refers in this connection to the intermezzi; but he may be pardoned for erroneously speaking of paintings instead of machines, for the machines which came out of the sky or the earth were indeed painted.

Mellini comments that Vasari created a sky vault above the prospect of Florence ("vn cielo a vso di mezza Botte"),[25] hence something that would have corresponded to our present-day cyclorama. He also states that within it Vasari mounted wooden shutters that were canvas-covered and painted with clouds on a blue background to match the hemispherical sky—a sky which, in Mellini's phrase, "giraua in tondo."[26] One must not mistake this phrase, as did Hans Tintelnot,[27] for an indication that *periaktoi* were being used; rather, one should translate "giraua in tondo" as "described an arc" or "followed the curvature," since the scenery was palpably laid out in a semicircle, "secondo che faceva tutta la Scena." Mellini ex-

22. Settimani, *Diario, 3,* 356, cited in Alessandro d'Ancona, *Origini del teatro italiano, 2* (Turin, 1891), 167, n. 4.

23. Antonio Francesco Grazzini, called Il Lasca, "Descrizione de gl'intermedj rappresentati colle commedia nelle nozze dell' Illustriss. et Eccelentiss. Sig. Principe di Firenze, e di Siena," printed in *Del Teatro comico fiorentino, 5* (Florence, 1750), App., p. 18.

24. Mellini, cited in Vasari, *Opere, 8,* 621.

25. *Apparato,* p. 9. Grazzini, p. 3, and Cini-Vasari, 8, 572, speak of a "concavo cielo."

26. *Apparato,* p. 9.

27. *Barocktheater und barocke Kunst* (Berlin, 1939), p. 24.

pressly designates this as an "inuention nuova," by means of which the setting obtained greater depth of perspective and the buildings themselves greater elevation. In other words, this ingenious arrangement "faceua sfuggire molto la prospettiua, & daua gran ricrescimento agli edificij di quella Scena."[28]

This setting created by Vasari and painted by Prospero Fontana did not change in the course of the performance. The five acts of the comedy, as well as Cini's intermezzi, were played against the Florentine background, although Timante managed to distract the spectators from time to time by causing the sky to open and scenic elements to rise from the traps.

The first intermezzo served as a prelude to the first act of D'Ambra's comedy. The concave sky opened over Florence. The shutters ("cortine di legname") were manifestly withdrawn, revealing a heaven beyond the sky ("un altro molto artifizioso cielo"),[29] from which Venus emerged in a gilded and bejeweled car drawn by two snow-white swans. Her following consisted of the three Graces and the four Seasons. Except for garlands of roses and myrtle blossoms, she was naked. The Graces appeared altogether nude, with loose and flowing hair. Winter wore a blue gown flecked with snowflakes. Spring had an iridescent dress covered with blossoms. Summer wore a yellow costume adorned with ears of corn. Autumn was dressed in red and laden with fruit. The goddess and her retinue sang a *canzone* in the manner of a *ballata*.[30] Slowly the cloud lowered, revealing a vision of divinities (probably painted) who stayed behind on Olympus. At the same time, sweet scents spread through the auditorium.[31]

Meanwhile, a winged and naked Cupid appeared, accompanied by the four passions that caused the greatest discord in his kingdom: Hope, in a green dress with a spray of blossoms on her head; Fear, recognizable by her pale gown and the hare motif that embellished head and legs; Joy, in a white and orange costume; Pain, garbed in black. These companions bore Cupid's weapons—the bow, the arrows, the burning torch, and the nets. The god of love and his companions came on foot ("per terra di camminar sembrando"). At length the cloud car touched down upon the stage, and the Graces and Seasons climbed out to form a group around Venus, who remained in her car and voiced her indignation in a song: men slighted her and revered only beautiful Psyche. She gave the god of love her man-

28. Mellini, *Apparato,* p. 9.

29. Cini-Vasari, *8,* 572.

30. Musicians behind the stage accompanied the song for eight voices composed by Alessandro Striggio with the following instruments: 2 *gravicembali,* 4 *violoni,* 1 *liuto mezzano,* 1 *cornetto muto,* 1 *trombone,* and 2 *flauti diritti.* Cf. Grazzini, p. 16.

31. Cini-Vasari, *8,* 573.

date to aim his shafts at Psyche, and the impudent Cupid forthwith shot a number of his arrows into the auditorium. Then the cloud returned to the sky, and the shutter closed the hole in the vault, without leaving a trace of where the aperture had been.[32]

The second intermezzo bridged the pause between the first and second acts of *La Cofanaria*, and was essentially a musical interlude, an allusion to the invisible voices with which Cupid sought to entertain his Psyche. A group of musicians filed onto the stage. They evidently came from the Florentine houses on the sides, since Cini comments that a little Cupid appeared "da una delle quattro strade, che per uso de' recitanti s'erano nella scena lasciate."[33] The *amoretto* held a swan in his arm, in which a violone was concealed, and this he played with a reed. Then the following persons emerged simultaneously from four streets ("per le quattro pre-scritte strade della scena"): enamored, winged Zephyrus in a blue dress covered with blossoms; Music, in a costume embroidered with various instruments and notes, playing on a large violone and escorted by a number of amoretti who were likewise playing instruments; and lastly Playfulness and Laughter. Together they sang a song in praise of Psyche. Instrumentalists concealed behind the stage accompanied the madrigal which Striggio had composed.

Cini chose the following situation for his third intermezzo. Cupid is so taken up with love for Psyche that he has no time to inflame the hearts of mortals, thus causing many frauds (*fraudi*) and deceptions (*inganni*). The stage floor, or *pavimento*, seemed about to burst open, and seven small hills ("*piccoli monticelli*")[34] arose from the traps, from which seven and again seven Inganni crept forth, wearing leopard skins. Their legs and thighs were covered with snake skin; they wore fox heads as headpieces, and held traps, rods, hooks, and prongs, beneath which were concealed the serpents (*storte*) on which they played. After a madrigal composed by Francesco Corteccia, they made their exits through the "quattro pre-scritte strade della scena."

Psyche had discovered Cupid's identity by the glow of an oil lamp: a drop of the hot oil dispatched the love god to the sickbed. As he now no longer minded his affairs, love died out in the human race, and the catastrophic consequences became the subject of the fourth intermezzo. Instead of the seven small hills, there now arose seven small gorges ("*piccole voragini*"),[35] probably open traps, from which

---

32. The sky "in un momento chiusosi, senza rimaner pur vestigio, onde sospicar si potesse da che parte la nugola e tante altre cose uscite ed entrate si fussero" (ibid., p. 574).
33. Ibid.
34. Ibid., p. 575.
35. Ibid., p. 576.

dark smoke billowed forth. Personifications of the evil passions then rose out of these chasms: first, Discord in shredded garments; Ire, with claws and a bear's head, joined her; next appeared Cruelty, with a tiger's head and crocodile feet, holding a torch; then came Rapine, scythe in hand, with a head covering in the form of a bird of prey, her feet those of an eagle; nor could Revenge forbear being present, appearing with a viper on her head and a short bloodstained saber in her hand. Next, two anthropophagi (the Laestrygones of Homer's *Odyssey*) made their appearance playing trombones. Each of them was escorted by two Furies carrying whips and other instruments of torture, another camouflage for musical instruments. The Furies' bodies were covered with wounds from which hot flames seemed to spit; they were girded with snakes, and their arms and legs were in chains. The figures on stage danced a galliard and sang a madrigal composed by Corteccia, with a brazen, warlike melody. Finally, they performed an extravagant morris dance and then ran off in wild confusion.

In the fifth intermezzo Psyche despairs because Cupid has forsaken her. She falls into the hands of the implacable Venus, who sends her down to Tartarus for the purpose of bringing back some of Proserpina's beauty in a box. Psyche appeared in utter desolation, "per l'una delle strade,"[36] accompanied by four figures of allegory: Jealousy, with four heads, in a dark blue dress embroidered with eyes and ears; Envy, with the snakes which she devours; Worry, with a vulture feeding on her intestines; Scorn, ill-clothed and with an owl perched on her head. The four figures then fell upon Psyche with blows. When they reached the middle of the stage, the floor opened at four places, from which fire and smoke poured out. Four horrible serpents emerged from these traps, in which four violinists were concealed; supported by trombones behind the stage, they played in accompaniment to Psyche's madrigal, composed by Striggio.[37] The sweet sadness of this music was such that few eyes remained dry. Then a much larger trap opened ("nuova e molto grande apertura nel pavimento") and three-headed Cerberus emerged against a background of smoke and flame. Psyche threw him one of the two sops she had taken along for safety on the trip to the underworld, having been warned by the speaking tower. Finally, hoary Charon appeared in some dark abyss ("in vna oscura voragine"), and Psyche climbed into his bark with her four tormentors.

The fifth act of *La Cofanaria* was followed by the sixth intermezzo, the final chapter in the story of Cupid and Psyche. Again there was not a complete change of scene. Instead, from a trap there arose a mountain covered with laurel trees and

36. Ibid., p. 577.
37. Ibid., p. 578.

flowering shrubs, and on its summit, winged Pegasus.[38] A group of amoretti, Zephyrus, Dame Music, and the reunited Cupid and Psyche descended in succession from Mount Helicon. Psyche had returned from the underworld unimpaired; Jupiter had interceded with Venus, whose rancor forthwith turned to grace. Even Pan appeared at the wedding, accompanied by nine satyrs who played on various instruments. At length Hymen came, and an epithalamium began, resulting in an effortless transition from Cupid and Psyche to Francesco and Joanna.

At the conclusion of the spectacle the guests withdrew to other chambers, while the great auditorium was transformed into a banquet hall. After the sumptuous *convito,* the guests again retired from the Salone dei Cinquecento, which the attendants now transformed with utmost haste into a ballroom, and there the couples gave themselves up to the pleasures of dancing until daybreak.[39]

Calvalcade of Dreams

On February 2, 1556, just after nightfall, a singular procession moved along the animated thoroughfares of Florence: the *Trionfo de' Sogni.*[40] Judging from an allusion of Cini, the hereditary prince may have got the idea for this parade at the imperial court on his visit to his bride and her brother, the Emperor Maximilian II.[41] It was a typically baroque conceit, in that it held the pursuit of fame, glory, beauty, and riches to be a vain groping after chimeras, which, when exposed, reveal the evanescence of all worldly enticements. Behind Love, Ambition, Beauty, Plutus, and Bellona, followed Madness, or Pazzia, with her retinue. Whoever yields to such phantoms ends a prisoner of folly. Yet this did not prevent the Medici from paying homage to Plutus, and Siena had still not recovered from injuries inflicted by a triumph of Bellona; Cosimo I showed no inclination to banish Camilla Martelli from his mind, and Francesco remained infatuated with Bianca Cappello. For the Medici, all captives of Pazzia, the *Trionfo de' Sogni* remained a pastime, another masquerade.

The cavalcade of dreams was opened by two sirens blowing trumpets; they were said to have the gift of appeasing storms at sea with their sweet song.[42] Following them were two figures, whose variegated garb (red and yellow, black and white) supposedly symbolized the four humors. Then came the standard bearers: on the

38. Ibid.: "si vide del pavimento della scena in un tratto uscire un verdeggiante monticello, tutto d'allori e di diversi fiori adorno."

39. For the convito, cf. Mellini, Apparato, pp. 24–26.

40. Our principal source, in addition to Cini, is the anonymous 1565 *Descrizione* mentioned in note 6.

41. Cini-Vasari, *8,* 581.

42. 1565 *Descrizione,* p. 5.

banner a griffin, half eagle, half lion, with the explanatory device: "I am neither eagle nor lion, but I share in both, just as sleep has its divine and its human aspects."[43]

Cupid, a naked child holding a torch, led the first swarm of *maschere,* a group of lovers. The allegoric figures Hope and Fear were also in his train, Fear wearing a grey costume and coiffed with a deer's head, Hope robed in green, his headpiece a chameleon. The retinue of the god of love wore gold costumes, richly embroidered with pearls. Riding on horses with gorgeous caparisons were the lovers, bound to each other by light golden chains.

Narcissus, wearing a dark blue costume embroidered with flowers, boots of green satin adorned with gold branches, and on his head a narcissus blossom, led the inebriates of Beauty, flanked by Youth and Proportion. The followers of Narcissus, like those of Fame, Riches, and the goddess of war, wore bat wings which characterized them as the abortive children of dreams, thereby underscoring the theme of the Trionfo—life is a dream.[44]

A third group consisted of Fame and her entourage. The goddess herself wore a robe of shimmering gold fabric with a bluish cast, and on her head a globe. Her wings were made of peacock feathers, and she held a golden trumpet with three bells. Two symbolic figures walked at her side, Glory and Prize of War. Fame's minions were ranked in three groups: emperors, kings, and dukes, all enveloped in the same gold fabric, but distinguished from one another by their crowns. They too sat astride their horses, with bat wings on their shoulders.

Plutus, god of riches, rode at the head of the next unit. Characterized as a blind man by his face mask, he held gilded and silvered branches, and his costume was exceptionally opulent. Greed and Rapacity were members of his retinue. Avarizia, in yellow, carried a wolf on her head, and Rapacità, in red, a falcon. The gold costumes of the rich were strewn with precious stones.

Bellona guided the brave, wearing a costume on which silver branches were appliquéd, and a helmet of silver fabric crowned with a laurel wreath. Her instrument was a trumpet of war, whose invention Pindar ascribed to Pallas Athena. Terror and Courage were the peripheral figures: Spavento in grey with a cuckoo as *impresa;* Ardire in red with the head of a lion. The bay horses had red harnesses and saddles.

The last group consisted of fools, led by Pazzia, whose costume was bright and

43. Ibid., p. 6.

44. "Avevano questi, e tutti gli altri dell'altre squadre, per dimostrazione che per Sogni figurati fussero, ciascuno (quasi che mantelletto gli facesse) un grande et alato e molto ben condotto pipistrello di tela d'argento in bigio su le spalle accomodato" (Cini-Vasari, *8,* 583).

variegated. So that everyone could see that clear thinking was patently not her forte, her hair was badly rumpled. She was attended by a satyr and a bacchante, both adorned with grapes. Folly and her cohorts did not wear bat wings, since they were not portraying insubstantial dream phantoms but reality, in contrast to the fancied values which are "nothing but dreams and disguises" ("sogni veramente e larve").[45]

Marching between the individual units were forty-eight witches, the first group of whom were joined by Mercury and Diana, wearing three heads—symbolic of Hecate. Priestesses were also marshaled into the procession at regular distances.

The finale consisted of the pageant of the god of sleep, who is responsible for all dreams. His car was drawn by six somnolent (according to Plinius) bears garlanded in poppies and guided by Silence, a haggard, bearded ancient, robed in grey, who symbolically laid his finger to his lips. Silenzio was attended by three women portraying repose, whose face masks made them seem fleshy and well-fed. Six nymphs strode alongside the Trionfo.

The pageant car was built in the shape of a hexagon. A giant elephant's head formed a cave in which the god of sleep, Somnus, was reclining, as Ovid had envisaged him, "cubitoque levatus"—that is, propped on his elbow.[46] His face white and chubby, thanks to a mask, he was garlanded with poppies and naked except for a grey loincloth. Four figures were at his side: Morpheus, ever capable of transformation, with four faces and a many-colored costume; his female counterpart; Icelus, an adept at changing into animals, as indicated by his mask, a mixture of horse, bull, lion, and tiger, and his costume, a patchwork of their skins and hides; and Phantasus, who, according to Ovid, could slip into inanimate objects, and thus wore a costume which resembled a field of flowers in front, a mountain behind, and fire and water on either side. Somnus had still other offspring, nameless sons in various disguises dispersed throughout the float.

At the highest point of the cave of sleep stood Alba, or Dawn, with blond hair and a silver costume, while under the mouth of the cave reclined the naked figure of Night, with a sleepy badger. The pageant car was decorated on all sides with graphic portrayals, all related to the common theme "Sleep and Dream." Bacchus was shown as the father of sleep riding on his car drawn by two tigers, accompanied by Ceres, the mother of Somnus, and Pasithea, his spouse. In one picture, Hermes lulled hundred-eyed Argus to sleep, whereas still another called to mind the salutary effects of sleep in the temple of Asclepius. Several reliefs emphasized that the

---

45. Ibid., p. 581.
46. "Posarsi in sul gombito destro" (1565 *Descrizione*, p. 17).

gods send vital messages to men in their sleep. Beneath, between, and above these pictures swelled a cascade of arabesques, putti, and figures in relief.

The cavalcade halted at the most important points of the city in order to give the sons of sleep on the *carro* an opportunity to sing a canzone,[47] alluding to the central theme of the Trionfo.

Genealogy of the Gods

On February 21, 1566, the great *Mascherata della geneologia degli dei de' gentili* unfolded in Florence. The route followed by this festival procession is not known to us. It is clear, however, that the majority of the 60,000 inhabitants of the city enjoyed the spectacle from grandstands which had been erected in two locations, the Piazza Santa Croce and the Piazza Santa Maria Novella.[48]

The pageant was based upon the idea that the pagan gods were coming to attend the nuptials of Francesco and Joanna, just as, in the mythical past, they had been present at the marriage of Peleus and Thetis.[49] Here the comparison ended, for an appearance of Eris in Florence was naturally dispensed with. The ideological foundations for the pageant were conceived by Vincenzio Borghini, the expert on mythological questions at the Medicean Court.[50] Giorgio Vasari designed the chariots and costumes.[51]

Jean Seznec[52] has compiled Borghini's sources with the help of Baldini's *Discorso*. The most important of all the authorities was, of course, Boccaccio, with his reference work *De Genealogia deorum*. Among later compendiums, the following were at the scholar's disposal: Lilio Gregorio Giraldi's *De Deis gentium varia et multiplex historia* (1548), the ten books of *Mythologiae* of Natale Conti (1551), *De Natura deorum* by Phornutus (1505), and above all, Vincenzo Cartari's *Le Imagini colla sposizione degli dei degli antichi* (1556). The Mascherata also

47. The text in the *Descrizione,* p. 3.

48. Agostino Lapini informs us in his *Diario fiorentino*, p. 151, that the parade took place at night, under the illumination of a thousand torches, on the "di di Berlingaccio"—that is, on the last Thursday of the carnival. The costs amounted to 30,000 scudi.

49. For a reconstruction of the Mascherata, see *Discorso sopra la mascherata;* Cini, *Descrizione.*

50. The best introduction to Borghini's way of thinking is his report to Duke Cosimo dated April 5, 1565, printed in M. Gio. Bottari, ed., *Raccolta di lettere sulla pintura, scultura ed architettura, I* (Milan, 1882), 125–204.

51. Approximately 150 of Vasari's original drawings are preserved in the Biblioteca Nazionale in Florence; many copies may also be found there and in the Gabinetto Disegni e Stampe degli Uffizi.

52. "La Mascarade des dieux à Florence en 1565," *Mélanges d'archéologie et d'histoire,* 52 (1935), 224–43. Cf. also Jean Seznec, *The Survival of the Pagan Gods* (New York, 1953), pp. 280–82.

drew on Hesiod's *Theogony,* Cicero's *De Natura deorum,* Ovid's *Metamorphoses,* Pausanias' description of Greece, Virgil, and the *Saturnalia* of Macrobius, to the extent that Boccaccio had not already used these sources.

Both descriptions of the festival, that of Baldini as well as Cini's, begin with the ornamental chariot of Demogorgone and conclude with the twenty-first car, that of Janus. At the end of his *Discorso,* however, Baldini reports that the chariot of Janus was first in the procession, while Demogorgone's float concluded the cavalcade.[53] Bacchus and Ceres evidently followed upon Janus, which accounts for floats number twenty and nineteen in the descriptions; for Baldini informs us that after Janus, there followed those gods "who were closest to the human race, those, moreover, who were best known, such as Bacchus and Ceres and the other earth divinities."[54]

Eight trumpeters in women's clothing opened the cavalcade and diverted the spectators with their *lazzi.*[55] Then came Hesiod, author of the *Theogony,* carrying a banner in five colors: brown signifying the earth, aquamarine the sea, white the air, red fire, and bright blue the sky. Hesiod was followed by the first car, the *Trionfo di Iano.* Four musical ensembles were enlisted in the procession: one attached to the Bacchus car, another to Pan, a third group of musicians preceding Venus, and a fourth marching in front of the float of Demogorgone.[56] Six *maschere* were marshaled into the parade to keep the proper order: a Mercury, an Iris, a Hercules, an Achilles, a Cassandra, and a Tuscan Atlas, to whom the founding of Fiesole was attributed.

For a more detailed description of the procession, we shall consider the twenty-one pageant cars as they passed in review and were presented to the spectators—that is, by reversing the sequence given in the two descriptions of the festival. It should be noted that the twenty-one gods to whom the individual cars were assigned were not portrayed by people in costume, but were statues which Vasari treated as part and parcel of the architecture of the floats.

The structure of the Janus car was conceived as a Janiculus, a hill with twelve altars, on which stood a statue of the two-faced god. Two white rams drew the vehicle. Sixteen escorts made up its train: two Prayers, Religion, Porrina and Postverta (from Ovid's *Fasti*), Good Favor (*Favore*), Favorable Outcome (*il buono*

53. Baldini, p. 129: "ma è da auuertire che nel mandar fuori la mascherata l'authore tenne ordine contrario à questo che ho tenuto io nello scriuerla, percioche primieramente furon mandati suoni Trombetti, dipoi lo stendardo, & poi innanzi à tutti gli altri il carro di Iano . . . di maniera che l'ultimo Triompho à passare fu quel di Demogorgone."

54. Ibid., p. 130.

55. Ibid., p. 128.

56. Ibid.

Evento), Anna Perrena, two *Fetiales,* a Roman consul, two senators, two soldiers, and Money personified.

Janus was followed by the car of Bacchus,[57] which was shaped like a silver ship (Figure 3). On its bow stood a statue of the god, in the form of a panther. A great staff of thyrsus served as the mast, on which hung an unfurled sail with depictions of the maenads. The ship-car seemed to be tossed about on the waves, with fish darting up from the billows. Because of the fact that a wine-gushing fountain could not be mounted, three bacchantes and three satyrs showered wine on the spectators from the car.[58] Surrounding Dionysus were twenty-three companions: on the float itself stood the Thracian King Maron, the three bacchantes, and the three satyrs; behind it followed the nymph Syca (a darling of Bacchus), Staphylus (a son of Silenus or Dionysus), Cissus (one of Bacchus' catamites), Silenus on an ass, Aegle, Chromis, Mnasyllus (from the sixth *Eclogue* of Virgil), Comus, Intoxication, Laughter, two men and two women (votaries of Bacchus), Semele, and Narceus (from Pausanias).

The *trionfo di Cerere* was decorated with nine paintings depicting episodes from the legend of Demeter. Two winged dragons drew the car, which was escorted by the following fifteen figures: two Eleusinian virgins, two boys, two girls, two men, two bashful matrons, three Greek priests, Triptolemus (astride a dragon), and Iasion, beloved of Ceres.

Diana's car was also adorned with nine paintings, whose motifs were derived from the myths surrounding the goddess. Two white stags made up the team of this float, which was encircled by Hippolytus and eight nymphs of the chase.

Cybele's car, drawn by two lions, was square-shaped[59] and decorated with four reliefs. Fifteen persons comprised her entourage: ten Corybants, two Roman matrons, P. Cornelius Scipio Nasica, the Vestal Virgin Claudia Quinta, and Atys, beloved of the Great Mother.

Four black horses were harnessed to the chariot of Pluto and Proserpina, which was guided by an infernal monster. At the feet of the underworld god lay Cerberus. The retinue of twenty-two consisted of three Furies, Nessus and Astilus (the centaurs), Briareus, Acheron, Cocytus, Styx, Phlegethon, Charon, Lethe, Minus, Aeacus, Rhadamanthus, Phlegyas, Sisyphus, Tantalus, Julius Caesar, Octavianus Augustus, Penthesilea, and Thomyris.

Pan's float (Figure 4) consisted of a "shady grove, executed with such skill that

57. Cini-Vasari, p. 612.
58. Baldini, p. 121.
59. Cini-Vasari, p. 609.

it looked natural and real" ("ombrosa selva, con molto artifizio fatta, aveva naturale e vera sembianza").[60] It was pulled by two billy goats. A cave sheltered the god, who had ten companions: two satyrs, two sylvan deities, two fauns, the nymph Syrinx, the nymph Piti, beloved by Pan, Pales (an old Roman agricultural deity), Bubona (goddess of cattle), Myiagros (god of the flies), and Evander, who introduced sacrifices to Pan in Italy.

Oceanos and Thetis shared a chariot made up of cliffs with the appropriate flora and fauna. Yoked to it were two whales. Fourteen figures thronged about the trionfo: Nereus, another Thetis (daughter of Nereus), three sirens, two Graeae, three Gorgons, Scylla, Charybdis, Echidna, and the sea nymph Galatea.

Drawn by two sea horses, Neptune's car, "capriccioso e bizzarro,"[61] was made of shells and volcanic limestone (Figure 5). Four dolphins supported a crab which served as the sea god's pedestal. Following in Neptune's wake were nineteen figures: Glaucus, Proteus, Phorcys, two Tritons, Aeolus, Zephyrus, Eurus, Boreas, Auster, Otus, Ephialtes, two Harpies, Canopus, Zetes, Calais (the Boreades), and Neleus.

The *carro di Junone* was drawn by two peacocks and decorated with five paintings. The goddess' cortege comprised eleven people: Iris, a comet, Serenity, Snow, Fog, Dew, Rain, three virgins, and Populonia, who averted catastrophes.

Two dogs drew Vulcan's car, which was modeled after the island of Lemnos. Three Cyclopes—Brontes, Steropes, and Pyragmon—headed a throng of fourteen others: Polyphemus, Erichthonius, Caccus, Caeculus, Servius Tullius, Procris, Orithyia, Pandion, Philomela, and Cacca.

Minerva's float was bronzed and had the shape of an equilateral triangle. Two owls, "grandissime e bizzarrissime,"[62] appeared to have the vehicle in tow. There were fifteen allegories: Virtue, Honor, Victory, Good Name, Faith, Health, Nemesis, Peace, Hope, Clemency, Opportunity, Repentance, Happiness, Pellonia (who drove out enemies), and Science.

Luna's car, drawn by one black and one white horse, was decorated with four reliefs. Eleven figures were in her company: Endymion, the Spirits of Good and Evil, the god Vaticanus, Egeria, Nundina, Vitumnus, Sentinus, Edulica, Potina, and Fabulinus.

Drawn by two storks, Mercury's float was in the shape of a pentagon, because of the fact that the god was being celebrated as patron of the arts, the arts are created

60. Ibid., p. 607.
61. Ibid., p. 606.
62. Ibid., p. 602.

by hand, and each hand has five fingers![63] Moreover, the car carried a heap of stones, because the ancients were accustomed to throwing a stone at the feet of the statue of Mercury whenever they passed one. Twelve figures followed in this trionfo: Argus, Maia, Palestra (or Lotta), Eloquence, the three Graces, two Lares, Art personified, Autolycus, and an hermaphrodite.

Two white doves were yoked to the car of Venus, on which four reliefs (or paintings) depicted the life of the goddess. Her cortege numbered seventeen: Adonis, two *amoretti*, Hymen, Talassio (the bridal shout!), the Art of Persuasion, Paris, Concord, Priapus, Manturna, Friendship, Honest Pleasure (*Onesto Piacere*), Dishonest Pleasure (*Inonesto Piacere*), the Goddess of the Bridal Girdle, Beauty, Hebe, and Charm (*Allegrezza*).

Three paintings and two statues adorned the chariot of Mars, which was drawn by two wolves (Figure 6). The god was attended by twenty-two companions: two Salii, Romulus, Remus, Oenomaus, Ascalaphus, Tereus, Ialmenus, Brittonia, Harmonia (wife of Cadmus), the legendary inventor Hyperbius, Aetolus (a son of Mars), Ire, Deception, Menace, Rage, Death, Spoils of War, two captives, Brute Force, and Cruelty.

Five scenes relating to the following themes were graphically depicted on Jupiter's car: the rape of Europa, the abduction of Ganymede, the adventure with Aegina, the tale of Danae, and the liberation of Saturn (Figure 7). Two eagles pulled the chariot, on which stood three statues, Helena, Epaphus, and Arcesius. The high seat of Jupiter, modeled after the throne of Zeus in Olympia, was designed to conform with the description of Pausanias. Even the details evoked Phidias' masterwork. Twenty-two figures were in Jupiter's retinue: Bellerophon, Perseus, Epaphus, Hercules, Scytha (a son of Jupiter), Castor, Pollux, Justice, four Penates, two Palici, Iarbas, Xanthus (god of the river Scamander), Sarpedon, a son of Zeus by Europa or Laodamia, four Curetes, and Fortune.

Apollo's car had a team of four winged horses guided by Speed. Seven paintings alluded to his legendary life: Phaëthon, Python-Dragon, Marsyas, the labors for Admetus, the transformation of the Delian into raven when horrified by Typhoeus, his metamorphosis into a lion, and his love for Daphne. There were twenty followers: the three Horae, Month, Year, Aurora, Aesculapius, Phaëthon, Orpheus, Circe, the nine Muses, and Memory.

Two black oxen drew the float of Saturn, which terminated in a double-tailed Triton in the rear. Saturn's suite numbered eleven: Modesty, Truth, the Golden

63. Baldini, p. 58.

Age, Repose, two dark-skinned priests (*Cirenei*), two Roman priests, Vesta, Chiron, and Picus.

Uranus' car was decorated with seven scenes from the life of the father of the Titans (Figure 8). It was pulled by two bears, a large one and a small one, alluding to the constellations Ursa Major and Ursa Minor. Uranus stood on a blue celestial globe strewn with constellations,[64] and was accompanied by twenty-one figures: Atlas, Hyas, the seven Hyades, the seven Pleiades, a Titan, Iapetus, Prometheus, and two Atlantides (a legendary people who venerated Uranus).

The finale came with the float of Demogorgone (Figure 9), the father of the entire race of gods, who owed his existence to a grammatical misinterpretation.[65] His chariot, pulled by dragons (Cini mentions two, Baldini four),[66] resembled a dark, double cave ("oscura e doppia spelonca").[67] Flanked by Eternity and Chaos, Demogorgone was visible in the foremost grotto. In the recessed part of the cave were Erebus, Night, and the Ether. The grottoes were vaulted over by a wooded hill representing Mother Earth.[68] Twenty-six figures encircled the trionfo or followed it in processional fashion: Discord, the three Parcae, the Pole, the Python, Envy, Fear, Obstinacy (Pertinacia), Ignorance, Poverty, Hunger, Lamentation, Sickness, Age, Hydra, the Sphinx, Licentiousness, Falsehood, Thought, Momus, Tages, Antaeus, Day, Fatigue, and Oath.

The approximately four hundred *maschere* in the procession may be divided into two groups: mythological figures and abstract allegories, some clear and some cryptic.

Among the figures of myth certain were easily identifiable: Hercules in a lion skin with his club, for example, or Orpheus with his lyre, Perseus with the head of Medusa, or Atlas, a dark-skinned man with a white headband holding a celestial globe. The grotesque with many arms could readily pass for Briareus; the infernal figure, holding a rudder, in the company of Pluto could only signify Charon; the young man wearing a wreath of marjoram blossoms as a headdress was recognizable as Hymen (Figure 10) because of the burning torch in his right hand. In fact, the god of nuptials might have stepped out of the sixty-first poem of Catullus because of the bridal veil in his left hand and the golden *socci* on his feet. The man in hunter's garb in the Venus retinue was, of course, Adonis; the shepherd, in

64. Ibid., p. 19.
65. Cf. C. Landi, *Demogorgone* (Palermo, 1930), pp. 14-17.
66. Cini-Vasari, p. 590; Baldini, p. 8.
67. Cini-Vasari, p. 590.
68. Ibid.

Luna's company, Endymion. The somber figure holding a torch in his right hand and a statue of man in his left immediately evoked Prometheus. The naked girl from whose limbs reeds seemed to sprout could be recognized without difficulty as Syrinx, especially since she was associated with Pan. The sacerdotal figure with the gnarled stick and the red snake, in the company of Apollo, could have been no one but Aesculapius (Figure 11). Although the nine Muses were betrayed from the beginning by their number, their costumes might have misled one into taking them for nymphs, were it not for the musical instruments they carried and the feathers they wore in their hair, recalling their victory over the winged sirens in the contest of song (Figure 12). Castor and Pollux, (Figure 13) could not have seemed too puzzling to the spectators, both wearing suits of armor, but one of the Dioscuri had eight stars on his helmet, the other ten; however, instead of the conventional plume, which might have been expected, flames burst from the tops of the helmets, recalling the St. Elmo's fire which, when it appeared on the masthead, promised rescue to sailors in distress.

On the other hand, a goodly number of the mythological figures could not have been identified without a sound knowledge of mythography. To cite a few examples: In Mars' entourage was a woman who seemed to be in the process of transforming herself into a snake. This, plus the fact that she wore a gold necklace, would have suggested Harmonia, a daughter of Mars, the spouse of Cadmus (Figure 14). Circe walked in Apollo's retinue in the costume of a matron with a regal headband; instead of a scepter, she carried larch and cedar branches, which she burned during her magic rites (Figure 15). A young man was attached to the Jupiter car who wore as his *acconciatura* the head of an elephant complete with tusks and trunk. The figure was conceived as Epaphus—that is, Jupiter's son by Io —and the elephant head was an allusion to the Egyptians, whose veneration Epaphus (Apis) enjoyed (Figure 16). Two groups of seven women dressed as nymphs marched in the Trionfo di Cielo. How could the spectators have identified them as the Hyades and the Pleiades? By their headpieces: the Hyades wore the head of a bull in their hair, whereas the Pleiades had fastened ears of corn to their forelocks, and the backs of their heads gave a hibernal impression. But this was a real challenge for the observers, for even Vasari could not keep the two groups separate: among his designs (Figure 18) the costume for the Pleiades is marked "Hyade," while the Hyade's costume (Figure 17) bears the notation "Pleiade."

But there were still more complicated visual puzzles to be solved. In Vulcan's entourage was a young man, with the feet of a dragon, who wore a crown with seven stars and carried a miniature chariot in his hand (Figure 19). Only a thorough knowledge of Virgil's *Georgics* could shed light on the meaning of this figure: he was Erichthonius, legendary King of Athens and son of Hephaistos, who was held to be the inventor of the quadriga. The dragon's feet alluded to a version of the legend, according to which the body of Erichthonius terminated in the form of a snake. There was in Mars' suite another man who held a quadriga in his hand, but in this case the chariot had been smashed. The figure wore regal garments and carried a scepter. Mars? King? A battered chariot? For the initiate this could only signify Hippodamia's father, whose chariot disintegrated in the race with Pelops. Baldini's humanist allusion[69] refers to Pausanias and his description of the figures on the pediment of the temple of Zeus. One figure associated with Jupiter was truly baffling: a regal apparition holding in his hand a small fire-spitting mountain full of serpents and lions (Figure 20). The answer to this rebus is Sarpedon, the Lycian king who came to aid the Trojans and was slain by Patroclus. The lions, serpents, and volcano alluded to the Chimera that dwelled on a mountain in Lycia until it was slain by Bellerophon. While the figure with the hundred eyes placed all over his body could be identified after some reflection as Argus, another figure in Mercury's retinue presented considerable difficulties. The face of this person was shrouded by a hood; he wore felt shoes and carried a lantern, a pick-lock, and a rope ladder. He was Hermes' son, the master thief Autolycus.

How did one attempt to distinguish the four underworld rivers in Pluto's following? Acheron appeared in a pale brown costume carrying a vase from which gushed water mixed with sand: Virgil had spoken of the turgid mud and sand which this stream carried along with it. Cocytus was dressed in black, black water streaming from his vessel. Phlegethon was represented as a stream of fire, whence his red costume and red water. A woman in dark blue dress, with water of the same color flowing from her vase, stood for the swampy Styx.

Other perplexing figures who could only be deciphered after exhaustive study were Neleus, Phorcys, Amymone, Atys, and Echidna.

Finally, there were figures in the procession whose mysteries only Borghini and his two hierophants, Baldini and Cini, ultimately understood. To this esoteric category one might relegate Pales and Myiagros, the fly-catching god, Astilus and Canopis, Orithyia and Vitumnus, Palestra and Maia, and scores of others. Which of the spectators, apart from Borghini, had ever heard of Palestra (or Lotta), who appeared in Mercury's train, since Philostratus had made her the daughter of this god? She appeared to be ephebic because of her underdeveloped breasts and short coiffure, and she carried olive branches, for she preferred this tree and its oil, with which men rubbed themselves before beginning the wrestling

69. P. 47.

31

bout (*lotta*). Maia, the mother of Hermes, also had a place among the followers of Mercury. The legend responsible for her costume derived from the *Saturnalia* of Macrobius, according to whom she was the daughter of Faunus—a legend complicated by the fact that the father had pursued his daughter with illicit proposals, beat her with a myrtle switch, and attempted to seduce her with wine in order finally to unite with her in the form of a snake. One would have thus needed a fair acquaintance with the sex life of Faunus in order to decipher the grapevine on Maia's head and the coil of snakes about her scepter. It is noteworthy that Borghini eschewed the familiar, taking real delight in the aberrant and obscure. One might have expected Persephone, for example, to have appeared in the entourage of Ceres-Demeter. But she was absent, and in her place Triptolemus and the still less known Iasion displayed themselves about the Ceres-float.

Alongside the figures of myth strode the abstractions—that is, Ignorance, Weakness, Joy, Hope, Friendship, Concord, and others. Mythological associations were of no avail here, and everything had to be achieved by symbolic costuming. The gamut of symbols extended from the precise to the abstruse. To begin with, there were abstractions which presented no difficulties to a society well-versed in emblematic imagery. Shoulders which sprouted white wings, a long trumpet grasped in the hand, unmistakably characterized the subject as Bona Fama. One allegory could have been unraveled with a passing knowledge of zoology: that of Ire, presented as a blind woman who foamed at the lips, wore a red robe and a rhinoceros headpiece, and rode a baboon. Explanation:[70] the rhinoceros is slow to take anger and then only when vexed, but at that time it becomes the "most irate" of animals; the baboon was considered to be, by nature, excitable to frenzy.

Memory (Figure 21) was personified by a woman in the flower of her maidenhood. The humanistic explanation for her youthfulness was based on Aristotle's observation that memory lapses with old age. But why the black costuming? Black was held to be the color of persistence, stability, and endurance. Memory held a black dog in her hand, as dogs were considered to have long memories in antiquity. Her headpiece was a hodgepodge of the most disparate objects, an allusion to the fact that the memory is capable of retaining a multiplicity of impressions at the same time.

Modesty (Figure 22) trailed along in the company of Saturn, her face concealed behind her veil, and in her left hand, an ermine. Her connection with Saturn was based on Juvenal's sixth Satire, which begins with the descent of Chastity upon the earth at a time when Saturn still held sway over it. The veil alluded to Pe-

70. By Baldini, pp. 47–48.

nelope, who, forced by her father to choose between remaining with him in Sparta and following Odysseus to Ithaca, blushed with shame and hid her face behind a veil. But what significance could be attached to the small white animal with the topaz neckband? It came from Petrarch's *Triumph of Death*,[71] in which he cites a snow-white ermine on a green background with a neckband of golden topazes as the animal emblematic of the virtuous woman.

Certain difficulties arose in the characterization of such lamentable figures, manifesting common physical traits, as the allegories Hunger, Care, and Disease. For Hunger, Vasari (Figure 23) took a leaf from the eighth book of Ovid's *Metamorphoses*, in which Fames is said to dwell in the Caucasus and to pluck the sparse tufts of grass from the stony soil with her nails and teeth. Ovid also envisaged Hunger as a hollow-eyed creature resembling a flesh-covered skeleton. To enable the initiates to relate her to Ovid, she carried a small mountain in her hand: the Caucasus! Representing Care was a woman in a tawny robe who wore a blue thrush for a headdress: the song of this "lonesome" bird was considered melancholy. For the allegory of Disease, Egyptian symbolism was invoked. Here the authority was Horapollo and his *Hieroglyphica*. The incarnation of sickness held an anemone in her hand and wore a garland of anemones in her hair, for the Egyptians regarded this flower as the symbol of disease.

Seznec[72] overestimated, in my opinion, the oriental admixture in the procession. To be sure, Borghini consulted Horapollo, and the bearded Apollo with the small basket which he wore as a head covering was no doubt modeled on the Assyrian Apollo of Heliopolis. But the direct source followed by Borghini here was the *Saturnalia* of Macrobius (1.17.66–70). The legends of Apollo depicted on the car itself were pure Hellenic lore, and the guide for the float, Velocity, wore a dolphin as headdress, because Aristotle had pronounced the dolphin the swiftest animal on land or in the sea.

One can scarcely assume that the spectators grasped the play on symbols in the allegory of Justice (Figure 24), who was in Jupiter's entourage: a pretty woman on horseback strangling a hag whom she belabored with a stick. One might have supposed that the subject here was cruelty, especially since there was a woman in Mars' float who was throttling a child and bore the name Crudelità. Investigation of this singular portrayal of justice, however, leads back to Pausanias, who, in his description of the famous Cypselus chest in the fifth book, mentions a relief of Dike who chastises the hag, Injustice, choking and beating her with a stick.

One of the puzzles strangest to the eye was the personification of Thought (Fig-

71. Baldini erroneously refers to Petrarch's *Triumphus Castitatis*.
72. "La Mascarade . . ." (1935), pp. 229–32.

33

ure 25), conceived as an old man. His headpiece consisted of peach stones, the skin of which was serrated by intersecting canals, "just as the human soul is lacerated by thought"[73]—a symbol drawn from Pierio Valeriano's *Hieroglyphica*. Thought's costume was covered with thorns, the prickles of which were directed against his body, since thoughts torture the mind as thorns do the flesh.

That this *Klassische Walpurgisnacht* left the great mass of spectators nonplussed is attested by Baldini, when he gives reasons for the copiousness of his commentary at the beginning of his *Discorso:* "The festival procession displayed such a wealth and variety of figures that in the short span of time available to the observer they could not be grasped by everyone, and this gave rise to criticism."[74] In order to dilute the pagan flavor of the pageant, Baldini concluded his description with a Christian twist: reproductions of the individual figures in the Mascherata would shortly appear in print, so that everyone might be convinced of the "vanity and futility of the fables and fabrications in which the ancient heathen believed."[75] Essentially, such a parade could only contribute, he felt, to strengthening belief in the one God and in the true religion.

Religious Afterpiece

The festivities concluded during the Lenten season with a *sacra rappresentazione,* a portrayal of the Annunciation scene in the church of Santo Spirito. Traditionally, the performance should have taken place in San Felice, where Brunelleschi had formerly created the machinery for it as described by Vasari. But Santo Spirito was larger[76] and could contain the numerous guests. Evidently Brunelleschi's technical mechanism was used here as well. Celestial Paradise was housed in Salvi d'Andrea's cupola,[77] which opened, revealing the heavenly hosts and angels as they moved in circles in various directions.[78] From this Paradise the Archangel Gabriel, escorted by eight small angels, descended into the chamber of the Virgin,

73. Baldini, pp. 15–16.

74. P. 5: "la Mascherata . . . fu tanto varia & tanto copiosa di figure, ch'e potrebbe essere ageouolmente, che in quel tempo, che ella durò a andar' fuori la non fusse cosi compresa da ognuno, & per questo forse da qualcun' biasimata."

75. Ibid., p. 131.

76. "Più capace e più bello" (Cini-Vasari, *8,* 616). Cf. also *Der literarische Nachlass Giorgio Vasaris,* eds. Karl Frey and Hermann-Walther Frey, 2 (Munich, 1930), 190.

77. "Dalla più alta parte della cupola di quella chiesa, ove il prescritto Paradiso era figurato" (Cini-Vasari, *8,* 617).

78. "Meraviglioso e stupendo ed incomparabile fu il Paradiso, che in un momento aprendosi, pieno di tutte le gerarchie degli angeli e de' santi e delle sante, e co' vari moti le diverse sue sfere accennando" (ibid., p. 616).

which was slightly elevated above the floor of the church, and after the Annunciation, he was again drawn upwards—a singular atavism in the life of a Renaissance society. But Joanna of Austria was a *religiosissima sposa* and had evidently set eyes on enough pagan deities in the course of the carnival to justify this final assertion of monotheism.

3. Décors by Baldassare Lanci

1568–69

In 1561 Baldassare Lanci da Urbino, a pupil of Girolamo Genga, entered the service of the Tuscan state and was twice given the opportunity to demonstrate his abilities as a set designer: for the baptism of Leonora, first offspring of the marriage of the hereditary Prince Francesco and Joanna of Austria, during the carnival of 1568; and for a state visit to Florence of the Archduke Karl in the spring of 1569. Both events provided an occasion for pageants, tourneys, and theatrical performances, for which Lanci was commissioned to design the décors.

CALENDAR OF EVENTS FOR 1568[1]

February 2: *Mascherata di Cacciatori;* music to *canzone* by Francesco Corteccia.

February 9: Joust in the Piazza Santa Croce.

February 12: *Mascherata in Cocchio,* parade of pageant cars, with music by Alessandro Striggio.

February 15: Serenade to music by Stefano Rossetto in front of the old Medici palace on the Via Larga, followed by a tourney.

February 23: Pageant of the Butterflies, with music by Striggio.

February 26: Allegoric pageant with a *Trionfo* of Fortuna, the music by Rossetto.

---

1. Sole primary source: Alessandro Ceccherelli, Descrizione di / tutte le Feste, e Maschera / te fatte in Firenze per il / Carnouale, questo / anno, 1567. / E insieme l'ordine del Battesimo della / Primogenita dell'Illust. & Eccell. S. / Principe di Firenze, e Siena, con / gl'Intermedij della Comme / dia, et dell'apparato / fatto per detto / battesimo. / Con licenza, & priuilegio, 1567.

The christening took place in the Battistero on the last Sunday of the carnival and was followed by a performance of the comedy *I Fabii* by Lotto del Mazzo,[2] with six interludes by unknown authors. *I Fabii* was performed in the "sala grande dipinta"[3] of the ducal palace—that is, in the Salone dei Cinquecento. Degrees for the ladies of the court were erected along the side walls; the Duke and his guests of honor sat on a dais in the middle of the hall, not far from the stage. The settings were by Baldassare Lanci da Urbino.[4]

After the candles were lighted in the auditorium, the curtain divided ("la tela ch'era tirata auanti la prospettiua . . . fu in vn tratto tagliata"),[5] and the audience was offered a view of the ducal palace and the surrounding structures "fino alla fine di Vacchereccia." Statues of *colossi* framed the stage to the right and left: on each side a Titan "in mirabili scorci," creations of the sculptor Giovanni da Bologna. Each of the giants held a torch in one hand and with the other seemingly gathered up the folds of a cloth which closed off his side of the stage. The comedy setting remained unchanged until the end of the fourth act. At a later point we shall discuss the change of décor for the fifth act. Smaller alterations, dictated by the intermezzi, took place within the framework of the Florentine city *veduta*.

FIRST INTERMEZZO: THE INFERNAL ABYSS

For the first intermezzo a hell-mouth formed like the jaws of a fire-spitting dragon[6] gaped in the rear of the stage. Through it emerged familiar figures of the underworld: the inevitable Furies, followed by Ixion, two Danaïdes, Tantalus, Tityos, Sisyphus, Salmoneus, Phlegyas, and a Lapith. The three Erinyes and nine transgressors having formed a semicircle on the stage, the inferno closed up and disappeared, while the shades sang the somber canzone of the first intermezzo, "Tratte del tristo abisso." After this madrigal, they made their exit "per tutte le strade della scena," and the first act of the comedy could begin.

A few remarks are in order on the costumes, which were possibly the work of Bernardo Buontalenti; in all events, he is mentioned one year later as a costume designer. The Furies, feigning nudity, wore soot-covered tights; serpents were coiled to form their hair and girdles, and they wore masks which suggested that they were screaming. Ixion, the first murderer, came forth with a drawn sword in a

2. On the title page of the original edition of *I Fabii*, the author is described as a "calzaiuolo fiorentino."

3. Ceccherelli, p. 17 r.

4. Ibid., p. 17 v.

5. Ibid., p. 18 r.

6. Ibid.: "da mezo il palco in dreto vna testa di vn mostro che s'assimigliaua à serpente, con lunghi, & acuti denti, e aperta la gola ne usciua fuoco, & fiamma."

bloodstained white garment, wearing a double mask that smiled good-naturedly in front and glowered furiously behind. The two Danaïdes were fittingly characterized by bottomless pitchers from which water poured. Tantalus, in regal attire, had a flame-spewing serpent dangling over his head, evoking fear of that eternal menace. Tityos displayed his liver, to which a vulture was clinging. Sisyphus, as the symbol of those who attempt the impossible, vainly tried to balance a ball on the tip of his scepter. Salmoneus was portrayed as the blasphemer who brandished a blazing torch at the heavens. And the sumptuously attired Phlegyas, with his crown of flames, figured as the symbol of betrayal.

SECOND INTERMEZZO: HERCULES AT THE CROSSROADS

After the conclusion of Act I, the young hero came from one side of the stage, wearing a dark blue cloak over his white costume, while Vice (Piacere) advanced toward him from the other, in a flesh-colored robe with veils and gold adornments, her breasts bared and her blond hair crowned with flowers. Next appeared the twelve monsters which the hero had to overcome. They formed a phalanx in the rear, while Hercules and Piacere sang their duet in the foreground. Identification of the monsters was made simple for the spectators: the Lernaean Hydra had seven heads that spewed flames; the body of the serpent was cut out of green velvet and covered with golden scales. Next came the Nemean lion, a man clothed in a genuine lion's hide ("vna pelle naturale di Lione, dentroui vn'huomo"), and two hybrid creatures, half men and half serpents, followed by various beasts from the realms of myth. At last Hercules drove out Dame Vice, and the intermezzo ended with a canzone of the monsters, "O giouinile ardire." Then began the second act of *I Fabii.*

THIRD INTERMEZZO: THE RAPE OF THE NYMPHS

This was a pastoral piece. Four shepherds led four nymphs onto the stage, in the middle of which a semispherical grape arbor appeared as a surprise effect ("in vn tratto") in the middle of a flowered meadow. The nymphs and shepherds withdrew into the bower to sing the canzone "In questi verdi prati." Four satyrs then charged into the scene, frightened away the shepherds, and abducted the nymphs. Meadow and arbor vanished "in vn subito." This partial change of scenery was technically accomplished by means of some sort of *ekkyklema.* The meadow on which the bower stood was a "piece of the stage floor" ("era di vn pezo del palco"), maintained in equilibrium by a pivot and swung out into the spectator's view by means of a winch ("bilicata con vn perno, per via di vno argano si voltaua").[7] Ceccherelli made the comment: "fu vna merauigliosa e stupenda cosa."

FOURTH INTERMEZZO: THE POWER OF CALUMNY

In this interlude with allegoric significance, suddenly, from the stage floor, arose a royal throne ("in vn subito vsci di sotto il palco"),[8] on which sat a king attentively listening to two women, Ignorance and Fear, whisper insinuations in his long donkey's ears. Still other allegoric figures appeared: Envy, Slander, Treachery, Deceit, Remorse, Truth, and four representatives of public opinion, who came forth in long, iridescent robes. Each representative of the people wore a clock dial over his black and rumpled hair—a symbol of inconstancy; Lack of Judgment and Fickleness were symbolized by still other attributes. The allegories formed a semicircle about the royal throne and sang a canzone. They then marched off, and the throne vanished into the trap.

FIFTH INTERMEZZO: THE MUSES AND GRACES

Cupid appeared, followed by Fear, Hope, Envy, Honor, Contentment, Fame, Reward, and Virtue. The group gazed up at the heavens, from which a cloud descended until it eventually covered the entire stage (that is, the setting with the ducal palace). In the middle of the cloud, on a bench, sat the three Graces and nine Muses. The safety of the heavenly apparitions was assured by an iron harness ("vna cigna di ferro").[9] In order not to shatter the cloud illusion, the safety belt had been camouflaged with cotton ("tutta piena di bambagia"). The cloud itself was painted on canvas ("di tela depinta"). Cupid and his female companions saluted the Muses and Graces by singing the canzone "Ecco dal Ciel le noue Sorelle," and the latter responded with the piece "Oh che non sol pur guerra." In the meantime the cloud had touched the stage floor, and the Muses and Graces descended. After two lyric numbers, the cloud vanished upward, and the spectators were presented with the prospect of a new segment of the city of Florence: the straw weavers' quarter across from the cathedral—the setting for the fifth act of the comedy.[10]

How did Baldassare da Urbino bring about this scene change? Evidently with the help of rotating prisms. The text of the description leaves no room for doubt

7. Ibid., p. 22 v.
8. Ibid., p. 24 r.
9. Ibid., p. 25 v.
10. In any case, the new veduta of the city differed altogether from the first one: "il qual volgere la faceua diuersissima da quello che alla prima era mutando tutte le case" (ibid., p. 18 r.).

that individual parts of the setting were changed by being rotated on their vertical axes: "tutti i pezzi erano bilicati sopra certi perni"[11]—i.e. the scenic elements were mounted on pivots and balanced so that a small child would have no difficulty turning them around ("che ogni minimo fanciullo con gran facilità la volgeua"). Ceccherelli's judgment was patently confirmed by all spectators: "vn artifizio merauiglioso!"

SIXTH INTERMEZZO: THE ASSEMBLY OF THE GODS

After the end of the fifth act the heavens parted over Florence, disclosing the gods assembled at a banquet, which, according to Plato's *Symposium*, had been ordained to celebrate the birth of Aphrodite. Poverty (Penia), who longed to have a child by Riches (Poro), approached the divinities in the hope of snatching some of their surplus abundance. Poro, stimulated by too much nectar, united with Penia in the garden of Zeus, and with her begat Eros. The heavens remained open for a while to enable the spectators to identify the painted papier-mâché gods ("Dei di cartoni dipinti").[12] Then they closed, and the twenty-nine gods (the stage could not hold more) now appeared in person. Leading the van, Eros and his parents took the middle of the stage, while the other deities formed a semicircle behind them and sang a dance lyric to a score by Striggio, who also composed the remaining musical numbers.[13] The lyrics were written by "due eccellentissimi rarissimi ingegni." From their verses one may infer that these unknowns possessed but modest poetic talent. Nevertheless, they were able to integrate the mood and allegoric meaning of each interlude with the events of the following act.

❦❦

In the spring of 1569 a state visit by Archduke Karl to Florence was expected. Malicious rumors concerning Francesco's philandering, which had spread to the imperial court, and the less than edifying spectacle of Cosimo's private life prompted the Archduke to make the journey and to talk matters over with his sister.

CALENDAR OF EVENTS FOR 1569[14]

April 27: Formal entrance of the Archduke into Florence.
April 29: *Calcio* match in the Piazza Santa Croce.

11. Ibid., p. 17 v.
12. Ibid., p. 27 v.
13. Concerning instrumentation, cf. Ceccherelli, pp. 30 v., 31 r.
14. Primary sources: Raccolto / delle feste / fatte in Fiorenza / Dalli Ill. & Ecc. Nostri Signori e padroni / il Sig. Duca, & il Sig. Principe di / Fiorenza, & di Siena. / Nella venuta del Serenis-

May 1: Performance of the comedy *La Vedova* by Giovambattista Cini, with intermezzi by the same author. Alessandro Striggio composed the music.

May 5: *Mascherata delle Bufole,* probably in the Piazza Santa Croce.

The performance of Cini's comedy took place in the Salone dei Cinquecento,
since the reference in the *Raccolto* could only apply to this hall: "grandissima e
veramente Realissima Sala che vn Paradiso sembra."[15] A stage was set up at the
south end of the hall[16]—that is, facing the *Udienza* opposite. At a certain distance
in front of it stood the dais for princely personages. The ladies of the court sat
round about on the *gradi,* and the courtiers were accommodated on the ground
floor.

Baldassare Lanci's setting for *La Vedova* (Figure 26) showed a particular segment of Florence, the Antellesi district, with the façade of the Palazzo Vecchio and
the statues of the three giants: Michelangelo's David and Bandinelli's Hercules and
Cacus.[17] The heavens over Florence could be opened, and an aperture in the stage
floor enabled underworld figures to emerge in the second interlude.[18] Moreover,
the stage picture was so arranged ("con tanto ingegno accommodata") that it
could be transformed by a single swift rotation ("in vno momento riuolta"), a
technical problem we shall investigate below.

FIRST INTERMEZZO: THE CHARIOT OF FAMA

Wreathed in foliage and pulled on stage by Past and Present, the gilded pageant
car of Fama appeared in the Florentine setting before the first act of the comedy.
Dame Fama,[19] wearing a costume of dark blue satin trimmed with gold, white
veils, golden shoes, and wings, stood erect on a globe, her gold headdress crowned
by a constellation. In her right hand she held a trumpet with three bells, "for the
three parts of the world"; in her left were three garlands, one a laurel wreath, another of oak, and a third of palm leaves. Several men and women escorted Fama's

---

simo Arciduca / Carlo d'Austria per honorarne / la presenza di sua Altezza. / In Fiorenza. /
Appresso i Giunti. 1569.

[Giovanni Passignani] Descrittione / dell' Intermedii / fatti nel felicissimo / Palazo del Gran
Dvca / Cosimo, & del suo illustriss. / figliuolo Principe di / Firenze, & di Siena. / Per honorar la
Illvstris. / Presenza della Sereniss. / Altezza dello Eccellentissimo / Arciduca d'Austria. / Il
primo giorno di Maggio, / l'Anno MDLXIX. / In Fiorenza, / Appresso Bartholomeo Sermartelli.

15. *Raccolto,* p. 9.

16. Ibid., "In testa della parte di Mezzodi era la Scena."

17. *Raccolto,* p. 10.

18. Ibid.: "per mandare fuori gente finti vscire d'inferno."

19. The following description is based on Passignani, Sign. A3 r and v.

Trionfo. Nine youths and nine young girls "à guisa di nimfe" appeared from the opposite side, the girls wearing robes of red and yellow satin. The interlude concluded with a musical exchange of views between Dame Fama and the eighteen lovers.

SECOND INTERMEZZO: ERICHTHO

Erichtho, the deadly Thessalian archwitch mentioned by Lucanus and Dante, dominated the interlude that followed the first act.[20] Attired in grey, she had an emaciated face of Stygian pallor, and wore a wreath of cypress leaves on her matted grey-black hair. One foot was uncovered. She drew a number of magic circles on the stage with her wand, while conjuring up a series of infernal shades, whose emblems variously identified them as poets, sculptors, painters, musicians, or alchemists, although they were all uniformly cloaked in grey taffeta. After the *Ombre* had sung their mournful song, the witch sent them back to Hades.

THIRD INTERMEZZO: CLOUDS AND WINDS

Clouds drifted over the stage as an echo from Aristophanes. They were portrayed by fair-haired women in costumes of silver, red, yellow, or green. The Clouds sang a sweet madrigal before they were driven off to the east by the sixteen Winds, who arose from a trap wearing wings and an abundance of veils, and were divided into groups. The four East Winds appeared in costumes of dark blue satin and wore white masks. One of them, Aeolus, was made recognizable as their king by his crown and scepter. Dressed in white and bright blue satin, the four North Winds were masked as old men. The four West Winds wore youthful masks and red and blue costumes. Green and chestnut-colored robes marked the four South Winds, who wore masks with wrinkled, chubby faces of swarthy complexion. All the Winds gathered in the west, simultaneously blowing away the Clouds in an easterly direction with their breath. Before they exited by the various alleys of the set ("le strade della Scena") they blew on silver conch shells and sang a canzone.

The third intermezzo, like all the preceding ones, was played in the Florentine setting.

FOURTH INTERMEZZO: LATONA

After the third act of the comedy, there was a change of scenery, effected by Baldassare Lanci with the help of *periaktoi*. Both descriptions of the festival men-

20. For the following, cf. ibid., A4 r and v.

42

tion the rotation ("dopo il terzo Atto voltatasi . . . la Scena";[21] "la Scena, la quale girata").[22] A third eye-witness report will be examined below.

Here the spectators were presented with a view of a rustic landscape: the region of Arcetri outside the walls of Florence. According to the *Raccolto,* they saw a great sheet of clear water with a group of peasants at work.[23] The *Descrittione* mentions[24] a swamp full of rushes. The peasants were dressed in their local costumes: orange doublets over long white shirts, and hats of a golden yellow. They sang as they marched up to the pond with their scythes and sickles. Latona appeared next in a dark green costume trimmed in gold, her hair enveloped in a dark veil, with a bat as her coiffure. She held two small children in her arms—a golden one in her right arm, a silver one in her left, symbolizing the sun and the moon. In a madrigal she asked the peasants for permission to drink water from the pond, but the Lycian-Tuscan natives forbade her. Leto then appealed to Zeus, the father of the divine twins, who promptly transformed the peasants into frogs, and very plausible frogs at that: "tanto simili à veri che piu simili non sono i naturali."[25] They hopped into the water, croaking and gurgling a song which transported the spectators to their spiritual homeland somewhere between Ovid and Aristophanes. The name of Bernardo Buontalenti, who created the frog-peasants' costumes of transformation, emerges for the first time in a description of the festival in which he is mentioned as an "ingegniere e pittore dello Illustrissimo Principe."[26]

FIFTH INTERMEZZO: DIANA AND HER NYMPHS

Diana appeared with thirty-six nymphs, all of whom were dressed in the same fashion, although in different colors. With long veils hanging from their head-dresses, they traveled barefoot and barebreasted, carrying javelins. Half the group danced, while the other sang a hymn in praise of Diana, the silver-haired goddess who stood in their midst in a costume of white satin and silver brocade.

SIXTH INTERMEZZO: ASSEMBLY OF THE GODS

After the conclusion of Cini's comedy, the intensely luminous heavens opened,[27] and a gathering of the ancient gods was disclosed, singing the final hymn. At the

21. *Raccolto,* p. 13.
22. Passignani, A7 v.
23. *Raccolto,* p. 13.
24. Passignani, A7 v.
25. *Raccolto,* p. 13.
26. Passignani, A7 r.
27. *Raccolto,* pp. 14–15; Passignani, Bl r.

apex sat Jupiter on a gilded throne. Somewhat below him were the other deities: Mercury, Mars, Bacchus, Diana, Cybele, Venus, Saturn, Apollo, Aurora, Juno, Vulcan, Pallas, Astraea, and Ceres. The lesser figures of the three Graces, Peace, Spring, and two of Vulcan's Cyclopes—Steropes and Pyracmon—also appeared. Four *amoretti* peered down from clouds.

LANCI'S ROTATING PRISMS

We shall now turn to a closer investigation of the change of scenery which occurred at the end of the third act. Both descriptions of the festival intimate that here Lanci was again working with periaktoi. The accuracy of our assumption is confirmed by the account of a third eyewitness: Ignazio Danti, the architect, mathematician, and cosmographer, who had attended the performance of Cini's comedy. At the time, he was working on the maps for the doors of the *Guardaroba nuova* cabinets in the Palazzo Vecchio. Fourteen years later, in 1583, Father Danti published his impressions of the theatre in his edition of Vignola's *Le Due regoli della prospettiva pratica*. Danti augmented the work with a supplement on the problems of stage perspective, including a section which dealt with the use of periaktoi. He maintained that rotating prisms were employed for the first time by Aristotile di San Gallo in setting up a stage for Duke Pierluigi Farnese in Castro. Danti conveys to the reader an impression of how the periaktoi were arranged in a diagram, in which he envisages two three-sided prisms at each end of the stage and a larger periaktos as the background. He then proceeds to discuss the performance of 1569:

> During the visit of the Archduke Karl of Austria in the year 1569, I saw a theatrical performance in Florence in a similar decor [using periaktoi]; it was in the ducal palace where the setting, designed by Baldassare Lanci da Urbino, was changed twice. At the beginning of the comedy the stage picture showed the bridge of Santa Trinità, and since it was evident from the play itself that the dramatis personae had to go to the village of Arcetri, a rotation brought the second plane of the prism into view (si voltò la seconda faccia); the stage was seen to be full of cottages and gardens, just as they are found in Arcetri; vineyards and the surrounding estates were also visible. But then the scene changed a second time (la seconda volta si rimutò la scena) and the Florentine quarter of Alberti was disclosed. While the setting turned (mentre che la scena si giraua), the stage was covered, and occupied by the loveliest interludes written by Giouambatista Cini, a Florentine nobleman to whom we were also indebted for the comedy. I recall that during the first change of

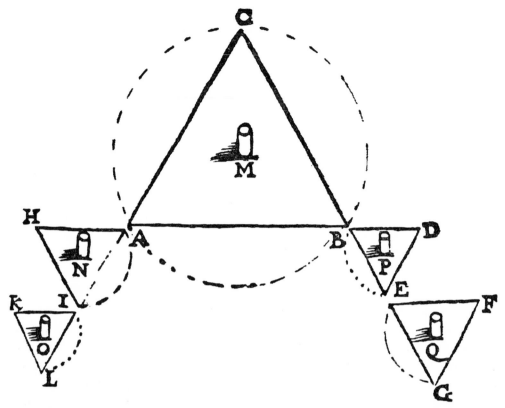

Ignazio Danti's periaktoi set, from his edition of Vignola's *Le Due regoli della prospettiva pratica* (1583).

scenery the heavens parted, disclosing a great number of gods up in the clouds who sang and played most delightful music. At the same time, a cloud descended to the feet of the gods, covering the stage while the rotation was accomplished (coprì la scena in mentre che si girò). When the cloud vanished upward, there appeared on the stage the landscape of Arcetri outside the Porta di San Giorgio, near the city walls. Meanwhile, the Trionfo of Fama swept across the stage, accompanied by several people singing a piece in response to music which resounded from the heavens. When the setting changed again by means of a second rotation (All' altra volta, che si girò la scena), it was likewise concealed behind a cloud which emerged, driven by winds, from the side (che di trauerso veniua), while the interlude took place.[28]

A comparison of this account with our primary source descriptions reveals that

28. Vignola, *Le Due regoli della prospettiva pratica*, ed. Ignazio Danti (Rome, 1583), pp. 91-92.

Danti had not retained the proper sequence of the intermezzi. He also mentions two changes of décor, for which we find evidence neither in the *Raccolto* nor in the *Descrittione,* but that is of no consequence here. The main point is that Danti recalled the performance of *La Vedova* in connection with a technical treatise on the periaktoi system, thereby providing the ultimate proof that Baldassare Lanci availed himself of those rotating prisms which Vitruvius described, albeit enigmatically, in Chapter 6 of the fifth book of his *De Architectura.*

The Bufolata

On the fifth of May a buffalo pageant was presented for the esteemed Austrian guest, a processional Trionfo with allegoric content. The symbolized figure sat or lay on the back of a disguised buffalo and was "hunted" by a troupe of figures rich in allegoric connotation who, on horseback, pursued the patient buffalo. A detailed description of the twelve buffalo groups would be tiresome to the modern reader. Yet a few details deserve attention, especially since the *bufolata* was an altogether typical element of the Florentine *Festkultur.*

The performance probably took place on the Piazza Santa Croce.[29] On one side of the piazza stood the grandstand for the guests of honor. Across from it an opening was made in the spectators' stands where a grove of oak and beech trees was planted, through which the first troupe of masqueraders entered the piazza. The buffalo was disguised as a hind and was ridden by a young lady who represented Human Life. She wore a white costume, cut *alla Ninfale,* with silver brocade over a green silk undergarment. Garlands of flowers served to adorn her. After Human Life had entreated the gods in a madrigal for protection against the onslaughts of the Seven Deadly Sins and the Furies, smoke began to rise from the glade, drifting partly over the piazza. The fire then flared up, and with a single thunderbolt the grove disappeared from the face of the earth. The way was now open for the Deadly Sins and the Furies to pursue Vita Humana, just as Aeschylus' Furies had once snapped at the heels of Orestes in the orchestra of the Theatre of Dionysus. They swarmed from the mouth of a cave, carrying trumpet-shaped instruments which spewed flames. The eighteen Furies, dressed in costumes simulating nudity, girdled with serpents, and flecked with blood, wore bat wings and held cypress branches from which spewed flames and smoke.

The procession, a *mostra* of the remaining eleven groups of the pageant, now began to file into the piazza. Sleep, on his bison, was pursued by the Sciences. Then

29. Our source for the *bufolata* is the "Descrittione / della Mascherata / delle Bufole," in *Raccolto,* pp. 17–79.

came Demogorgone on a buffalo disguised as Cerberus, accompanied by witches in extremely bizarre costumes, made up in part as alluring sirens and in part as hideous serpents. In order to facilitate identification for the public, they carried burning candles in one hand and books of magic in the other. Next followed a buffalo which was made to resemble a she-wolf ("pareua veramente vna Lupa"). It was ridden by a youth dressed as a woman, representing Prodigality, and heavily laden with finery. Six "Plutoni" on horseback and twelve pages comprised the entourage, of which six were costumed as Furies and six as Harpies. Another group portrayed Night, who was "hunted" by six Apollos. Then came Pestilence on her buffalo, followed by six figures disguised as Vulcan's smiths and representing Fire, with which Pestilence is purged. Next appeared Dame Discord on her beast of burden, pursued by six "Cavaliers of Concord." Discordia wore the costume which Ariosto had given her in his *Orlando furioso*. On the tenth buffalo rode Chimera, with the head of a lion or tiger, the breast of a goat, and the tail of a dragon, followed by Bellerophon and Nemesis along with the four Cardinal Virtues. The eleventh *Mascherata* offered a considerable challenge to the spectators' knowledge of mythology: the blind King Phineus was being pursued by Harpies who had stolen a portion of his sustenance, so that he suffered incessantly from hunger. Riding on his buffalo in a saddle of violet-colored velvet shaped to resemble a throne, he had before him a small table with simulated dishes. His inlaid gold scepter served as a goad. Six Harpies on horseback followed behind, disguised as fantastic birds with pale and haggard masks. From their open beaks protruded fangs.

In the center of the last pageant, which Cosimo himself had evidently devised, stood Beauty on a buffalo that had been transformed into a hind. Bellezza, looking very much like Diana or one of her nymphs, had six companions who in various ways allegorically portrayed the "Pursuit of Beauty." First came Delight, "natural vittoria, & honoratissima d'Amore," represented by the figure of a youth who resembled Narcissus. He wore two swan's wings as a headpiece, symbolic of the transformation of Zeus into this "suaue vcello." Then followed the figure of "Devoted Loyalty," who did not entice her lover with her natural beauty, but rather grew close to him through years of devotion. Riches and Flattery were also found in Beauty's train, Riches bearing a clear reference to the rain of gold. Finally, there appeared Deceit and Brute Force, the latter with the head of a bull in reference to the Rape of Europa. Brute Force was the last resort when the other arts failed to conquer Beauty. Escorting this retinue were pages disguised as dogs. Our anonymous commentator, who describes the bufolata in no less than sixty

47

printed pages, was forced to admit that the meaning of all these *concetti* was accessible only to those who had studied the figures carved on the cameos that were worn as decoration. The spectators, of course, had no opportunity to do so.

Meanwhile, as evening approached, a gilded chariot with a circular *teatro,* on which the nine Muses sang a canzone to Honor, made its entrance. The pages of the twelve groups then lighted their torches, and the procession filed through the darkening streets so that the Muses could repeat their canzone at various points throughout the city, while Archduke Karl and his sister sat pensively in a coach.

4. The Sbarra for Bianca Cappello

1579

In April 1578 Joanna of Austria died, thus leaving the Grand Duke Francesco I free to marry a Venetian, Bianca Cappello. Before two months had passed, he secretly made her his wife, and on October 12, 1579, married her publicly. It was an altogether unpolitical marriage, dictated by passion alone.

The festivities[1] began with the entrance of the Venetian envoys, who formally elevated Bianca to the "vera, & vnica figliuola della loro Republica, e di San Marco."[2] Tournaments were held on October 4 and 11 in the Piazza Santa Croce, and on the twelfth the coronation of the new Grand Duchess took place in the Sala

---

1. Principal source: Raffaello Gualterotti, Feste nelle nozze / Del Serenissimo Don / Francesco Medici Gran / Dvca di Toscana; / Et della Sereniss. sua Consorte la Sig. / Bianca Cappello . . . Nuouamente Ristampate. Firenze 1579. This edition contains the "disegni de' carri, & inuenzioni comparse all sbarra." The first engraving bears the inscription: "le inventioni e disegni di queste stampe sono del Sig. Raffaello Gvalterotti. Intagliate da Accvrsio Baldi e Bastiano Marsili." An earlier edition appeared in the same year without plates. A second primary source, although quite unproductive, should be referred to: [Cosimo Gaci], Poetica / Descritione / d'intorno all' inuentioni / della Sbarra / Combattuta in Fiorenza nel cortile del / Palagio de' Pitti in honore della / Sereniss. Signora / Bianca Cappello / Gran Dvchessa di Toscana. In Firenze, 1579. Leo Schrade has examined the festival from the standpoint of a music historian in his study "Les Fêtes du mariage de Francesco dei Medici et de Bianca Cappello," in Les Fêtes de la Renaissance, ed. Jean Jacquot (Paris, 1956), pp. 107–31. Karl Sälzle's reconstruction, in Richard Alewyn and Karl Sälzle, Das grosse Welttheater (Hamburg, 1959), pp. 82–90, is inaccurate. Also unsatisfactory is the essay by Hugh Edwards, "The Marriage of Francesco de' Medici and Bianca Cappello," The Art Institute of Chicago Quarterly, 46 (1952), 62 ff.

2. Gualterotti, p. 7.

del Consiglio. A hunt in the park of the villa at Poggio a Caiano followed next day, and finally on the fourteenth, the great Sbarra took place in the courtyard of the Pitti Palace, consuming a large part of the 300,000 ducats which the nuptials were said to have cost the Grand Duke.

The spectators were accommodated on three sides of the Pitti Cortile. *Gradi* were erected under the arcades, thus providing space beneath each arch for some thirty to forty ladies. The men stood in the courtyard behind the lists, which enclosed the tiltyard on three sides. Only in front of the main entrance and on the south side facing the garden were there no barricades. Guests from abroad were accommodated on the north side. A larger grandstand for Bianca and her guests (principally, family from Venice) was erected beneath the central arch on the east side. To the west sat the judges, among them Francesco de' Medici. Other guests observed the spectacle from windows and balconies.

A cloth was stretched over the courtyard at roof level. Seventy winged putti, bearing gilded candelabra with burning candles, hung down on wires from this artificial heaven. Between the putti gilded vessels were suspended. Further sources of light were installed beneath the arcades and on the balconies, and over 1,800 were counted in all.[3] At the south end of the courtyard Bastiano Marsili had painted on canvas figures of reclining river gods holding garlands, vases, and candelabra. This piece of decoration filled the space above the grotto to the height of half the second story. The space between the upper edge of this decorative strip and the ceiling cloth was left open for ventilation. An engraving (Figure 27) is attached to Gualterotti's expanded description showing the interior aspect of the courtyard. The print is practically worthless, since it creates the impression that the courtyard, apart from the visible barriers, was without any decorative elements whatever. Such, however, was by no means the case. On the contrary, scenic elements were built up at certain, although not precisely determinable, points in the courtyard, but are not mentioned by Gualterotti until well into the course of his description. Thus there stood in the courtyard two huts (*capanne*), in each of which an elephant was concealed. Also, a mountain had been constructed, probably at the edge of the tilting area, and, somewhat farther removed, a city laid by the sea; between these was a temple ("Era in su i confini dello steccato vn monte, e piu lontano appariua vna città in terra, e vicino al mare, tra la città, e'l monte vn bellissimo tempio").[4] The mountain was conceived as Helicon, the temple as the

3. Ibid., p. 12. Gaci (p. 5), also, speaks of the "altro nouello giorno" which all these lights created.

4. Ibid., p. 17.

shrine of Apollo, and the city as Delphi. Within the mountain, musicians were concealed. The temple was large enough so that Apollo's car could emerge from it drawn by two lions. Across from Parnassus stood another mountain, which, on being hit by a bolt from Apollo, opened and enabled the Maga and the five-headed dragon to appear from a cave. Mount Aetna, which opened for the Cyclopes' scene, was located beneath the loge of the arbitrating judges. In the case of these scenic set-pieces, entirely medieval *loca* were used and scattered over the *cortile* stage.

At the same time, however, the Renaissance demand for perspective scene-painting had to be taken into consideration. Of the three entrances on the grotto side, the two lateral ones were closed off by means of "prospettiue" with representations of the sea. On each side of the middle entrance to the right and left stood a statue of a colossus behind a fountain. These giants were conceived as symbols of the virtue which slays vice. Even the fountains had their significance, since the virtues are the springs, as it were, of the Muses. The middle entrance to the grotto was closed off by a curtain. When it was drawn aside, the spectator was granted the view of a seascape with waves and surf, and in the distance, the outlines of the City of Venice: "The sea was painted, and the painter had imitated the billows of the sea and its white breakers on the rocks with the greatest faithfulness to nature. Even the crags that rose from the water seemed to be genuine. But still more natural was the rising and subsiding of the foam after the waves had broken. Many lovely things could be seen upon the sea. *One* view was particularly beautiful: the prospect of the wonderful City of Venice . . . with some of the islands that surround it."[5] Here we have the element of Renaissance scene painting produced by illusionistic means. In 1579 the theatre found itself in a period of transition: on the one hand there were the surviving medieval loca, and on the other, an already new stage of illusion—a hybrid form which assumed importance two years later in the *Ballet comique de la Reine* in Paris.[6] There in the Pitti court, as in 1581 in the Petit-Bourbon, the majority of the participants made their entrance in ornamented chariots which, in Florence, were most likely drawn through the main

5. "Il mare era dipinto, & il dipintore haueua fatto l'ondeggiare al mare, si ch'ei pareua, che veramente si mouessi, e frangessi, e franto biancheggiasse d'intorno a gli scogli; e gli scogli pareuano veri, & a viua forza vscir dell'acque; ma piu vero pareua il farsi, e'l disfarsi della schiuma, che nasceua dall' onde rotte; in questo mare si vedeuano molte cose belle; ma vna bellissima, e questa era la marauigliosa città di Vinezia . . . con alcune delle sue isolette d'intorno" (ibid., p. 13).

6. Cf. my "Sixteenth-Century Continental Stages," *Shakespeare Quarterly,* 5 (1954), 366.

entrance into the cortile. The much-admired form of the *Ballet comique* was thus altogether foreshadowed in Florence in 1579.[7]

The Florentine spectacle began at one o'clock, when two men dressed in Persian fashion and two small Ethiopians made their entrance through the curtain that sealed off the grotto, striding up to both of the previously-mentioned huts and drawing out from them two elephants. Although they were not real elephants, they did resemble living animals in their movements. The two Persians led them across the tiltyard (*campo*), while the two small Moors swung on top of the elephants' heads. Scarcely had the animals disappeared into the grotto than it opened to drum rolls and fifes, exposing to view the surging sea and distant Venice. The drummers and pipers swarmed out of the grotto, followed by tourney pages with helmets and shields. Then came the seconds of the Tuscan party and the three seconds for the Persian challengers.

At this point it is probably well to explain the presence of the Persian element. Three Persian knights had found themselves in Florence on the occasion of Francesco's wedding and were ready to prove with lance and sword that the damsels of Persia were more beautiful, charming, and courageous than all the other women in the world. Spurred by this challenge, the Florentine knights arranged the tournament in honor of the Tuscan bridegroom and his Venetian bride.

The three Persian knights made their entrance on a pageant car drawn by two elephants (Figure 28). Finished in white and gold, the car was oval-shaped in front and rectangular behind. Foliage and sphinxes provided the ornamentation. The rear wheels represented the sun and the moon, and the front wheels were star-spangled. The three Persians descended from their elevated seat and were received by the master of the lists, who escorted them to the places provided for them.

Then the eyes of the spectators turned to the main entrance, through which a procession of foreigners slowly moved into the courtyard. Among these wayfarers one figure, who stood out for the rich finery of her dress, introduced herself forthwith as Damigella di Dalmatia. As the procession moved crosswise through the courtyard, halting in the vicinity of Helicon (the Temple of Apollo at Delphi), it was accompanied by "vna dolcissima armonia" played by musicians hidden in the mountain.[8] Then the lady from Dalmatia stepped in front of the loge of the Grand Duchess and proceeded to tell her, as well as others within earshot, her tale, which appeared to have originated in a courtly prose romance with echoes of Ariosto. It would seem, from the remark, "mandò sul palco tale scrittura," that the Dalmatian

7. Apart from the scenic hybrid form also in details of motif, as the story of the Maga who holds the heroes captive.

8. Gualterotti, p. 17.

52

handed the text of her story to the Grand Duchess; and the later assertion that Striggio's music resounded "mentre che tale scritto si lesse" likewise indicates a written notation. On the other hand, the command at the beginning of the tale of woe: "ascoltate con cortese animo in quale stato io mi ritrouo,"[9] points to an oral delivery. It is scarcely imaginable that only Bianca should have been initiated into the mystery, since the other wedding guests would not then have understood at all what was going on in the course of the tournament spectacle. One must probably suppose that the Damigella recited her story of misfortune aloud, underscored by Striggio's music in the background, thus explaining Gualterotti's remark on the "non inteso canto."

The lady hoped to obtain understanding from the wedding guests for her sad plight. Here in brief is her story: After a short period of wedded bliss, the Dalmatian bride lost her beloved knight Uliterio as the result of the machinations of an evil sorceress. Uliterio had been shipwrecked on one of his tilting journeys in a tempest aroused by the Maga. Having brought himself and two pages to safety on the coast of a strange land, he was accosted by the sorceress, disguised as a shepherdess lamenting her woes: her lover was held prisoner in a cave watched over by a five-headed dragon. Uliterio took pity on her and went forth to do battle with the dragon—a monster with four snakes' heads and a lion's head, on which it wore a crown. When Uliterio, on the advice of the Maga, jumped onto the back of the dragon, the latter folded its wings around him. Now Uliterio was held captive and could only be freed if the crown on the lion's head were given over to the "most worthy princess of the world." After this had been recounted to the Dalmatian by the two surviving pages, she—a singular case of syncretism—turned to the Oracle of Apollo in Delphi. Affected by her prayer, the god dispatched her to Florence, where she would again find her Uliterio.

Scarcely had the Damigella finished her story than the gates of Apollo's temple opened. There emerged the god in his car drawn by two lions: it had the shape of a tripod and was decorated with graphic representations of the Apollo legend (Figure 29). Apollo himself was a blond youth in golden attire, crowned in laurel, with sunbeams about his head, and a lyre and plectrum in his hand. The car halted before the Grand Duchess, and Apollo cried in a loud voice that a thunderbolt would cleave the mountain, revealing the sorceress and her dragon; whereupon the mountain was indeed rent by a flash straight as an arrow. After the fireworks had subsided, the Maga rode forth from the fissure on a fantastic beast (Figure 30). She wore a silver-violet costume with veils waving from the bizarre *acconciatura;* in

9. Ibid., p. 18.

53

her hand she held a distaff. Her beast of burden had the feet of a bird, the back of a serpent, the tail of a scorpion, the head of an old woman, and the horns of a billy goat; the monster's mouth spat fire, and two arms stretched out of the ears, each hand holding a lantern (doubtless manneristic impulses at play). The Maga was followed by the five-headed fire-spitting dragon. On Apollo's behest, the Dalmatian took the crown from the lion's head of the dragon, which obligingly bent to the ground. At this point the monster opened its wings, whereby Uliterio, portrayed by Count Ulisse Bentivoglio, was set free and reunited with his Damigella. The crown, decorated with precious stones, was conveyed to the Grand Duchess. Apollo sang a five-strophed madrigal in homage to the bridal pair, and Bentivoglio was escorted to his seat on the steps.

The next *carro* belonged to Night (Figure 31). Drawn by two black animals, it was surrounded by sedge and resembled a rock rising out of a swamp. Ether, a son of Night, acted as guide to the car, wearing a flame for a headpiece and carrying a blue sphere embellished with two falcon's wings on which the sun and the moon were depicted. In the middle of the car dark figures danced. Dame Night lay in the background enveloped in a silver cloth, enclosed by dark veils, and holding a bunch of poppies. At her side were two sleeping figures, Repose and the Dream. On the highest point of the rock, upon a cloud, stood Cielo, a young man holding the zodiac in one hand and a torch in the other; his headpiece was a celestial globe. When the car halted in front of Bianca, Night—whose voice was that of the celebrated Giulio Caccini—began to sing a madrigal composed by Piero Strozzi. Then several participants of the tournament and pages descended from the car and made their way to their appointed places.

The next pageant was drawn by two swans and guided by two beasts of the sea with human heads (Figure 32). It belonged to Dame Venus, who sat on a throne (to judge from the engraving; Gualterotti speaks of a rock), with *amoretti* swarming about her. Portrayed in graphic representations on the sides of the car was the love life of the goddess. Gualterotti mentions here[10] the name of the artist who attended to the outfitting of the car: Bastiano Marsili, who was probably also responsible for the other scenic elements, perhaps together with Accursio Baldi. The *trionfo* was chased in silver, with gold embellishments. Reliefs of naked women stood in the four corners. One of the *amori* declaimed verses before the Grand Duchess, and a group of amoretti sang a madrigal, which was followed by the madrigal of two warriors. Both pieces of music were composed by Piero Strozzi. Venus gave the golden apple she had received from Paris to one of the amoretti, with the commission of presenting it to the Grand Duchess. As Bianca took pos-

10. Ibid., p. 27.

session of the apple, it opened and transformed itself into a royal crown. Additional participants in the tournament then descended from the chariot.

A silver shell, in which sat two ladies and two knights, now slid into the courtyard (Figure 33). Europa and Africa were personified by ladies who had come, escorted by two cavaliers, to uphold the honor of European and African women against the Persian-Asiatic challenge. One of the ladies played on the lute, while the other sang and the two gentlemen listened. The shell-car was drawn by two "huomini acquatici" and was encircled by sea gods. After a madrigal in front of the Grand Duchess, the two knights descended and, escorted by their pages, paced off the tiltyard.

Three further participants in the tournament were introduced in most peculiar and laborious fashion: "Entrò nello steccato vn monte di terra."[11] Because of its weight, the mountain (Figure 34) could not be shoved out into the yard, but instead came to a standstill right at the lists, with the result that not all the guests could see how it was decorated. Nor, when it opened, could they see the hunt scene with wild animals ("ma per essersi male accomodato nel campo non si videro i fuochi lauorati, e le caccie, che vi si fecero, che furono tutte cose in se, e fuora di se bellissime; ma o non vedute, o poco vedute almeno").[12] Figure 35 gives a notion of the "unfolded" mountain and of the wilderness to which three knights, who had not been granted a hearing by their ladies, had retired. Having heard of the Persian challenge, the three had made the decision to defend the honor of the female sex at the jousts in Florence. In order to give the scene an even greater fantastic quality, the knights indicated that they had addressed themselves to the great magician Filaneo and asked him to transport them to the courtyard of the Pitti Palace. Filaneo had obviously granted their request, for they descended from the mountain grotto onto the tiltyard, where their pages and seconds appeared simultaneously.

The next car was a gigantic dolphin, actually a whale (Figure 36), which, tossing on the billows, was pulled in by various scaly creatures of the sea. The whale moved, breathed, turned its eyes, and opened its jaws. The sea creatures were from the Adriatic and Tyrrhenian Seas. Three sea gods sat on the head of the whale and, in honor of Bianca, sang a madrigal in which the voice of a soprano was conspicuous. Drummers, pages, and seconds then descended from the jaws of the whale (among them was Count Giovanni Bardi) along with two knights, all enveloped in costumes the color of the sea and decorated with marine motifs.

This *mostra* was followed by the second appearance of Venus (Figure 37). Eight

11. Ibid., p. 34.
12. Ibid.

55

Tritons opened the procession, some of them blowing on conches and others brandishing torches. The three Graces then appeared, followed by three nymphs, their supposed shadows. At this point the trionfo of Aphrodite Anadyomene made its entrance drawn by two doves which appeared to fly over the sea. The car itself was in the shape of a golden shell swimming on a silver sea. Venus was encircled by six torch-bearing amoretti. In her right hand she held a golden scepter, and led Amor by her left. Fire-spitting Furies in chains followed the car, while the Venus group sang a madrigal. The goddess born of foam had come to present two knights from the famed daughter of the sea, the City of Venice. She handed her scepter to one of the Graces and bade her strike the mountain with it. Installed under the judges' grandstand, the mountain, conceived as Aetna, opened to rumbling and fireworks, exposing to view a representation of Vulcan's smithy in the interior. There the cyclopes, busy at their forges, sang a madrigal composed by Maffio Veniero, "in a strange and solemn tone."[13] At the conclusion of the song five Cyclopes emerged from the cave followed by pages, seconds, and the two Venetian participants in the tournament whom Venus wished to usher in.

In the next scene Mars presented himself in person: he too wanted to defend "sua carissima Fiorenza" against the Persian challenge. He made his entrance on a scorpion (Figure 38). Two half-naked men, representing the Adriatic and Tyrrhenian Seas, strode in front of the procession, their loincloths made of aquatic flora, and their wigs of algae, coral, and shells. Two lions came behind them, one with the Venetian coat of arms, the other with the Tuscan. A fourteen-year-old boy rode on the Venetian lion, representing the Adriatic, and on the Florentine sat a fifteen-year-old who stood for Tuscany. Both boys wore women's clothing. The scorpion was 14 *braccia* in length and moved in the most natural fashion. On it stood Dame Fama (portrayed by a still beardless youth) and the god of war. Fama recited two eight-line stanzas before the Grand Duchess.

A procession of sea gods (Figure 39) made its way into the arena, preceded by trumpeters whose instruments resembled conches. Pages were carrying shields modeled after the bony armor of the sea turtle. Dame Adria, the "Queen of the Seas," came in dressed in a kind of coronation array, sitting on a dolphin. She was escorted by armed "nudi huomini marini" wearing grotesque face masks which evoked fantastic fish; their bodies ended in dolphins' tails. When the "maritima pompa" (staged by knights from Siena) halted before the Grand Duchess, the dolphin-tailed mermen made their obeisances with their tails, and Dame Adria sang a madrigal written by Girolamo Bargagli.

13. Ibid., p. 42.

At this point the onlookers would seem to have had almost enough ("Pareua, che la festa cominciasse a inuecchiare, e diuenir noiosa").[14] It was time for the last mostra, a Venetian galley drawn by four sea horses and guided by Neptune (Figure 40). Four sea nymphs walked in front of the gilded ship-car. On the stern stood Count Germanico Savorniano under a purple baldachin. He had come as a Venetian cavalier to defend the unique beauty and towering virtue of the women of Venice in the tournament. Small-bore cannon on board ship were fired during the entrance into the courtyard. Then, after yet another madrigal was sung for Bianca Cappello, this time with music by Claudio Merulo, the actual tourney, with jousting and sword fighting, began. In order to put an end to the battle, artificial beasts of prey were dispatched into the yard, spewing fireworks from their eyes and nostrils. Finally, the judges distributed the prizes for the best jouster, the best sword fighter, and the most beautiful mostra. First prize was awarded to the "marittima pompa" that had flocked about Queen Adria.

14. Ibid., p. 51.

5. Opening of the Uffizi Theatre

1586

Before becoming the morganatic spouse of Cosimo I, Camilla Martelli presented him with a daughter, Virginia de' Medici. Upon the death of the first Grand Duke, Francesco banished Camilla to a convent, which she was permitted to leave only once during the rest of her life, in February 1586, to witness the marriage of Virginia to Cesare d'Este.[1] The Duke of Ferrara arrived in Florence on February 3. On the sixth the nuptials were celebrated without great pomp.[2] All the magnificence was reserved for the performance of the comedy *L'Amico fido,* by Count Giovanni Bardi,[3] on February 6, in the new Uffizi Theatre. Count Bardi had also furnished themes for the six intermezzi and composed the music for the concluding one. For the first, second, and fifth interludes the scores were written by Alessandro Striggio; the third and fourth were composed by Cristofano Malvezzi. Bernardo Buontalenti, who built the auditorium and stage in the east wing of the Uffizi beneath the ducal art gallery, also provided the settings.

When Grand Duke Francesco pondered ways of celebrating the union of his half-sister to the House of Este,[4] he sensed that the diversions—the tourneys, *sbarre,*

1. For a chronicle of events see Lapini, *Diario fiorentino,* pp. 248–49.
2. Ibid.
3. Primary source: [Bastiano de' Rossi] Descrizione / del magnificentiss. / apparato. / E de' maraviglioso intermedi / fatti per la commedia / rappresentata in Firenze / nelle felicissime Nozze degl' Illustrissimi, / ed Eccellentissimi Signori / il Signor Don Cesare D'Este, / e la Signora Donna / Virginia Medici. / In Firenze, Appresso Giorgio Marescotti. / l'Anno MDLXXXV.
4. The following account is based on Rossi's *Descrizione.*

bufolate, and *mascherate*—which had been offered the guests on former occasions had grown somewhat stale. He wanted to give them something new, and for him this meant presenting a comedy with intermezzi more splendid than had ever before been seen, "senza alcun riguardo di spesa." Lapini informs us in his diary that the performance cost 25,000 scudi.[5] Francesco himself selected the best men to shoulder the burden of the enterprise: Count Bardi di Vernio, head of the *Camerata* in which opera was cradled, and Bernardo Buontalenti, the great architect and engineer, who had already given proof of his abilities on earlier occasions and now for the first time assumed responsibility for the over-all design of the production.[6] Buontalenti chose the most qualified artists and craftsmen available, more than four hundred of whom are said to have been involved in the undertaking.[7] Personally supervised by Count Bardi, the rehearsals, "esercitazione," were the longest and most intensive that the Florentines had ever witnessed.[8]

The performance took place in the new hall of the Uffizi,[9] which was ninety-five braccia long, thirty-five broad, and twenty-four high. The floor inclined toward the stage, descending approximately 2⅛ ells,[10] so that the spectators enjoyed an unobstructed view of the stage situated at the lower end of the auditorium. The stage itself occupied twenty ells of the length of the hall. Buontalenti installed six *gradi* against the longer sides of the auditorium and along the short side opposite the stage: in the Italian terminology of the day, he had created a "Teatro." In the middle of the hall, thirty braccia from the stage, approximately beneath the *Tribuna* of the present art gallery, a dais (*palco*) was erected which measured twelve ells square and rose fifty-eight centimeters above floor level in front. This was reserved for persons of princely rank and was upholstered accordingly in dark red velvet and lavishly gilded. Between the princely dais and the gradi, benches were set up for the male guests. The ladies sat on the rows of six luxuriously carpeted steps, which ran along the three walls. In front of the gradi Buontalenti erected at equal intervals twenty-four pyramids that gave the impression of having

5. Lapini, p. 250.
6. Rossi, p. 1 v., calls Buontalenti an "archittetore eccellentissimo, e nell' opere dello'ngegno, e di matematica, e d'altro, da agguagliarsi agli antichi: e che con viuezza del suo intelletto, alquale niuna cosa impossibile e faticosa, ha potuto ritrouar cose, che, e da'naturali, e da'matematici si reputaua, che trascendessero le forze vmane, e dell'arte."
7. Ibid., p. 2 r.
8. Ibid.
9. Ibid., p. 2 v.: "nella magnifica ed eccellentissima fabrica, che in Firenze de' Magistrati s'appella." According to Filippo Baldinucci, *Notizie de' professori del disegno, 8* (Milan, 1811), 41, the theatre was situated "sopra gli Uffizi nuovi dalla parte di verso la Piazza del Grano"— i.e. on the second story of the east wing.
10. The measurements are given by Rossi, p. 2 v.

59

been made of metal. As the level of the floor declined, the height of the pyramids progressively increased toward the stage, the highest measuring five ells. On the apex of each pyramid stood an urn in which white wax tapers burned, brightening the auditorium without obstructing the view of the stage. The urns seemed—and here everything was semblance—to be made of serpentine stone. Staircases leading to the gradi were situated between the pyramids. Above the degrees rose a gallery, the balusters of which appeared to have been chiseled from the finest marble. Scattered throughout the hall between the balustrade supports were ten fountains which also seemed to have been made of marble. Above each gold-ornamented fountain was the statue of a boy, again of imitation marble or metal. A trellis of myrtle blossoms stretched over the gallery, and above it were luxuriant leafy plants laden with fruit; hares and deer peered through the foliage. There were birds perched on the plants, some of them poised for flight, others having just paused to sing, and several birds whirring aloft. The trellis was divided into squares, with each division marked by columns atop which gilded fruit baskets had been placed. These baskets, apart from their aesthetic value, also functioned as receptacles to catch the wax that dripped from the chandeliers, lest it fall on the ladies seated below. The baskets also contained a surprise: as the princely persons took their places, live birds were released from them. As finishing touches to the décor, festoons of foliage and fruit were suspended across the middle of the auditorium from window to window, and statues of the gods were placed before the shutters, as if the pagan deities had come in by the windows out of curiosity, in order not to miss the Medici spectacle.[11] The ceiling of the auditorium was decorated with rosettes and heraldic emblems. From each rosette hung a chandelier formed by six Harpies, each of which carried a torch. Altogether there were ninety-six Harpies holding two hundred and eighty-eight torches. At each of the two terminating points of the gradi stood a painted figure six ells high—the river god Po on one side, the Arno on the other. The guests entered the hall through an archway above which two charming putti supported an armorial shield.

An ornamental frieze, on which naked children gamboled amidst festoons, concealed the mechanism of the curtain, which was of red velvet and evidently divided into two parts. When the Grand Duke gave the sign for the festival to begin, the curtain was lowered. Rossi uses the word "cadere" but adds that each curtain half, as it dropped, changed into a side border, framing the stage laterally.[12] Next to

11. The conceit originated with Rossi.

12. Rossi mentions "curtains" in the plural, p. 4 v.: "le cortine, che copriuan la Scena, è parue, che si conuertissero in due ricchissimi, e gran panni di velluto rosso, con bellissimi, e gran napponi d'oro, e di seta, che eran dall' vna, e dall' altra banda."

each drape stood a figure of simulated marble: on one side the personification of the art of architecture, and on the other, that of the art of perspective, with the motto: "Deception through shadow—but I too reveal the truth" ("Con ombra inganno, anzi dimostro il vero").

The stage was elevated five ells above the floor of the hall.[13] A staircase and three fountains were painted on the front wall concealing the trap room. So convincing was the effect that after the performance, the spectators were tempted to climb these steps onto the stage. Two wild lions crouched before the staircase, guarding the approaches.

Florentine Veduta

The first setting showed Florence, the locale of Bardi's comedy. In plain view were the cupola of Santa Maria del Fiore, the *Campanile,* the Uffizi, the Palazzo Vecchio with its singular tower, the Loggia de' Pisani, the Church of Santa Maria Novella, and the Arcade of San Paolo. The buildings were so perfectly imitated that one could have mistaken them for reality. Rossi extolled the scale and peculiar lighting the architect had given to his structures.[14] Everything harmonized to complete the visual deception and give the stage picture a depth ("sfondato, lontananza") hitherto unattained. Here and there people moved across the stage, some on foot, others on horseback, still others in coaches, "tutte finte," although giving an impression of absolute reality. Moreover, the stage sky ("il Cielo della Prospettiua") had the color of the dawn, reminding Rossi of Boccaccio, for whom the colors of the sunrise ranged from scarlet to orange. Finally, perfumed smoke arose from Buontalenti's chimneys and wafted out into the auditorium, while concealed musicians played a gentle symphony to introduce the first intermezzo.

Count Bardi had originally intended to tell a coherent story in the six interludes, but he dropped this idea for the sake of offering his audience greater variety. Nevertheless, his six entr'actes were unified by a single theme: each of the intermezzi was related to the wedding of Cesare and Virginia. In the first interlude Jupiter sent down the Greatest Blessings upon the earth for the occasion of the nuptials; in the second, Evil was banished; in the third, Flora inaugurated Eternal Spring; in the fourth, Neptune appeared with his sea creatures to pay homage to the newlyweds; in the fifth, Juno contributed her felicitations; and in the final intermezzo the Tuscan shepherds joined in the general rejoicing.

13. Ibid., p. 18 r.: "cinque, che tanto, e non più, aueua la scena alto il palco."
14. Rossi mentions, p. 5 r., that Buontalenti was the first to find a method for illuminating it: "il nostro Architettore è stato il primiero, che abbia trouato il modo d'illuminarlo."

FIRST INTERMEZZO: THE RETURN OF THE GOLDEN AGE

After the décor of Florence was disclosed, the heavens above the city were opened by the Horae, and a large cloud supporting Hymen and the Greatest Blessings (Beni) appeared in the center. Jupiter, surrounded by all the gods, was seated on another cloud. The assembled gods were arrayed in perspective foreshortening ("in iscorcio"), so that the heavens appeared to have a depth extending into the eighth sphere. In a madrigal Mercury gave the Beni his mandate to go down to earth and there, on the occasion of the princely nuptials, inaugurate the Golden Age. Mercury's solo was accompanied by viols, lutes, gravicembali, and an *organo di legno*. As the cloud carrying the Beni descended, its occupants sang a madrigal. Having touched down upon the stage, the Beni alighted and the cloud disappeared, as though blown away by the wind, where no one could tell.[15] The Florentines had never seen anything like it. (On earlier occasions—in 1565 and 1569— the spectators had been able to watch the empty cloud return to its point of departure,[16] and the suspending apparatus, or "appiccagnolo"—literally, a hook— had been visible to all.) Once the cloud had vanished, the Beni made their exit "per diuerse strade per la Città," and the *prologus* came forth, giving the signal for Bardi's comedy to begin.

Bastiano de' Rossi gives us a detailed description of the costumes worn by the gods (Jupiter, Saturn, Apollo, Mars, Mercury, Venus, Cupid, Pallas, Diana, and Hymen) and the Beni (Virtue, Honor, Faith, Beauty, Youth, Pleasure, Happiness, Health, Peace, and Success). Without going into detail, it should be noted that they were fashioned chiefly out of satin, the finest sendal, and gold fabrics, and that an effect of veils gave each one its special quality. Pearls, precious stones, and cameos were used in abundance. While it was only natural that gems embellished the crown of Jupiter, even the crest that towered above the war god's helmet was bejeweled; Saturn's tawny satin cap was not merely edged in fur but was ornamented with gold and precious stones; and jewels adorned Apollo's gilded quiver and his veil-covered boots. The goddesses displayed their breasts, insofar as this could be reconciled with their mythological reputations. Cupid and Pleasure were portrayed by handsome boys feigning nudity in leather skin coverings. Buontalenti's taste was for sharply contrasting colors: Apollo, in a gold face mask, wore a doub-

15. Ibid., p. 7 r.: "e parue che'l vento l'auesse fatta sparire: perciocchè non si vide andare, ne ritornare in luogo veruno."

16. Ibid., p. 7 r.: "Perciocchè in quella [nugola], che, nelle nozze della Serenissima Giouanna d'Austria Granduchessa di Toscana, di felicissima ricordanza, fu opera di questo Artefice rappresentata, e in quella, che per opera di Baldassare Lanci, nell'onoranza dell'Arciduca Carlo fu fatta, si videro suso ritornar vote."

let of flesh-colored satin, with sleeves of cloth of gold and green silk, a surcoat of iridescent turquoise and yellow sendal, a cloak of bright blue satin, and silver satin trousers, the whole accented with veils.

SECOND INTERMEZZO: THE DAMNATION OF EVIL

After the first act of Bardi's comedy began the second intermezzo, which led into the realm of the Stygian Jupiter. As if by magic ("quasi miracolosamente"), boulders appeared on the stage, and with them, the monstrous figures of the Evils. These Mali sat in a semicircle on the rocks, where they expressed their torment through gestures: Ingratitude, Deceit, Envy, Discord, Ire, Hunger, Pestilence, War, Furor, Terror—all were despondent, since in view of the Florentine nuptials they had been banished from the earth and condemned to dwell in Hades. Suddenly the floor of the stage opened ("in vno stante fu veduta la terra aprirsi"); a horrible cavern gaped wide, and as the boulders vanished behind it, the city of Dis emerged in a fiery glow, amidst flames and billows of smoke, dismal mires, and muddy streams. The Furies howled shrilly on the battlements of the burning towers, brandishing tangled serpents. What the spectators beheld was the scene Dante described in the ninth Canto of his *Inferno*. Two misshapen devils then appeared, leading a host of twenty others, all wearing ghastly masks. Their hair was green-black, and their leather costumes gave the impression of nudity. Holding smoking torches, they gave the scene a spectral glow. A bark plowed through the lead-colored sludge, ferried by Phlegyas, whom Bardi's audience recalled from Dante's eighth Canto. A horrible old man with a scraggly beard, naked and covered with flames, he sang a song once he had brought the boat to a standstill. Trombones and bass viols lent a suitable accompaniment. He then readied his bark to receive the Mali. While he rattled his chains, the Evils sang a madrigal of lamentation. Phlegyas had difficulty steering his craft. As soon as he dipped his flaming rudder into the Stygian flood, smoke billowed up, and the current soon bore him off in all directions. Buontalenti, who could have made things much easier for himself, had evidently spared no pains. At length the boat was moored fast, and the Mali were forced to embark. The Evils howled furiously as Phlegyas cast off. The devils hurtled after them; the city of Dis was swallowed up, and the cavern closed. Thus ended the second intermezzo.

Rossi's description of the costumes reveals a knowledge of this field which presumably was not shared by the audience. Whereas he had evidently scrutinized each individual costume at his leisure before the performance, the spectators could hardly have been expected to grasp the symbolic significance of all the Mali. To be sure, the allegory of Discord presented no difficulties. Buontalenti had given her all the features that might have been anticipated: one part of her coiffure was gold, the other silver; one part smooth, the other rumpled. The colors of her satin costume were as variegated as possible: red, yellow, chestnut, silver, dark blue, and pink. She held judicial briefs under one arm, and books and manuscripts in her hand. Those versed in iconology could have taken the figure wearing the head of a hippopotamus for the allegory of ingratitude, just as they had related the rhinoceros headpiece to Ire. But it was more difficult to distinguish Furore from Terrore, even though the latter wore a lion's head and the former only a confused mass of hair. Deceit, represented by a striking blonde in a robe of violet satin, expressed her true nature simply by a scorpion's tail. Envy, Hunger, and Pestilence were more or less aged hags with sagging breasts.

THIRD INTERMEZZO: THE INAUGURATION OF ETERNAL SPRING

At the beginning there appeared a landscape with mountains, fields, and all kinds of trees, but everything was dry and barren and bare of foliage. Some of the trees were withered, others broken by storms. Then Zephyrus emerged from a cave in the west with his bride, Flora. Slowly they proceeded to the middle of the stage, where Flora sang a solo by Malvezzi, accompanied by a lute and a harp. In a short reply Zephyrus heralded the approach of Spring.

And Primavera was on her way with her retinue of two amoretti, three light breezes (*Aurette*), two nymphs, two satyrs, and the demigods Pan and Priapus. The votaries of Spring began to dance as the trees slowly sprouted leaves *à vista*. Everything turned green, and the rivers and lakes were filled with water. Nightingales started to sing, and other birds joined them to the accompaniment of lutes, harps, muted cornets, trombones, and dolcians. Supported by the chorus of nymphs and satyrs, Primavera sang her madrigal, in which she related the coming of spring to Cesare and Virginia, leaving the last word to the singing and cavorting nymphs. Then the primaveral throng and the landscape disappeared, to the astonishment of the spectators, who were at a loss to explain the rapid technique that had produced the transformation.[17] And once again the décor of Florence was revealed for the third act of *Amico fido*.

The costumes of Flora, Primavera and the two nymphs were richly decorated with floral motifs. Pearls, precious stones, and spangles glittered in their blond hair, about which fluttered veils. The beauty of their breasts was generously displayed. Pan had a long beard and the ears and horns of a billy goat. He wore black

17. Ibid., p. 16 r.: "ne si vide in che maniere . . . la gran macchina del giardino si potessero, senza veder come, leuarsi con tanta prestezza dauanti agli occhi de' marauigliati ragguardatori."

leather tights, a cloak of hide, and his feet were splayed like those of a goat. In his left hand he held a gnarled stick, in his right a shepherd's flute.

FOURTH INTERMEZZO: TRIUMPH OF THE SEA GODS

Here the audience was transported from the Florence of the third act to a sea-coast. At the outermost edge of the stage ("nell' estremità del palco") rose, "subi-tamente," impassable reefs, between which trickled real springs framed by shells, corals, and marsh plants. Thetis emerged between the rocks, while Tritons and other creatures of the sea formed a round. All of them were dripping as they came to the surface, and the monsters sprayed perfumed water from their conches. As Thetis' entourage encamped on the reefs, the goddess invoked Neptune in her solo. The entire stage was now inundated by the most natural-looking waves ("Tutta la scena era circondata dall' onde, le quali agitantesi si mostrauan natu-ralissime"). New sea monsters with wild eyes, scaly ears, and puffed cheeks emerged, agitating the sea, so that ships in the distance seemed to dance on the billows. Neptune angrily ascended, shaking his head and his trident. Accompanied by lutes, harps, trombones, and transverse flutes, he sang a madrigal in which he commanded that calm be restored to the sea. The twelve sea-nymphs on the chariot of the god transmitted his order to the monsters, who promptly submerged, causing the sea to be serene once again.

The Naiads then alighted from Neptune's car onto the land in two groups. During their responsive singing the reefs vanished, and in their place a flowering meadow appeared, where the nymphs gathered flowers. This gave the spectators time to admire Neptune's chariot, a *carro* ten ells high and just as wide, and to be astonished at seeing so tall a structure rise from the trap room, which itself was only five ells high.[18] The machine had the shape of a shell, on top of which stood Neptune, and below him, on steps, the Naiads. Dark sapphire was the color of the shell, its gilded frame ornamented with corals, snails, and pearls. Buontalenti had also mounted four paintings, but the spectators were too far removed to admire the details. Rossi describes them for us: On one of the panels Amymone was being molested by a satyr, and Poseidon appeared as her savior. Another spun the tale of Amphitrite's flight to Atlas, and a third her return to Poseidon. Finally there was portrayed the inundation of the city of Thebes.

18. Ibid., p. 18 r.: "si mostrò il carro marauiglioso agli occhi de' riguardanti, primieramente per la bellezza, e poscia per la grandezza, perciocchè la sua altezza era dieci braccia in quella di cinque, che tanto, e non più, aueua la scena alto il palco, si nascose, con grandissima marauiglia di chi lo vide."

No doubt the onlookers were far more vividly impressed by the four horses that pulled the Sea God's chariot. These artificial quadrupeds were entirely capable of functioning just as their live counterparts: they whinnied, chewed foam-covered bridle bits, and plowed the waves with their forelegs. Even the wheels of the car made the expected movements until Neptune reined the horses and brought them to a halt. After some of the nymphs had plucked flowers and others caught gleaming, wriggling fish, they returned to the car, which now began to sink. Rossi praised the designer because the vehicle sank into the waves without rumbling or rattling ("non si sentì strepito ne cigolamento"), noises which were invariably produced on such occasions ("come in sì fatte cose suole auuenire"). As soon as the nymphs had climbed in, the meadow once more transformed itself into the reefs of before, with Thetis and her sea gods swimming about and splashing each other in the water.

Thetis had dark blue hair adorned with pearls and corals. On the tip of her *ninfale* she wore a silver shell in which two coral branches were planted. Several blue veils cascaded from the shell down to her shoulders, yet leaving room for a garland of reeds. Her costume was fashioned of thin, bright blue taffeta trimmed in gold and decorated with emblems of the sea. An ornamental ribbon circled her bare breasts, over which veils were draped. She was nude down to her waist. Her foot covering was colored blue and gold, relieved by blue veils and sea ornaments. The twelve Naiads differed from Thetis in the greater modesty of their costumes. The Tritons, both male and female, had blue tails with silver scales, and evidently wore masks.

FIFTH INTERMEZZO: JUNO AND HER NYMPHS

At the end of the fourth act of the comedy, the sky grew dark over Florence. Flashes of lightning stabbed from the clouds. Subsequently, a bright cloud appeared, carrying a car drawn by two peacocks. In it sat Juno, Iris, and fourteen nymphs, one of whom represented the siren of the day, and the other that of the night; the heads of the remaining twelve nymphs were adorned with the signs of the zodiac. While the peacocks spread their tails, Juno sat on her elevated seat, the nymphs below her on steps. The chariot was gilded, and the spokes of the wheels glinted like sunbeams as they turned. Bolts of lightning streaked like incandescent arrows through the rain and hail. At last the storm subsided, and a most convincing rainbow formed about Juno's cloud. To the accompaniment of lutes, harps, and gravicembali, the goddess invited her nymphs to brighten the heavens in view of the wedding in the house of the Medici. And as they sang, the skies cleared. By a veritable feat of Buontalenti's stage magic, the cloud with Juno and her nymphs disappeared. It seemed to vanish into the depths of the stage and was finally supplanted by a smaller cloud seemingly occupied by the same figures that had inhabited the large one.

Throughout, Juno and Iris wore basically the traditional nymph costume, although the former had a crown on top of her ninfale. The twelve nymphs were divided into four seasonal groups, and were dressed accordingly: the zodiac group of spring wore floral decorations, the summer group golden ears of corn, the autumnal trio fruit, and the hibernal nymphs snowflakes.

SIXTH INTERMEZZO: A PASTORAL AFTERPIECE

Now the stage transformed itself into a flowered meadow with sylvan glades. A magnificent palace stood next to a grotto surrounded by caverns which had collapsed. Pines, cypresses, oaks, and chestnut trees seemed to touch the heavens with the tops of their branches. Artificial animals prowled between the trees, provoking wonder and delight in the spectators. Then appeared two groups of Tuscan shepherds and shepherdesses, nineteen in each band, singing a *ballata*. Lutes, harps, dolcians, shawms, bass, soprano, and tenor viols, flutes, transverse flutes, straight and coiled cornets, rebecs, and large flutes provided the musical accompaniment composed by Bardi. During the choral piece the Maga of Fiesole had come out of the palace, as if attracted by the as yet unheard melody. She finally contributed a madrigal of her own, alluding to the princely nuptials. The performance ended with singing and dancing by the pastoral couples. Four shepherds, the *Pastori Eroi*, and four shepherdesses were fantastically attired, while the others wore simpler costumes. But even with costumes that approximated Tuscan native dress, ample use was found for satin, taffeta, and pearl and gold ornamentation.

No drawings or engravings of the interludes of 1586 have been discovered. Aby Warburg[19] has attempted to relate a pen-and-ink drawing (Figure 41) signed by Buontalenti to the first intermezzo. The design shows Jupiter enthroned on a cloud, with eighteen deities scattered on four other clouds. Standing on the stage with Apollo (?) and Pallas (?) are the Muses. Stage center is a large eagle between whose wings five putti are visible. Since neither the Muses nor the eagle appeared in the first intermezzo, Warburg assumed that Buontalenti's drawing referred to an original conception for the first intermezzo, an idea Bardi had discarded when he let his Jupiter send the Beni down to earth in place of the Muses.

In conclusion, a few remarks should be made concerning the technical problems that Buontalenti had to solve. His stage was twenty ells deep and thirty-five

19. "I Costumi teatrali per gli intermezzi del 1589," *Gesammelte Schriften, 1* (Berlin, 1932), 425.

ells wide. The dimensions of the proscenium opening cannot be determined. The height of the trap room, however, has been verified: five ells. As the putto-frieze was at least two ells high in a hall which measured twenty-four ells from floor to ceiling, we may assume that the height of the proscenium opening was approximately seventeen ells. The side scenes diminished in size progressively toward the background, whereby Buontalenti gained gridiron space for his machinery, winches, drums, and counterweights, all of which permitted clouds to appear in the first and fifth intermezzi. In the trap room were located the windlass, notched bar, and vertical groove by means of which Neptune's chariot was elevated, perhaps by that process for heaving aloft a mountain which was described by Nicola Sabbattini (*Pratica,* Bk. II, Chap. 24). For the inferno of the second intermezzo the great trap was probably operated in the way Sabbattini recommended for hell scenes (Bk. II, Chap. 23). It is no longer possible to determine which method Buontalenti utilized for his seascape. Sabbattini described (Bk. II, Chaps. 27–29) three methods, the first of which could not have been applied here, since people had to rise up between the waves. Be that as it may, the upper two-thirds of the stage toward the backdrop, what Furttenbach called the *hintere Graben,* were allotted to the "water surface," while the remaining third along the front edge of the stage was occupied first by reefs, then by a flowering meadow, and again by reefs. Buontalenti's stage magic of 1586 could be technically mastered with the help of such machinery as Sabbattini later described. This does not necessarily suggest that Buontalenti only applied solutions such as we find described in Sabbattini's treatise. An artist of Buontalenti's stature might well have hit upon a number of inventions of which that staunch practitioner Sabbattini, who in 1638 was still unaware of flat wings, had no inkling.

We are entirely dependent on conjecture in seeking to establish which method Buontalenti did employ for his *à-vista* scene changes. Rossi does not even give us a hint and merely stresses the rapidity with which the changes were accomplished. Serious consideration should be given to the possibility that Buontalenti was already working with wings (in the sense of flat frames) and had achieved his *à-vista* transformations in this manner. A complete change of scene, with altered sides and backdrops, took place in the second, third, fourth, and sixth intermezzi. The first and fifth interludes took place in the main Florentine setting, which was partly concealed by clouds. Supplementary scenic transformations occurred during the second, third, and fourth entr'actes: in the second, the city of Dis emerged from the initially rocky landscape; in the third, the barren garden scene changed into a spring landscape; in the fourth, reefs first appeared in the foreground, then a flowered meadow, and finally the reefs again, each time with the sea as a background.

The Grand Duke no doubt breathed more easily once the performance was over. None of the invited guests surmised that Francesco I had been in a state of trepidation when he gave the signal for the spectacle to begin. They were not aware that he nurtured the suspicion, based on a prophesy, that the hall would cave in during the performance. While his guests were gathering, he had searched the quarters of the city officials downstairs for concealed explosives, and not only the rooms but the cabinets and bookcases as well. Having convinced himself that all was in order, he locked the rooms, posted sentries in front of the doors, and returned to the auditorium.[20]

20. We learn these details from Settimani's manuscript diary, quoted by Corazzini in his edition of Lapini's *Diario,* p. 250, n. 1.

6. Intermezzi for *La Pellegrina*

1589

Political considerations prompted Grand Duke Ferdinando I to seek his bride in France. He hoped thereby to strengthen his position, even though he was binding himself to a country debilitated by internal crises. His choice fell on Christine of Lorraine, the favorite granddaughter of Catherine de' Medici. The wedding by proxy took place in Blois. On the twenty-third of April, the flotilla bringing the new Grand Duchess from Marseilles to Tuscany landed in the harbor of Livorno. The journey continued via Pisa to Poggio a Caiano, where Ferdinando for the first time saw the young bride who was to make him a fine wife. Christine, adaptable and vivacious, knew how to win the hearts of the Florentines. The dazzling nuptials,[1] which enraptured the city for three weeks, were an auspicious beginning.

---

1. Primary sources: [Bastiano de' Rossi] Descrizione / dell' Apparato, / e degl' Inter- / medi. / Fatti per la Commedia rappre- / sentata in Firenze. / Nelle nozze de' Serenissimi Don Ferdinando / Medici, e Madama Cristina di / Loreno, Gran Duchi di / Toscana. / In Firenze. Per Anton Padovani M.D. LXXXIX.

Diario / descritto / da Giuseppe / Pavoni / Delle feste celebrate nelle solennissime Nozze delli Serenissimi Sposi, il Sig. Don Ferdinando Medici, & la Sig. Donna Christina di Loreno Gran Duchi di Toscana. / Nel quale con breuità si esplica il Torneo, la Battaglia nauale, la Comedia con gli Intermedÿ, & altre feste occorse di giorno in giorno per tutto il dì 15. di Maggio. MDLXXXIX. Alli molto illustri, & miei Patroni osservandiss. li Signori Giasone, & Pompeo fratelli de' Vizani. / Stampato in Bologna nella Stamperia di Giovanni Rossi, di permissione delli Signori Superiori. 1589.

Raccolta di tutte / le solennissime Feste / nel Sponsalitio / della Serenissima / Gran Duchessa / di Toscana / fatte in Fiorenza il mese di Maggio 1589. / Con brevità raccolte da Simone Caval-

CALENDAR OF EVENTS

April 30: Christine's processional entry into the festively decorated city, followed by a banquet in the evening.

May 1: Accompanied by a band, young peasants from Pretola carried a Maypole festooned with Whitsuntide greenery into the city in homage to the newly married couple. The highlight of the day's entertainment was a musical soirée preceded by a ball.

May 2: Performance of Girolamo Bargagli's comedy *La Pellegrina,* by the Intronati, an acting ensemble of "giovanni nobili" from Siena. The production took place in the Uffizi Theatre.

May 3: Day of the Finding of the Holy Cross. The Grand Duke and his bride received communion. Toward evening, Christine drove in a carriage to the Church of the Santissima Annunziata, where the miraculous fresco of the Virgin was unveiled. There was also an instrumental concert.

May 4: The traditional *calcio* game in the Piazza Santa Croce with a hundred participants in the match, of whom fifty, the party preferred by the Grand Duke, entered wearing flesh-colored satin, while the other team, favorites of the Grand Duchess, appeared in light blue. The flesh-colored players gallantly lost the game.

---

lino da Viterbo. / All' Illustriss. et Reverendiss. sig. Patriarca Alessandrino, Caetano. / In Roma / Appresso Paolo Blado Stampatore Camerale 1589.

[Anon.] Li / sontuosissimi / apparecchi, / trionfi, e feste, / fatti nelle nozze / della Gran Duchessa / di Fiorenza: / Con il nome, & numero de Duchi, Prencipi, Marchesi, Baroni, & altri gran Personaggi: postovi il modo del vestire, maniere, & livree. / Et la descrittione de gl' Intermedi rappresentati in una Comedia nobilissima, recitata da gl'Intronati Senesi. / Aggiontovi l'ordine, & modo che s'è tenuto nel Coronare l'Altezza della Serenissima Gran Duchessa. / Stampata in Fiorenza, & in Ferrara per Vittorio Baldini. / Et ristampata in Venetia per Lodovico Larduccio. 1589.

A German observer at the performance of *La Pellegrina* was one Barthold von Gadenstedt (1560–1631), who traveled through Italy in the years 1587–89, and whose manuscript journal has been preserved in the Herzog August Bibliothek in Wolfenbüttel (Cod. Guelf. 67.6 Extrav. fol.).

Warburg, in *Gesammelte Schriften, 1,* 259–300, with addenda by the editor, Gertrud Bing, on pp. 394–422, and with excerpts from the *Memorie e ricordi* of Girolamo Ser Jacopi (in the Archivio di Stato in Florence).

Angelo Solerti, *Gli Albori del melodramma,* 2 (Milan-Palermo-Napoli, 1904–05), 17–18: excerpts from Settimani's *Diario* (in the Archivio di Stato in Florence).

Emil Vogel, *Bibliothek der gedruckten weltlichen Vokalmusik Italiens 1500–1700, 1* (Berlin, 1892), 382–85, with references to the musicians who collaborated in the "stampa musicale" edited by Cristofano Malvezzi: Canto / Intermedii / et Concerti, / Fatti per la Commedia rappresentata in / Firenze / Nelle Nozze del Serenissimo / Don Ferdinando Medici, / e Madama Christina di Loreno, Gran Duchi di Toscana. / in Venetia, / Appresso Giacomo Vincenti. / M.D. XCI.

May 5: Good Friday, hence a pause in the festivities.

May 6: Performance of the improvised comedy, *La Zingara,* by the Gelosi troupe in the Uffizi Theatre.

May 7: A Sunday. High Mass in San Lorenzo. In the evening a thirty-two course banquet in the Salone dei Cinquecento. Instrumental music was played throughout the evening.

May 8: Animal baiting in the Piazza Santa Croce. Lions, buffaloes, bulls, bears, tigers, and foxes were put into action. A terrified mule diverted the spectators until it was torn to pieces by lions. There was even a small "satyr play," a battle between cats and rats, in which the latter emerged victorious. The galleries were amused.

May 9: The relics of St. Antoninus, the first Archbishop of Florence, transferred in a procession from one chapel in San Marco to another, along a route that covered half the city.

May 10: The tilt at the quintain in the Piazza Santa Croce.

May 11: Nocturnal jousting at barriers and naumachy in the courtyard of the Pitti Palace.

May 12: A Friday.

May 13: Performance of *La Pazzia* by the Comici Gelosi in the Uffizi Theatre.

May 15: According to Settimani's *Diario,* the performance of a comedy in the Salone de' Magistrati—that is, in the Uffizi Theatre—so that the Venetian envoys and others who had come late could have an opportunity to see the play.[2] It cannot be determined from this entry which of the comedies was repeated, although presumably it was *La Pellegrina.*

The principal theatrical event of this "Maggio Fiorentino" was the performance of Girolamo Bargagli's comedy *La Pellegrina,* or more accurately, the attendant six intermezzi. As in 1586, Count Giovanni Bardi was commissioned to invent the ideas for the interludes. Warburg's investigations[3] furnish proof that on this occasion the Count succeeded in working out a coherent plan for the content of the six intermezzi, with the influence of music in the lives of gods and men providing continuity of theme. Emilio de' Cavalieri was entrusted with organizing the spectacle. Execution of the set designs once again lay in the hands of Bernardo Buontalenti.

2. Settimani is occasionally confused. Thus he erroneously locates the performance of *La Zingara* in the "gran Salone del Palazzo Vecchio." He gives the "Regio Salon grande di Palazzo" as the locale of the performance of *La Pellegrina,* but he indicates dimensions appropriate to the Uffizi Theatre. The Settimani passages were reprinted by Solerti, *Albori, 2,* 18.

3. Warburg, in *Gesammelte Schriften 1,* 425.

The performance took place in the Uffizi Theatre.[4] The seating arrangement was the same as three years before, and the auditorium was again surrounded by degrees ("tutta circondata di gradi"), except, of course, for the side along the stage. Situated in the middle of the hall was the dais for princely personages. The décor of the auditorium, however, differed from that of 1586. Lorenzo Francini and Francesco Rosselli contributed new paintings. Ideas for the new statues, in which the various arts of poetry were given concrete form, were conceived by Giovambattista Strozzi.[5] And when all of the torches in the hall seemed to light up by themselves,[6] the spectators were apparently stunned.

An oval staircase four ells high led up to the raked stage, which, at its highest point in the rear was elevated five ells above the auditorium floor. This time the stage had a depth of twenty-five ells, making it five ells deeper than in 1586. The breadth of the stage could not have exceeded thirty-five ells. A balustrade ran along its edge, with lamps built into the balusters[7] to illuminate the stage floor— in other words, footlights. The stage was closed off on each side by a gigantic statue of a river god: on one side, the Arno with the winged heraldic lion and the lily; on the other, the Moselle, which irrigated the homeland of the new Grand Duchess. The latter was surrounded by herons, and a heron motif embellished the sixteen chandeliers (each with eighteen tapers) in the hall.

Before the performance began, the stage was draped across by a red house curtain.[8] Once this hanging had dropped,[9] the spectators viewed a painted prospect which contained the Corinthian architectural elements and gold tones of the auditorium, thus creating an "anfiteatro perfetto." Shortly afterward the second curtain likewise descended, exposing the first décor. We learn from Rossi's description that the audience was presented with a *veduta* of Rome, and that Buontalenti, thanks to the skill of his perspective scene painting, was able to set the stage with the most imposing structures of the ancient and modern city.[10] It is notable that neither Giuseppe Pavoni nor the anonymous chronicler mention the Roman per-

4. The following account is based on Rossi, *Descrizione dell' apparato.*
5. Ibid., pp. 8, 11–14.
6. Ibid., p. 15. Baldinucci, *Notizie, 8,* 53, states in his chapter on Buontalenti that these torches seemed to ignite themselves, and that no trace of "fuoco lavorato" was in evidence, causing no little astonishment among the spectators.
7. Rossi, *Apparato,* p. 35: "ogni balustro nascondea un lume."
8. Ibid., p. 16: "paramento incarnato"; Pavoni, p. 14: "tela rossa."
9. Pavoni, pp. 14–15: "mandate giù."
10. Rossi, *Apparato,* p. 17: "aueua l'Artefice con l'eccellenza dell'arte saputo adombrare il uero, e con lo sfondato allontanarne dagli occhi i più nobili e più superbi edifici antichi e moderni della sourana città."

spective but refer instead to a "blue curtain"[11] which provided the backdrop for the lowering of a cloud machine.

FIRST INTERMEZZO: HARMONY OF THE SPHERES

The prelude to the first intermezzo evidently made use of the Roman background. In a downstage position stood a Doric temple built of ashlars. A cloud descended from the heavens, and on it sat the Doric Mode (Armonia Doria), accompanying her madrigal on a lute. On a lower level she was flanked on each side by three women who appeared to be attentive to her song. These were the six other Modes, the Phrygian, Lydian, Mixolydian, Hypodorian, Hypophrygian, and Hypolydian. The "Harmonies" were painted with the utmost verisimilitude.[12] Several sunbeams burst forth from behind the cloud, which was so altogether "convincing" that the spectators were at a loss to say how it moved as it gradually floated to the earth, headed toward the temple, and then vanished into it, along with Armonia Doria. Immediately afterward, the temple also disappeared, perhaps into a trap, and the scene changed ("sparì la scena di Roma") for the second part of the first intermezzo.

After a "cambio di case" the starry heavens appeared, with four clouds rising up. So realistic were these imitations that one might have expected rain at any moment. Sitting on the low-hovering clouds were the eight Platonic sirens, plus two others who belonged to the ninth and tenth spheres.[13] Following their madrigal, the heavens parted in three places, and three clouds issued from these openings. On the central cloud sat Necessity on her throne, holding the spindle of the cosmos between her knees. She was encircled by the three Parcae. Seated on the other two clouds were the seven Planets (Luna, Venus, Mars, Saturn, Mercury, Jupiter, and Sol) and Astraea. The celestial background glowed brilliantly through the three apertures, at least toward the zenith; in the lower regions its luminescence was dimmed by the colors of the rainbow. On high were twelve heroes divided into pairs to portray the six virtues: Justice was represented by Numa Pompilius and the Egyptian Queen Isis; Religion by Masinissa and a Vestal Virgin; Piety by Aeneas and a devout young girl, who was noted by Valerius Maximus; Conjugal Love by Tiberius Gracchus and Portia; Magnanimity by Hieron, King of Syracuse, and by Busa, the Apulian woman who fed the Roman soldiers who had fled to

11. Pavoni, p. 15: "tela azurra." Barthold von Gadenstedt also fails to mention the Roman décor in his journal (fol. 671), but he does refer to the "blaue seidene Decke."

12. Rossi, *Apparato,* pp. 18–19: "con tal rilievo dipinte, che elle parean uiue."

13. To Gadenstedt (fol. 672) these were all simple *"Engell."*

Canusium after the battle of Cannae; Valor by Lucius Siccius Dentatus and Camilla.

The cloud-borne sirens ascended to the heavens, singing a musical exchange with the Planets. As the clouds rose from the lower part of the stage, sunlight streamed in, while in the upper regions night was swiftly approaching. After a concluding madrigal sung by the sirens, the Planets, and the Parcae, the seven clouds dispersed, the heavens closed, the stars grew pale, sunlight flooded the sky, and, as if by magic, a view of the city of Pisa appeared upon the stage. How did this scenic change take place? Rossi declares[14] that the clouds of the first intermezzo had concealed the Pisa setting and then merely disappeared. Thus the perspective of Pisa would have been built up behind the cloud décor, which had concealed ("coprieno") the veduta until the scene was changed. Pavoni,[15] however, describes the process as follows: "Et in vn tratto si voltò la Scena, apparendo in prospettiua la Città di Pisa." According to the anonymous account: "subito si uolta la Prospettiua tutta e apparisce la Città di Pisa." The use of the verb *voltarsi* may point to the utilization of a turning mechanism. And the German word, *umwenden,* employed by Barthold von Gadenstedt, tends to confirm this view.

We can trace the idea of the first intermezzo, the musical harmony of the cosmos, to concepts that Plato expounded in the tenth book of his *Republic:* a diamond spindle turns between the knees of Necessity, and on each of its eight whorls stands a siren, giving forth a tone to harmonize with the tones of her sisters, thus creating the harmonious music of the spheres. The Moirai, daughters of Necessity, sit at their mother's feet, accompanying the harmony of the sirens with their song. Lachesis sings of the past, Clotho of the present, and Atropos of the future. Even the celestial heroes were prefigured by Plato, and the invigorating Doric mode was admitted as a prelude to the intermezzo, because in his Utopia Plato gave it preferred status.

Count Bardi put such high demands on his audience that, in fact, only classical philologists could have followed him. As Rossi's erudite commentary did not appear until after the performance, we should not be surprised that Pavoni took no cognizance of the Platonic cosmos, but saw merely "il Paradiso."[16] Nor did he even grasp the Armonia Doria, but saw only "vna donna" sitting on a cloud and singing, "molto soauemente," a madrigal that ended in adulation of the bridal couple. To be sure, Pavoni recognized the Planets and could identify the sirens as

14. *Apparato,* p. 35: "sparite uia le nugole, che la [prospettiua] coprieno."
15. P. 25.
16. P. 15.

well, probably because they were partly dressed as birds. Of Necessitas and the Parcae, however, he makes no mention. To the anonymous chronicler Armonia Doria was simply an "Idra," "quale canta sola eccellentissamente." Simone Cavallino da Viterbo noticed only "una donna da angiola vestita," and admired the singing of Vittoria Archilei.[17] As Warburg has pointed out,[18] not even the cultivated spectators could grasp the obtrusive symbolism of the costuming. But that would scarcely have perturbed Count Bardi, who may have shared the sentiments of Ben Jonson, as expressed, twenty years later, in his *Masque of Queens*: "A Writer should always trust somewhat to the capacity of the Spectator, especially at these Spectacles; Where Men, beside inquiring eyes, are vnderstood to bring quick eares, and not those sluggish ones of Porters, and Mechanicks, that must be bor'd through, at euery act, with Narrations."

As to the costuming, a few examples should suffice here. Bardi envisaged Armonia Doria as a woman of imposing majesty. Thus she wore a dress of dark green velvet with ornaments of solid gold. Her girdle was set with precious stones, and seven jewels adorned her golden crown. For the attributes and the costume of Necessitas, Buontalenti followed the description of Horace, in his Ode to Fortuna (C.1.35): bronze hands holding two stout nails, such as one might use to fasten beams together; wedges (the "cunei" of Horace) and strong but light fetters, similar to the catgut with which criminals were bound; hooks and molten lead painted on her throne; a robe of grey satin with silver embellishments and a cypress crown; between her knees, the diamond spindle. The Parcae were dressed in white and wore headbands, just as Plato had pictured them. In order to heighten the effect,[19] Buontalenti embroidered some additional details. Each of the planets had his particular "house" and was surrounded by an aureole which formed a kind of *mandorla*. Mars, for example, had his seat over a scorpion. His gilded armor, adorned with monsters, corresponded to Statius' description in the *Thebais*: a glowing helmet that seemed to be ablaze; a shield that appeared in a blood-red light. Painted on the seat was his chariot, drawn by the two horses, Fear and Terror, mentioned by Homer. Winged Fama stood on the prow of the car as described by Virgil in the fourth book of the Aeneid. Ptolemy, Claudian, and Ovid were cited as authorities for the planet Luna, as were Suda and Pausanias for Jupiter.

It was impossible to grasp the significance of the heroes in the Platonic heavens without commentary. How should the spectators have identified the nobleman

17. Cavallino, p. 3. Neither did Barthold von Gadenstedt identify the Doric Mode, but he was transported by the loveliness of her singing.
18. Warburg, in *Gesammelte Schriften, 1,* 281.
19. Rossi, *Apparato,* p. 25: "perchè facesser più bella vista."

armed in African fashion, who wore a crown-shaped helmet and a purple cape over his sky-blue robe? The key to this baffling figure lay in the two elephant tusks in his right hand and the statue of religion in his left: he was Masinissa, a portrayal of the religious man who restored the tusks which had been stolen by one of his captains to their rightful place because sacrilege was abominable to him. With Aeneas, on the other hand, the spectators should have had less difficulty, for he carried an old man on his shoulders, a small child on his arm, and in his free hand held a naked sword.

Pictorial documentation for the first intermezzo is fairly extensive. A pen-and-ink wash drawing (Figure 42), preserved in the Victoria and Albert Museum, conveys an overall impression of the setting in impressionistic form. James Laver[20] is of the opinion that this is an original sketch by Buontalenti. There exists also an engraving by Agostino Caracci (Figure 43) which, in contrast to the design, was executed with a strict central perspective. Necessitas and her spindle are identifiable both in the design and the engraving, while the remaining figures, the sirens, Planets, and heroes, are not recognizable as such. Details of the Planets' costumes, however, can be gleaned from two of Buontalenti's drawings in the Florentine National Library in which the attributes of the gods and Astraea are clearly intelligible (Figure 44). Other original sketches by Buontalenti for Necessitas and the Parcae (Figure 45), as well as for individual sirens, the Vestal Virgin of the heroes' heavens, and Armonia Doria (Figure 47), are also preserved in Florence. For the first intermezzo forty-five costumes in all were fitted, as indicated in the *Libro di conti*,[21] which has been examined by Warburg. This account book, in the Florentine municipal archives, contains a summary of the fabrics used, daily notations of the tailors' wages, and entries concerning the production of the plays. The two tailors, Oreto Belardi and Niccolò Serlosi, were responsible for sewing the costumes with the help of fifty assistants. The account book yields information only concerning those singers who participated in the first intermezzo.[22] With the exception of Armonia Doria, sung by Vittoria Archilei, all the roles were filled by male singers. The Planets, sirens, Parcae, heroes, and Necessitas were portrayed by members of the court chapel of the Grand Duke or by singers from Bernardo Franciosino's musical academy. A few independent artists also took part. Masks were prepared for all the participants. Moreover, in order to rid the singers of their masculine appearance, papier-mâché breasts and chests ("poppe e petti di

20. "Stage Designs for the Florentine Intermezzi of 1589," *Burlington Magazine, 60* (1932), 294–300.

21. Warburg, in *Gesammelte Schriften, 1,* 275–76.

22. Cf. the list in Warburg-Bing, in ibid., p. 398.

cartone") were fitted on them.[23] The sirens' costume (Figure 46) presented a special problem: as they were birdlike creatures, feathers were required, but real plumes would have been too costly. Therefore, the tailors were instructed to fashion them out of canvas and paint them accordingly.[24]

Gertrud Bing has disclosed one of the most important sources of the performance in her supplement to Warburg's essay. This contains excerpts from the *Memorie e ricordi* by Girolamo Ser Jacopi, the engineer-commandant of the fortifications, who was entrusted with supervising the technical production of the intermezzi. His notes permit us to take a look behind the wings. Ser Jacopi took Buontalenti's directives and noted the wishes of Emilio de' Cavalieri, functioning as an intermediary between the set designer and stage manager on the one hand, and the craftsmen and stage crew on the other. Buontalenti chose the technicians who were to operate the machines of the first intermezzo. According to Ser Jacopi's entries, some of the crew members were responsible for setting the cloud of Signora Vittoria in motion; others had to man the windlasses ("arghani") by means of which the clouds holding the sirens were lowered; a third detachment stood ready by the grooves in which the shutter was pushed to expose the central opening in the heavens.[25] Other workers were posted expressly for the purpose of lighting and watching over the oil lamps ("lucerne"); they were admonished to exercise the utmost care in trimming the wicks and refilling ("riempiere") the lamps. One of the artisans was commissioned to camouflage the ropes ("canapi") and beams ("travi") of the clouds with felt. One painter had to add another coat of paint to the spindle to give it a more diamond-like brilliance. Even the musical instruments were embellished with golden rays. In his notes Ser Jacopi never refers to the right or left sides of the stage but rather to "the side where the rooms of the *zanni* are located"—i.e. where the dressing rooms were, or to "the side toward the corridor."[26]

The lyrics of Armonia Doria's madrigal, written by Giovanni Bardi, were set to music by Emilio de' Cavalieri.[27] Vittoria accompanied herself on a *leuto grosso*, supported by two *chitarroni* played backstage by her husband and Antonio Naldi.[28] The texts of the subsequent madrigals were written by Ottavio Rinuccini, with music by Cristofano Malvezzi.[29]

23. Warburg, p. 431.
24. Ibid.
25. "Le guide della bucha del mezzo nelle aperture del cielo."
26. And where the musicians, also, played.
27. Rossi, *Apparato*, p. 19.
28. Vogel, *Bibliothek, 1*, 383.
29. For the instrumentation, cf. ibid., pp. 383–84.

The Setting for *La Pellegrina*

Pisa supplied the locale for Bargagli's comedy. The spectators saw the cathedral with its leaning tower, the Church of San Giovanni, the noble edifice of the Campo Santo, the palace of the Knights of the Holy Order of St. Stephan and its church, and many other structures designating the quarter known as Lungarno, all of them "maestreuolmente contrafatte."[30] Concealed illumination ("nascosi lumi") intensified the effect of perspective depth ("la lontanezza che procedeua dallo sfondato"). Everything was calculated to gently deceive ("dolce inganno") the spectators' senses. Buontalenti achieved this through a combination of curved and straight lines ("linee rette"): into the rectangular open space issued curved lanes ("le strade di linea curva"). Rossi assures us that Buontalenti was the first set designer to build a décor using a combination of straight lines and curves. He mentions further "tre fori," which enable us to posit the existence of a back scene constructed in the form of a tripartite screen. The downstage houses ("le prime case") were twenty ells high. Further upstage the height of the houses was scaled down as demanded by the vanishing point ("suo punto"). The style of architecture was Tuscan, mixed with Doric, Ionic, and Corinthian, or an amalgam of these elements.

During each intermezzo this "great machine" ("così gran macchina") was transformed *à vista*. In this way, the architect displayed seven settings ("prospettiue") with rapidity and ease and without the slightest incident, so that the spectators had the feeling that it was all taking place as in a dream (Rossi). In addition to the lightning-swift ("come baleno") transformations, there was the astonishing effect of the flying machines which rose out of the earth and into the heavens, thence to descend earthward again, frequently after soaring over the stage in all directions. These maneuvers were all the more astounding in that the clouds were always loaded with performers. Buontalenti took every precaution to place the costumes designed by him in their proper light. Each flying machine contained an abundance of lamps. The lateral décor pieces for the intermezzi were illuminated by lamps mounted on the back walls of the houses in the Pisa setting ("appiccati alle case"); these light sources were movable ("mobili") and could be rotated ("uoltando"). When permanently attached to the main setting, such lamps are hardly compatible with the use of periaktoi, whereas they could be reconciled with an embryonic flat-wing system. We would thus find a fixed Pisa setting, in which the side houses would be covered ("coprire") during the intermezzi by projecting frames of painted canvas. This explains how the lamps, fastened to the rear of the

30. Rossi, *Apparato,* p. 33.

permanent Pisa elements, cast light on the intermezzo wings. Rossi also informs us of the method used to light up the heavens ("Cielo"). For reasons of ventilation, the sky was perforated ("tutto sfondato"). In each of the apertures lamps were concealed, so that the heavens could be made to shine with the brightness of day. I assume that Rossi here uses the expression "Cielo" in the sense of a gridiron. The chimneys of the city smoked ("fumicanti, quasi naturali, cammini"), but it was a perfumed smoke, the aroma of which was wafted out into the audience. The addition of chimneys to the houses created some difficulties. From Ser Jacopi's notes[31] we discover that during a rehearsal Cavalieri objected that "le case della prospettiva" had been improperly set up, thus marring the view of the clouds. A carpenter was commissioned to install practicable doors in the first two houses, thus enabling the actors ("istrioni") to make their entrances and exits.[32]

SECOND INTERMEZZO: CONTEST OF THE PIERIDES AND THE MUSES

Now the Pisa veduta transformed itself into a garden "which covered the houses [of Pisa],"[33] so that no part of the city remained in view. Orange and lemon trees grew in the garden landscape, as did cedars, with many trees in blossom and others already laden with fruit. Perfumed water was sprayed in order to sustain the illusion. Vine leaves were entwined in trellises; low hedges ran along the ground; aromatic plants were set in ornamental urns; jasmine was planted between the rose bushes; and flowers sprouted from the lawn. Apart from the luxuriant flora, there were also representatives of the animal kingdom: hares, hedgehogs, tortoises, and, perched on the trees, birds whose song was deceptively imitated. Moreover, a "Sinfonia" was played by "dua [sic] Arpe, due Lire, un Basso di viola, due Leuti, un violino, una Viola bastarda, & un Chitarrone."

The spectators were given time to feast their eyes on Buontalenti's scenery. Then the stage floor opened, and from the trap arose a mountain, overgrown with vegetation, attaining the impressive height of twelve ells. This seemed all the more astounding in that the trap room itself was only about five ells high. On this Mount Helicon sat sixteen hamadryads on stony seats covered with blossoms. Before the machine had risen to its full altitude, a moss-covered grotto opened on each side.[34]

31. Warburg-Bing, in *Gesammelte Schriften, 1,* 402.

32. Ibid., p. 401.

33. Rossi, *Apparato,* p. 37: "che ricoperse in modo le case." Pavoni, p. 15, only has: "Si muta la prospettiua."

34. The anonymous description mentions 18 "musichi" who sat on the mountain and sang. During the madrigal, "subito si uolta la prospettiua da due bande, e ne nasce due antri," with 12 musicians in each one. The "subito si uolta" indicates that Buontalenti was here working with miniature revolving stages, a method which was later adopted by Inigo Jones as *machina*

In the right grotto sat the nine daughters of Pierus, and in the left, the nine Muses, for this was the intermezzo in which the song contest between the Muses and the Pierides, as well as the eventual metamorphosis of the haughty challengers into magpies, took place. The tree nymphs officiated as judges. After a madrigal by the Pierides came the song of the Muses. The texts for these madrigals were written by Ottavio Rinuccini, to music by Luca Marenzio. The Pierides were transformed into magpies in full view of the spectators. Croaking and chattering, they hopped about before taking off for the forest, just as Ovid had related in the fifth book of his *Metamorphoses.* We thus have an *à vista* change of costume such as Buontalenti had already successfully carried out in 1569, when, in the Leto intermezzo, peasants were metamorphosed into frogs. At length the mountain vanished, probably by sinking into the trap room, and the garden "dissolved" ("dileguarsi").

The sixteen hamadryads, musical instruments in their hands, wore satin costumes of a single cut but varying iridescent hues: dark blue, red, purple, white, green, yellow, sky blue, and orange. Their blond locks cascaded over their shoulders, and their headdresses consisted of gold or silver veils. They wore chaplets of oak leaves because, according to Ovid's fable of Erysichthon, they dwelled in oak trees. Buontalenti added embroidery to give their tucked-up costumes a barklike appearance. The Pierides wore satin costumes of varying colors richly trimmed with embroidery. To emphasize their vanity, they were laden with gold ornaments and jewelry. Since they wore masks, they could be ranked by age, the youngest being about fifteen years old, the eldest twenty-three. In contrast to the Pierides, the Muses were dressed with simplicity: cloaks of green velvet; inner garments of a pink and white iridescent material, embellished with a beautiful border; and a "simple" headdress, but one which glittered nonetheless with gold and jewels, and, of course, had a veil. Their headpieces were made of colorful sirens' feathers, and they carried musical instruments.

Buontalenti's pen-and-ink wash drawing for the second intermezzo (Figure 48) has been preserved in the Victoria and Albert Museum. In the center we see the mount of the hamadryads, with the Pierides on one side and the Muses on the other. The side grottos are not visible. We also possess Buontalenti's detailed design for the hamadryad's mountain (Figure 49). Only twelve of the nymphs are provided for in this sketch, while Rossi mentions sixteen, and the anonymous chronicler eighteen. Further costume designs for a Pieride, a Muse, and a magpie (Figure 50) may be found in the Florentine National Library. In 1592 Epifanio

versatilis for his *Masque of Queens* (1609) and by Tommaso Francini for his *Ballet de la délivrance de Renaud* (1617). Barthold von Gadenstedt mentions the fact that at the end the two side grottoes closed again: "und die 2 kleinen berge auch wieder vmbgewendet."

d'Alfiano made an engraving (Figure 51) which differs essentially from both the original design and Rossi's description. Warburg[35] has pointed out the differences and accounted for them by the fact that the picture was engraved three years after the event. It shows Apollo on the peak of the mountain, with the Muses sitting in three rows, and beneath them in a grotto, the Spirit of the Castalian spring. Nine other deities are situated in two grottoes to the right and left, perhaps the hamadryads, while the Pierides, transformed into magpies, frolic about.

We learn from Ser Jacopi's entries that the crew stood ready to uncover the stage ("scoprire il palco")[36] so that the mountain could be raised. Other workers operated a small winch ("verricellino") in order to thrust up the "beginning of the mountain ("il principio del monte"). A much larger windlass was probably required to lift the main bulk of the mountain; in any case, supports ("puntelli") were used to hold it in place after its ascent.

THIRD INTERMEZZO: APOLLO'S SLAYING OF THE PYTHON

After the disappearance of the mountain and the garden, the Pisa setting returned ("ritornò la scena al primiero modo"), and the second act of Bargagli's comedy began. At the end of this act "the houses were again covered" ("furono ricoperte le case"), this time with oak, chestnut, beech, and other trees, and the entire stage was transmuted into a sylvan glade ("tutta la scena diventò bosco").[37] Rossi's wording, "ricoperte le case," again indicates that painted frames were shoved out in front of the Pisa scene, for we may not assume that Buontalenti was here following the method described by Sabbattini in Chapter 5 of the second book of his *Pratica*.[38] In the middle of the boscage was a gloomy, rocky cave, from which the surrounding vegetation seemed to have been burned off, in contrast to the trees standing farther away, which were green and heavy with fruit, and whose tops seemed to touch the sky.[39]

Eighteen Delphic men and women entered in couples from the left, in pseudo-Greek robes that differed from each other only in color and ornamentation. In their madrigal they alluded to the dragon that was devastating the countryside. As they sang, another nine couples appeared from the opposite side, and in their mad-

35. In *Gesammelte Schriften, I*, 298–99.
36. Warburg-Bing, in ibid., p. 403.
37. Pavoni, p. 16, simply states: "Si muta la Scena a guisa di selua."
38. Sabbattini recommended this method only when the upper ridges of the house frames were straight; in any case, no chimneys could be tolerated; Buontalenti's Pisa houses, however, had chimneys. Neither could this be achieved by Sabbattini's second method of changing scenes, but it was possible to attain the effect by pushing forward painted flats.
39. Rossi, *Apparato,* p. 42.

rigal they likewise made mention of the Python. Then the beast itself emerged, thrusting its ghastly head out of the cavern's mouth to sun itself for a while.[40] Perceiving the "drago d'inestimabil grandezza," the Delphic couples began to pray for liberation from the monster. With a single thrust, it issued from its lair and spread its wings, which were spangled with mirrors. Its body was a color between green and black. Its gaping jaws were set with three rows of teeth. Catching sight of the humans, the Python began to emit flames, and its tongue glowed. But Apollo, armed with bow and arrow, was already soaring down from above. Now began the Pythian combat as described by Julius Pollux. Five stages could be distinguished. At first, Apollo scanned the terrain to determine whether it was suitable for doing battle. In the second phase he antagonized the dragon. In the third, he fought in iambic rhythm. The fourth part of the struggle was conducted in spondaic rhythm, ending with the triumph of the god and the death of the monster. In the concluding stage Apollo executed a swift victory dance. The spectators marveled at the rapidity with which Apollo descended from the heavens: a ray of light could not have traveled more swiftly; and their astonishment was all the greater in that they were at a loss to discover how the god—a puppet— had been kept aloft. The "Apollo finto" landed behind the stage, and promptly a dancer personifying the god appeared to carry out the combat in pantomime. Apollo wore a golden robe. In order not to impede the dancer, the traditional aureole was omitted. In the recognition sequence he danced with consummate skill about the dragon from a certain distance. He then made his challenge, posing valiantly as the beast hissed, gnashed its teeth, and beat its wings. The actual fight was waged once again through the medium of the dance. Apollo drove his arrows into the dragon's back, and the monster broke them off as inky blood gushed from its wounds. The howling serpent pursued its antagonist until it finally expired. At the end of his dance of victory, Apollo planted his foot on the dragon's head. Four Delphians who had been following the struggle from the edge of the forest now approached the beast, which lay in a pool of black blood. They summoned their companions and sang a hymn to Apollo. Meanwhile, the dragon was removed from the stage, and Apollo began a dance of joy. The intermezzo concluded with a second hymn by the Delphians, composed by Luca Marenzio.

Count Bardi had prescribed Hellenic costumes ("abiti tendenti al greco")[41] for the choral singers, but gave Buontalenti freedom to choose his colors, leaving them to the "discrezion dell' Artefice." Just as in their own day the theologians had stood guard over the use of symbols in Christian art, prescribing the elements

40. Rossi mentions, p. 43, "lo splendore della così bene allumata scena."
41. Ibid., p. 46.

of iconography for medieval artists, so Bardi, the "theologian" of ancient myth, kept strict account of every detail, insisting that the Delphic couples be distinguished by some sort of "cose marine," whether headpieces of coral branches or sea-shell ornamentation. For Bardi was aware that the Pythian combat had taken place in Delos and that certain writers ascribed the founding of Delos or Delphi to Delphus, a son of Neptune, whence the "cose marine."

A pen-and-ink wash drawing by Buontalenti for the third interlude (Figure 52) is preserved in the Victoria and Albert Museum in London. The Florentine National Library possesses the artist's drawings for Apollo and the dragon (Figure 53), as well as designs for the costumes of the Delphic couples (Figure 55) and for an Apollo costume. Apollo's assault from the air was given permanence in an engraving by Agostino Caracci (Figure 54). While Caracci's monster shows great similarity to Buontalenti's original, the engraver's Delphic couples bear no resemblance to the costume designer's sketches. Thirty-eight costumes were sewn for this third intermezzo.

A few technical details for which we are indebted to Ser Jacopi: stage hands were directed to push the shutter ("sportello") away from the opening through which the dragon emerged;[42] a skeleton ("ossatura") was made for the monster, with head and paws fabricated out of papier-mâché, a task assigned to Valerio Cioli, who had acquired a reputation as restorer of antiques; the dragon's head was 1¾ ells long and 1⅛ high; the paws were 1½ ells high;[43] and the "Apollo finto" was suspended by an iron wire.

FOURTH INTERMEZZO: THE INFERNO

After the third act of the comedy, before the setting changed ("auanti che si muta la prospettiua"),[44] a kind of prelude to the fourth intermezzo took place still within the Pisa veduta. A sorceress in the person of Lucia Caccini appeared on a flying machine.[45] Her golden chariot was set with precious stones. She wore an unbelted robe of green velvet, her tangled hair fell down around her shoulders, and a bright blue veil billowed from her head down to her unshod feet. In her right hand the Maga held a lash, and with her left she curbed two (according to Gadenstedt, three) winged dragons which stuck out their tongues, spewing flames.

42. Warburg-Bing, in *Gesammelte Schriften, I,* 403.
43. Ibid., p. 400.
44. Rossi, *Apparato,* p. 49.
45. Pavoni, p. 17: "in aria." Barthold von Gadenstedt mistook the sorceress for the goddess Juno.

This was intended to give the impression that the monsters were panting with effort. When the car reached the middle of the stage, the sorceress forced the animals to halt. She reached for her lute, which she kept in the chariot, and began to accompany her own song. At the same time, she crossed over the stage to conjure up the fire demons to which Plato alludes in several passages. After her madrigal of conjuration, she climbed back into her car and lashed the dragons, which shook their heads madly, champing their bits.

The car withdrew and a fiery sphere ("un monte di fuoco") appeared in the air, which, having reached the middle of the stage, opened to form a crescent.[46] In it stood the demons whom the Maga had conjured up, singing a madrigal. Their red taffeta wings were spangled with silver and trimmed with blue feathers. Their long crinkly hair seemed to be made of silver and fire. An intense glow was seen on their faces (probably masks). Their silver brocade surcoats reached down to the middle of their thighs, and their undergarments of gold fabric and green silk came to the knees. Their azure foot-coverings were worked in gold. The overall impression was one of angels from paradise. After the madrigal, the cloud closed and withdrew, thus ending the prelude.

In an instant the stage was covered ("la scena in uno stante fu coperta tutta")[47] with fiery rocks, chasms, and caverns, from which flames leapt and smoke billowed up. The stage floor opened ("s'aperse il palco"), disclosing an inferno from which two hosts of demons and Furies emerged. These were melancholy devils who sat on the rocks (which must, therefore, have been three-dimensional), with tormented looks, lamenting their fate in a madrigal. Two of the Furies wore tights of a sooty flesh color, making them appear naked. Their unclean, sagging breasts were entwined with serpents, and their hands and faces were smeared with blood. They shook their snaky locks with wild abandon. Instead of girdles, they wore serpents to cover their pudenda. The winged devils had eagles' claws on their hands and feet, and wore silk costumes that gave the appearance of snakeskin. Two horns projected from their unkempt hair. Distinguished from the Furies by the fewer number of serpents coiled on their bodies were two other female *maschere*. The devils and Furies stood on the right side, while on the left stood a similar group of lemures.

The hell itself was "tutto fuoco e fiamma." Souls stood in the crackling flames undergoing torment by devils. Charon was visible in his bark at the mouth of hell, just as Dante described him in the third canto of the *Inferno:* with a white beard

46. According to Pavoni, however, p. 18: "facendo la vista sua triangolare."
47. Rossi, *Apparato,* p. 51.

and flaming wheels for eyes, he kept striking at recalcitrant souls with his fiery oar. In the midst of the inferno stood Lucifer, with his torso rising out of a circular lake to a height of eight ells—another echo from Dante (*Inferno*, Canto 34, vv.55–60), whose visions guided the designer. Lucifer had three faces, the foremost red as blood, the one over the left shoulder black, and the right one white and yellow. Beneath each of the faces were two bat wings, and over the forehead was a great comb, borrowed from Dante. The Prince of Darkness was sheathed in a furry garment of sooty appearance. While he was busy devouring souls, an activity also alluded to by Dante, two of them, portrayed by agile children ("certi fanciuletti assai destri"), slipped out of his maw. They were soon recaptured, however, by two small devils, one of whom impaled one of the fugitives on a kind of pitchfork and stuffed him into Lucifer's jaws, while the other seized the second soul with his claws, and since he could not reach up to those same jaws, clambered onto Lucifer's wooly flanks and climbed until he could cram the soul into one of his other mouths. At Lucifer's right stood Geryon, king of the legendary island of Erythea, who, by his friendliness, lured strangers to his table and then slew them. Dante also includes him in the seventeenth Canto of his *Inferno*. Buontalenti had been advised by Bardi to give that giant a kind-looking face but the tail of a serpent and scorpion (again as envisaged by Dante). Minos, too, was in the Uffizi inferno, wearing a purple robe and a royal crown on his head; his unusually long tail was derived from the fifth Canto of the *Inferno,* in which it figures as a signpost for the damned. Harpies and Centaurs also inhabited this hell, as well as the Minotaur, Cerberus, and their ilk. The souls were held fast in the frozen lake, some of them immersed up to their necks, others up to their breasts; here and there individual limbs projected from the ice. Scarcely had the demonic singers on the rocks finished their mournful song than they plunged howling into the abyss. Lucifer too was swallowed up, and the inferno closed ("si richiuse lo'nferno"). The rocks and chasms "dissolved" ("dileguarono"), and the Pisa setting returned for the fourth act of the comedy.

No original sketches exist for the fourth intermezzo,[48] but, fortunately, we are in possession of an engraving by Epifanio d'Alfiano (Figure 56) which brings the hell scene to life for us. Soaring aloft are the demons of the region of fire. In the middle

48. For the Prelude to the fourth intermezzo the Cabinet des Dessins of the Louvre possesses a drawing (pen and ink, with watercolor) ascribed to Buontalenti. The attribution is questionable. If we are to accept the Buontalenti drawings in the Victoria and Albert Museum as genuine, the Louvre montage can hardly be claimed as typical of the artist's style. A reproduction of the Louvre design may be found in Jean Jacquot, ed., *La vie théâtrale au temps de la Renaissance* (Paris, 1963), Pl. 8, facing p. 95.

stands the Maga on her dragon car, and beneath her, three-headed Lucifer, encircled by devils who torment the singers. Here again we have a composite design, with the scenes which unfolded in temporal sequence placed in simultaneous juxtaposition.

A partial record of the tasks allocated to individual stage workers is contained in Ser Jacopi's *Memorie*. The stage had to be uncovered ("scoprire il palco") so that Lucifer, drawn up by means of a winch ("verricello"), could emerge from the trap. However, since the trap was so large that one could see into it, the trap room had to be painted so as to simulate another part of the inferno ("Dipignere l'inferno di dentro cioè sotto il palco"). Some members of the crew were directed to open the mouth of hell ("Per aprire la bocha del Inferno").[49] Others cut figures out of pasteboard ("dintornare").[50] At a rehearsal it was discovered that the Maga's cloud did not stand out boldly enough from the celestial background; hence its outlines had to be accentuated by further painting. The viols and trombones were camouflaged to resemble serpents. Forty-two costumes were fashioned for the fourth intermezzo. Giovambattista Strozzi wrote the texts to the madrigals. The Maga's song was set to music by Giulio Caccini,[51] the subsequent madrigals by Cristofano Malvezzi, and the dirge of the mournful demons by Giovanni Bardi.

FIFTH INTERMEZZO: THE RESCUE OF ARION

Once again "la scena si coperse tutta,"[52] this time with side scenes on which reefs had been painted. The stage floor ("il palco") transformed itself into a surging sea contained by the lateral reefs. Small barks were visible in the distance, tossing on the waves; thus depth of perspective ("lo sfondato") was achieved. A mother-of-pearl shell, five ells wide and three high, emerged from the sea. It was drawn by two dolphins which bounded ahead, squirting perfumed water in the air. In the shell sat Vittoria Archilei as Amphitrite in a seamless flesh-colored sheath, which, for feigned nudity, left nothing to the imagination. She wore a blue-green cape embroidered with snails, shells, and fish, a headdress of coral branches, a mother-of-pearl crown, and shoes that resembled fish with silver scales. Pearls adorned her neck and ear lobes, and coral hung on her arms.

Fourteen Tritons and an equal number of naiads arose simultaneously with the shell. The Tritons wore garlands of sedge in their blue hair, which dripped as

49. Warburg-Bing, in *Gesammelte Schriften, I*, 405.
50. Ibid., p. 403.
51. Rossi, *Apparato*, p. 50.
52. Ibid., p. 55.

they came up between the waves. Their tails were of turquoise-colored satin, trimmed with silver scales. The nymphs were as "nude" as Amphitrite, but they wore neither crowns nor pearls. The sea gods carried instruments on which they began to play. Amphitrite accompanied herself on a lute, alluding in her madrigal to the Medici nuptials. A musical compliment to the newlyweds was also paid by the naiads. Finally, the Tritons amused themselves by splashing each other in the water.

At length the water gods submerged, and a well-fitted galley appeared, its crew plowing through the waves with their oars. The vessel was completely equipped with mast, yards, sails, oars, and anchor. It was fifteen paces ("passi andanti") long, and correspondingly broad and high. With its crew of forty, the ship executed various maneuvers: for example, it pointed its prow toward the princely personages in the auditorium; and all sails were struck in homage to the bridal couple. Arion was aboard the vessel, returning to Corinth. This role was played by Jacopo Peri, who also sang "con mirabil attentione de gli ascoltanti,"[53] an aria which he himself composed. Here Bardi followed the narrative in Plutarch's *Moralia*. The singer stood on the gilded poop with his harp, attired like the ancient poet in red-gold brocade and the customary laurel wreath. When the crew was just about to pounce on him with their knives, Arion plunged into the sea, and the water sprayed high in the air. He emerged again, riding on the back of a dolphin. But the sailors believed him dead and sang a merry tune, feeling themselves secure in the possession of his treasure. According to Pavoni,[54] the ship executed a few more turns before departing through the "strada" by which it had entered.

We are in possession of Epifanio d'Alfiano's engraving of this décor (Figure 57). Six of Buontalenti's costume designs relating to the intermezzo are preserved in the Florentine National Library; the costume for Arion (Figure 58) and one for a sea nymph (Figure 59), as well as four costume sketches for sailors (Figure 60). Ser Jacopi informs us that the dolphin was four ells in length, fabricated of papier-mâché, and covered with silver foil ("Stagnuolare con argento il delfino").[55] Arion-Peri's harp was made of pasteboard. The naiads' musical instruments were fashioned to resemble shells. The ships tossing about in the distance were cut from pasteboard and moved in grooves ("canali in sul palco"). Once again the texts for the madrigals were furnished by Rinuccini, with music by Cristofano Malvezzi (except for Arion's solo).

53. Vogel, *Bibliothek,* p. 384.
54. P. 21.
55. Warburg-Bing, in *Gesammelte Schriften, 1,* 406.

SIXTH INTERMEZZO: ASSEMBLY OF THE GODS

After the last lines of the comedy had been spoken, the stage was filled with clouds ("ricoperta tutta la scena"). The heavens opened, revealing a consistory of some twenty pagan deities which shone so radiantly that Rossi was reminded of some verses from Dante's *Paradiso*. Seven clouds appeared through openings, each of them adorned with blossoms, alluding to Dante's "nuvola di fiori." Five clouds descended to earth, and two remained hovering aloft. The cloud in the central aperture was larger than the others and held Apollo, Bacchus, Harmony, and Rhythm. On a second one, next to the first but somewhat lower, stood the three Graces. The Muses were scattered over several. Here the myth as told in Plato's *Laws* was brought to visual realization: taking pity on the harassed human race, Jupiter had given Apollo, Bacchus, and the Muses his mandate to dispatch Harmony and Rhythm to earth, so that men could obtain relief from their burdens in singing and dancing. As the five clouds descended in a slow tempo, a host of winged *amoretti* held fast to their festoons of blossoms, thus giving the impression that they were supporting the clouds. The first madrigal was sung by Apollo; the second by the three Graces and three of the Muses, and the third by the six remaining Muses scattered on the two lower-hanging clouds. Twenty pairs of mortals simultaneously appeared in pastoral dress. Lured by the sweet music issuing from the clouds, they came on stage from four directions. As soon as the clouds touched down upon the stage, the gods alighted and the clouds disappeared "as in a flash" ("come baleno"). A ballet of nymphs and shepherds concluded the evening.

A pen-and-ink wash drawing by Buontalenti (Figure 61) is preserved in the Victoria and Albert Museum, and a sketch for an Apollo (Figure 63) in the Florentine National Library may have been drawn for this intermezzo. Gertrud Bing discovered a Fortuna design by Buontalenti in the London collection of Henry Oppenheimer.[56] In all events, ninety costumes were prepared for the final intermezzo. Epifanio d'Alfiano has captured the spirit of the scene in an engraving (Figure 62).

The texts for the madrigals were composed by Rinuccini and the music by Malvezzi. For the final dance *canzone,* set to music by Emilio de' Cavalieri, the words were contributed by Laura Lucchesini. One could hear the voices of Vittoria Archilei and Lucia and Margherita Caccini in the *terzetti.*[57]

❦

56. Ibid., Pl. 53, Ill. 94.
57. Vogel, *Bibliothek,* p. 385.

On the sixth and thirteenth of May the intermezzi were repeated, but no longer in connection with *La Pellegrina*. Since the Comici Gelosi, then the most celebrated of the commedia dell' arte troupes, had arrived in Florence, the Grand Duke proposed that the impromptu comedians perform a comedy "à gusto loro."[58] The choice of a piece presented difficulties, inasmuch as the troupe then had two prima donnas, Isabella Andreini, a permanent member of the Gelosi, and Vittoria Piissimi, who had evidently left the Confidenti troupe temporarily and joined the Gelosi. As was to be expected, the rivalry between the two leading ladies was pronounced, with the result that Vittoria insisted on appearing in her star role in *La Zingara*, while Isabella wished to display her talents in her showpiece, *La Pazzia*. Finally, the problem was solved by permitting Vittoria to appear in *La Zingara* on the sixth of May, while the thirteenth was reserved for Isabella's *La Pazzia*. On both occasions Bardi's intermezzi were repeated.

Pavoni calls Vittoria's portrait of the gypsy woman a "cosa rara & marauigliosa,"[59] but the real sensation was Isabella's "madwoman." Pavoni outlines[60] the plot of the *Pazzia* as follows: Isabella, the only daughter of Pantalone de' Bisognosi, and Fileno, a stalwart young man, fall in love. Isabella's maid and Fileno's man-servant do the same. Meanwhile, a student by the name of Flavio loses his heart to Isabella, but his love goes unrequited, as she cares only for Fileno. When Fileno sends a confidant to Pantalone to ask him for the hand of his daughter and is informed that he is too young to marry Isabella, the lovers resolve to flee. While they are discussing the means for carrying out the elopement and agree upon a sign of recognition for Fileno, Flavio overhears them. Somewhat before the scheduled rendezvous with Fileno, Flavio appears and gives the stipulated sign. Isabella comes out of her father's house and flees with Flavio, whom she believes to be Fileno. A few moments later, when Fileno appears in front of the house, he finds —instead of his beloved—the maid, vainly searching for her mistress. Fileno grows frenzied, and Isabella likewise loses her reason when she discovers that her abductor is Flavio. In her madness, she begins to soliloquize in various tongues—Spanish, Greek, and French. To the great delight of Christine of Lorraine, Isabella also sang in French. She then imitated her fellow actors by speaking in the accents of Pantalone, Gratiano, the Zanni, and Il Capitano. At length a potion is given to her which restores her sanity. Then she proclaims "con elegante & dotto stile" the joys and torments of love. The eloquent art of Isabella Andreini absolutely transported the spectators.

58. Pavoni, p. 29.
59. Ibid., p. 30.
60. Ibid., pp. 44–46.

On the eleventh of May, in the Pitti Palace,[61] the tourney and sea battle took place. A red ceiling cloth closed off the cortile above (Figure 64). 600 white tapers and 410 oil lamps provided the illumination. Grandstands for the ladies were set up beneath the loggias. Guests by invitation had to establish their identities upon entering with "segni di Porcellana." In front of the arcades and along the Boboli side a bulkhead was built up to a height of three ells and calked with pitch ("bittumata"), so that no open joints remained. This was to prepare for the naumachy that followed the tourney. On the garden side, a fortress was constructed which was to be defended by Turks. Just as the tilt was about to start, a thundershower broke out which lasted for an hour and played havoc with the scenery. Worst of all, the downpour prematurely inundated the cortile. Two hundred bags of sawdust were procured to dry it out. After this delay, the tilt could begin. The participants rode in on *carri trionfali,* which brought with them an abundance of scenic surprises. On one of the cars a sorcerer appeared, muttering conjurations. Another chariot, in which musicians were concealed, was pulled by a large dragon. The challenge in front of the Turkish fortress was executed by the Duke of Mantua and Pietro de' Medici. For the next surprise, a mountain conceived as Aetna was shoved into the arena. As it opened to face the bride, two knights descended. After a brief jousting prelude, other cars were drawn into the cortile, decorated with fountains, clouds, shrubbery, animals, ships, boulders, sirens, giant birds, and elephants. One of the vehicles was drawn by two "lions" and two "bears." Cavallino informs us[62] that for this purpose four donkeys were covered with bearskins and the hides of lions. Don Virginio enjoyed himself in the role of Mars, making his entrance on a vast mountain pulled by a crocodile. But the greatest excitement was caused by a garden which, propelled by invisible forces, moved into the courtyard and unfolded on all sides to the twittering of birds. In the garden were imitations of towers, fortresses, pyramids, ships, horsemen, and animals, all made out of greenery ("fatto di verdura"). A cloud of birds swarmed up before the Grand Duchess, and one of the animals landed in the bride's lap, a good omen. Then began the joust with pikes and rapiers, concluded by fireworks that suddenly blazed up from the barriers.

While the spectators retired to the palace to fortify themselves with a repast, the cortile was transformed into a basin. Water gushed into the courtyard from subterranean aqueducts until it reached a level of approximately five feet.[63] An

61. For the following, cf. ibid., pp. 35–43.

62. P. 43.

63. "forse cinque piedi" (Pavoni, p. 40). According to Cavallino, p. 44, the artificial sea had a depth of 4 braccia. But this seems incredible.

etching by Orazio Scarabelli gives us an impression of the eighteen galleys of various sizes that floated upon this sea.[64] After a round of cannon shots had lured the guests from the buffet back into the courtyard, the sea battle between the Turks and their besiegers could begin (Figure 65). The Christians were victorious and conquered the fortress with the help of rope ladders.

64. According to Cavallino, 22 vessels were involved.

7. Buontalenti and the New Opera

1600

For many years dynastic speculation focused on Maria de' Medici, a daughter of Francesco and Joanna of Austria. It appeared for some time that she would be married off to Spain; then came rumors of a possible match with Emperor Rudolf. Political maneuvers and divinations ended abruptly when on April 30, 1600, Grand Duke Ferdinando I proclaimed the betrothal of his niece to King Henri IV of France. The wedding by proxy took place in Florence.[1] Ferdinando's ambitions were flattered, and the Florentines had yet another cause for rejoicing.

Following the nuptial ceremonies on October 5 was a banquet in the great hall of the Palazzo Vecchio, where the musical interlude *La Contesa fra Giunone e Minerva* was inserted in an essentially culinary feast. On October 6 Jacopo Peri's *Euridice* (libretto by Ottavio Rinuccini, and a few musical pieces composed by Giulio Caccini) had its premiere in the Pitti Palace. On October 9 the opera *Il Rapimento di Cefalo* was performed in the Uffizi Theatre. Giulio Caccini set Gabriello Chiabrera's libretto to music, and Stefano Venturi del Nibbio, Luca Bati, and Piero Strozzi contributed choral songs.

1. Primary source: Descrizione / delle felicissime / Nozze / Della Cristianissima Maestà di Madama Maria / Medici Regina di Francia / e di Nauarra. / Di Michelagnolo Bvonarroti. / In Firenze / Appresso Giorgio Marescotti. MDC. Further principal sources in excerpt in Angelo Solerti, *Musica, ballo e drammatica alla Corte Medicea dal 1600 al 1637* (Florence, 1905) pp. 23–27 (from the diaries of Settimani and Tinghi). Rinuccini's *Euridice* libretto is reprinted in Solerti, *Albori, 2,* 105–42, the text of Chiabrera's *Cefalo* in *3,* 9–58.

Quarrel between Juno and Minerva[2]

We may pass over the Lucullan pleasures of the banquet, although it is note-worthy that theatrical elements figured in the dessert, the grand-ducal confec-tioners having turned their talents to scene design. Their "winter landscape," a snowy forest with animals and hunters, all in icing, was particularly appreciated. The master bakers had, to a certain extent, collaborated with technicians to pro-duce sugared animals that could move and change their shapes.

For the musical interlude *La Contesa fra Giunone e Minerva*, a scenic frame-work had been devised. At one end of the Salone dei Cinquecento stood two grottoes, from which two luminous clouds emerged during the course of the banquet, and soaring aloft, slowly opened. On one of the clouds sat Juno in her chariot drawn by peacocks; on the other, the goddess of war was seated in a car pulled by a unicorn. Simultaneously, a rainbow vaulted across the hall. Then be-gan the *Contesa*, devised by Giovan Battista Guarini, with music by Emilio de' Cavalieri.

Juno expressed her displeasure at the warrior goddess' decision to be present at so serene an occasion. After an exchange of words, the goddesses agreed that valor, no less than the other virtues, must be presumed to dwell in such an illustrious pair as Henri IV and Maria de' Medici. In any case, both goddesses had come to attend the "superhuman banquet of the demigods" ("soprumano conuito di Se-midei"). After singing a hymn in praise of the newlyweds, they set out on their re-turn to Olympus.

Peri's *Euridice*

Peri's opera was performed on the sixth of October in the Pitti Palace. Buonar-roti says simply: "nel Palazzo de Pitti"; the envoy from Modena refers to a "saletta nella parte di sopra del palazzo a Pitti";[3] and Cesare Tinghi[4] gives as the locale of the performance "su alle stanze del sig. Don Antonio Medici a Pitti." Nowhere is the set designer mentioned; yet one may venture to assume that Buontalenti was at work, even though the opera was "simple," requiring no machines. The archi-tect had designed a proscenium frame referred to by Buonarroti as a "grand' arco," with a niche on either side. In one of these niches stood the statue of Poetry, in the other, that of Painting. The setting was concealed at the beginning by a curtain.

Rinuccini's libretto was divided into a Prologue, sung by Tragedy, and six

2. Our account follows Buonarroti's *Descrizione*.
3. In a letter to the Duke of Modena, reprinted in Solerti, *Musica*, p. 27.
4. In ibid., p. 25.

scenes. The first three were played in "magnificent forests" ("selue uaghissimi") that were partly three-dimensional and partly painted on flat surfaces ("e rileuate, e dipinte"). So skillfully were the light sources distributed that the stage seemed to be flooded with daylight ("per li lumi ben dispostiui piene di una luce come di giorno"). The fourth scene was played in an underworld setting of forbidding rocks, defoliated trees, and lead-colored plants ("orridi massi si scorsero, e spauenteuoli, che parean ueri, soura de' quali sfrondati li sterpi, e liuide l'erbe appariuano"). Farther in the background the burning city of Dis with its leaping flames, blazing turrets, and a glowing, copper sky became visible through a cleavage in the rocks ("per la rottura d'una gran rupe la Città di Dite ardere vi si conobbe vibrando lingue di fiamme per le aperture delle sue torri, l'aere d'intorno auuampandoui di vn colore come di rame"). At the end of the Hades scene Rinuccini's libretto states: "Si rivolge la scena, e torna come prima." The verb *rivolgersi*, used here in its primary meaning, that of "turning itself about," may point to the utilization of periaktoi. In any event, the first setting was brought back for the fifth and sixth scenes.

Extant accounts of the performance refer to the singers and instrumentalists.[5] Francesco Rasi, a tenor in the service of the Duke of Mantua, sang Aminta; Melchior Palantrotti, Pluto; Jacopo Giusti, "con molta grazia," Dafne; and Antonio Brandi (Il Brandino), the shepherd Arcetro. The latter was eulogized by Marco da Gagliano in the Preface to his *Dafne*: "His voice is a contralto; his enunciation is superb and his charm in singing equally admirable; not only were his words clearly audible, but he excited rapture beyond words through his gestures and movements."[6] The prima donna at the Court of the Grand Duke, Vittoria Archilei, sang the role of Euridice. Peri called her the "Euterpe dell'età nostra," and in his Foreword to *Euridice* added: "Not only has she embellished my music with trills and long simple and double runs ("giri di voce"), which her lively artistic mind constantly invents (more to comply with the taste of our time than in the belief that only herein lay the beauty and power of our singing), but she has also adorned it with those graceful and charming turns which no amount of notation can express and which, if written down, cannot be learned from writing." Jacopo Peri, the composer, sang the role of Orfeo, and Marco da Gagliano later commemorated his performance when he wrote: "One cannot grasp the charm and power of his music without having heard him sing it himself. For he endows it with such con-

<hr>

5. Cf. Peri's Foreword to *Euridice*, in Solerti, *Albori, 2,* 110. Outstanding instrumentalists played behind the stage ("dentro alla Scena"): Jacopo Peri (gravicembalo), Don Garzia Montalva (*chitarrone*), Giovanbattista Jacomelli (*lira grande*), Giovanni Lapi (*liuto grosso*).

6. Gagliano's Preface to *Dafne,* in Solerti, *Albori, 2,* 72.

summate grace that he is able to convey the total emotional content of the words to the listeners, swaying them at his will to feel joy or lamentation."[7]

Caccini's *Il Rapimento di Cefalo*

On the evening of October 9 an audience of up to three thousand men and eight hundred women gathered in the great hall over the Uffizi to attend the performance of Caccini's opera, for which Buontalenti had created the settings.

The red silk curtain with gold fringe was decorated with lilies, foliage, and heraldic spheres. It was divided in the middle and drawn to the sides, where two female figures, personifications of Theory and Practice, closed off the stage. The proscenium terminated above in a frieze supported by amoretti, with the coat of arms of the Medici in the center flanked by Dignity and Magnanimity.

The setting for the Prologue was a mountain almost twenty ells high, covered with trees and bushes. Its base extended over the entire stage. Clouds hovered in the background. On the summit stood a winged white horse, Pegasus, whose hoof stroke had caused the spring of Hippocrene to well forth on Mount Helicon. The spectators actually saw water from the source trickle down the slope of the Muses' mountain. Apollo sat in the shadows of the laurel and myrtle trees with the nine Muses, and in their midst was the incarnation of poetry, a woman crowned with laurel, hair cascading to her shoulders, holding a lyre in one hand, and a plectrum in the other. Veils in four colors hung from her girdle, an allusion to the four most noble arts of poetry; on one foot she wore a sock, and on the other a cothurnus. She slowly descended a winding mountain path, displaying her costume from various angles. Walking up to the front edge of the stage, she made her curtsy and began to sing "con diuina voce." First she presented herself as Poetry, and then proceeded to sing the praises of the new French queen, predicting great deeds for Henri IV and his successors.

Once the Prologue ended, the mountain sank away before the eyes of the spectators. Buonarroti uses the expression "deflate" ("sgonfiandosi"), probably to indicate that the mountain collapsed like a deflated balloon. As the peak slid into the trap, the Muses sang in chorus. Helicon must thus have consisted of a firm scaffolding to support the considerable load of trees and masquers, as well as of canvas pieces lightly propped up from beneath, which were nonpracticable and had merely to give the illusion of bulk and breadth.

Scarcely had the mountain disappeared than the first act of the opera began. The stage floor and the first wings were "unveiled" ("il piano della scena, e le prime prospettiue scopertesi"), revealing broad plains, deep caverns, and shady

7. Ibid., 68–69.

96

forests. The stage was barely illuminated at all, since there was still not a glimmer of dawn. Hunters sat about on rocks, waiting for daybreak with their greyhounds and ornamented hunting gear. One of them, Cephalus, more sumptuously attired than the others, was still asleep. On the side facing east, opposite the sleeping hunter, a pink cloud bordered in gold and silver appeared in the heavens. Descending slowly to earth, it opened to reveal a pretty young woman with shining face and golden wings. She was none other than Aurora. Smaller clouds detached themselves from her cloud and fluttered about the goddess of dawn, who appeared in an iridescent white robe with a reddish cast. As she floated down, she sang a song, and perfumed air wafted out into the auditorium. Immediately after her landing on the stage-meadow ("su gli scenici prati"), she guided her glowing feet with graceful steps over to the sleeping Cephalus and confessed her love to him. Meanwhile, growing smaller and smaller, the cloud closed and withdrew into the heavens, an effect that left the spectators duly amazed. At the same time, the appearance of the setting changed ("le scene si trasformarono"), and areas which had hitherto been dark were illuminated. The painted hillocks ("le dipinte piaggie"), mountain peaks, and tree tops were bathed in a golden glow. It may be that Buontalenti was here using transparent screens illuminated from behind. After singing a duet, Aurora and Cephalus withdrew while the hunters remained behind to sing a choral piece (composed by Stefano Venturi del Nibbio) before departing.

The jealous Tithonus, with disheveled beard and grey-white hair, now appeared on a large cloud. He was lamenting the loss of his beloved, and searching the whole stage for her. As his cloud traveled through the air, it underwent several metamorphoses: first it grew larger, then shrank again; at one point it resembled a dolphin, and at others, a horse, a forest, or a mountain. At length the many-layered cloud ("doppia per molte falde") vanished behind the other clouds, and the scene changed ("il tutto cambiar si vide") for the second act.

In place of forests and plains there now appeared the sea. Far in the background ("per profondissime lontananze") a number of islands and hazy blue mountains emerged. To achieve this effect, Buontalenti had chosen a fairly low vanishing point ("per lo punto assai basso posto di quella prospettiua sfugente"). One could see the billows foam and hear their roar. From one side came a whale, fourteen ells in length, and from the other, the chariot of Helios, drawn by four horses; at first one saw only their heads, then as they slowly worked their way up, they finally came into full view, panting and shaking their heads, almost impossible to bridle. The golden car was set with precious stones and embellished with the following reliefs: the pursuit of Daphne by Apollo; the transformation of the nymph into a laurel tree; Apollo slaying the dragon; and the twelve signs of the zodiac. The driver of the car stood erect, a radiant youth with glowing robes and golden hair.

The whale was a "grandissima bestia" with silver scales and an uneven back, on which, precariously balanced, was the aged Oceanus, his bristly beard streaked with moss, wearing a royal crown (for according to Thales, water was the fountain-head of all things), and on his shoulders, a soft cape decorated with marine orna-mentation. Not only did the whale have quills which it could thrust out and re-tract again, but it could flap its ears, roll its great yellow eyes, and submerge its head and raise it dripping to the surface, spouting jets of water. White fangs projected from red gums over its wrinkled lips, crunching the gleaming fish which leapt from the waves. Tritons swam about the whale, rough creatures of the deep, with scaly bluish-green skin, blowing their conches and lashing the water with their forked tails. Clouds scudded across the sky. In short, the spectators were in-trigued by the "caos di macchine" which Buontalenti had conjured up.

With fury in his voice, Oceanus asked the sun god to explain the delay of daybreak. As if in answer to this question, Cupid now appeared aloft, a winged, blindfolded boy with an arrow in his hand, the quiver slung across his chest, soar-ing like a bird through the air on his cloud, flying this way and that ("con moto distorto"). Two swarms of amoretti escorted him, holding hands and dancing a round in mid-air ("facessero a mezza l'aria, vn solo coro tondo"). The sea monster with its rider now submerged, immersing first its head and then its curved back, splashing water high into the air. Even Helios—without the dawn, no day—sank back into the deep, and his horses had to take an unaccustomed course. The heavens were deprived of sunlight, and a melancholy mood settled over the entire scene. Even the waves assumed a glassy look. But Cupid and his chorus of amoretti celebrated the triumph of Aurora's new love, and then vanished, along with the seascape.

Once again a sylvan landscape appeared, different from that of the first act. This gave Aurora and her lover the opportunity to sing a duet. After their depar-ture, the entire stage grew dark "in vn tratto" and the scene was then varied to a forbidding, rocky landscape full of ruins and dark trees. In the further part of the stage ("nell'vltimo confino") Night appeared, wreathed with poppies and sheathed in black veils and a blue mantle spangled with stars. Black wings sprouted from her shoulders. She held two small children in her arms, one white, the other black. These were her sons, Sleep and Death. She evoked the impression that she had just risen from the Cimmerian caves. Her chariot, drawn by two owls, was of bur-nished gold. Its four wheels had no rims, and only the radiant spokes were visible, diverging to form stars, hence symbolizing the four nocturnal vigils. As Night's chariot ascended, the stage grew darker and the heavens lost their blue color. The amazement of the spectators reached its climax when the lights in the auditorium were also dimmed and reduced to the size of small stars. A large moon ascended, its shape a crescent to prevent too much brightness; as clouds passed over it, its color changed. The signs of the zodiac, arranged in a semicircle, arched above Dame Night. Over each sign hovered a seraphic boy, an indication that the cycle of nature stood under divine influence. The youths had been selected for the beauty of their voices, since they had to sing while executing their circular movement with great adroitness. Night disappeared a few times behind the clouds, emerged again, and was finally seen no more, having ascended to Jupiter to complain of the latest Aurora scandal. It then grew brighter on stage, and the fourth act began.

Now the earth trembled and crevices cleaved open. The spectators were once more spellbound as they watched "tanto di voto sotto la scena." The stage resembled a mine with lodes of metal and stones of the most divers colors. Hidden springs babbled and mists arose, their scented vapors wafted out into the auditorium. A mass of earth in the shape of a small mountain heaved up from a caved-in hollow and was moved from within, as though burrowed through by moles. At length the shell of the mountain burst open, revealing a female figure portraying the goddess Berecyntia, the Great Mother of all life. She wore an earth-colored robe and a mural crown. Berecyntia lamented that, as a result of Aurora's dalliance with Cephalus, the sun would not come up, depriving the earth of its needful warmth. Suddenly Cupid appeared in a cloud car which differed from the one in which he had originally been seen. The god of love predicted a favorable development in the Aurora affair, whereupon Berecyntia disappeared.

Mercury with his winged helmet and caduceus appeared in an opening in the heavens. With Jupiter's mandate, he commanded Cupid to bring Aurora to her senses so that the continued existence of the world might be assured (without the dawn, no sunrise, without the sun, no life). Cupid was incensed by this order and made ready to take flight. This resulted in a charming "contrasto di macchine" as Mercury began to pursue the love god through the air. At length, the divine messenger managed to lay hold of Cupid and draw him onto his own cloud, Cupid's cloud expanding for the maneuver. Both now flew up into the heavens, which were filled with clouds. The great cloud in the middle seemed to rupture, striking radiant beams from its fissures, and as it opened, it disclosed an assembly of twenty-five deities. By now the clouds filled the entire stage, and the gods sang a choral piece composed by Luca Bati.

The fifth act of the opera began without further change of scene. Cupid and Mercury had arrived at the feet of Jupiter, who sat upon his eagle in the midst of the lesser deities. It was Jupiter's wish that Cupid go down to earth and grant the lovers eternal fulfillment of their love. To bring Aurora into the heavens on a cloud, he descended. When Cephalus arrived with his hunters, he was likewise borne off into the heavens on a cloud which had arisen from the earth ("uscente di sotto terra") and during the ascent assumed the shape of an urn with no base. The opera concluded with a hunters' chorus composed by Caccini and incorporated into his "Nuove Musiche."[8]

Now followed the afterpiece. The stage was transformed into a semi-oval "gran Teatro" in Doric style, with gilded columns and statues. This "onstage auditorium" was conceived as an extension of the actual auditorium. Heroes took their places on the gradi, their eyes turned in expectation of the arrival of the goddess of fame. A bulky machine ("graue macchina") arose out of the trap ("sorse di sotto la scena"), surpassing all of its predecessors in height.[9] On top of this "carro magnificentissimamente ornato" stood Dame Fama, with great wings and flowing hair, holding the traditional trumpet and an olive branch. Her robe was wrought all over with eyes. One of her feet was planted on the globe, the other raised as if to dance. Beneath her sat sixteen women representing the eighteen cities subject to Grand Duke Ferdinando: Florence sat on a lion and wore the royal crown and a gold cape; Siena, dressed in black and white, sat on a crowned she-wolf, her bosom covered with silver armor in the ancient Roman fashion. As the chorus of cities extolled Ferdinando, Fama was whisked away on a cloud into the heavens. The machine now began its slow descent. As a scarlet lily blossomed in the background, with red balls clustered about it, the sixteen ladies, instead of descending into the trap, alighted from the sinking car and formed two rows on stage to the left and right. The spectacle ended with singing and dancing. Buonarroti declared that it could be confidently compared to the spectacles of ancient Rome. This may explain the boundless praise that Bernardo Buontalenti and his assistant, Alessandro Pieroni, earned from their contemporaries.

8. The singers and musicians, 75 in number, were grouped in a semicircle ("in mezza luna"); solo passages were sung by Melchior Palantrotti, Jacopo Peri, and Francesco Rasi.

9. The audience could not fathom how a machine with a height of 25 braccia could rise out of a substage which was only one sixth as high ("che ben per tre doppi era piu eleuato di tutta l'altezza del palco").

8. Giulio Parigi and the Wedding of Prince Cosimo

1608

In the autumn of 1608 the nuptials of the hereditary Prince Cosimo, eldest son of Grand Duke Ferdinand, and the Hapsburg Archduchess Maria Magdalena were celebrated in Florence.[1]

CALENDAR OF EVENTS

October 18: Festive procession of the bride into the city, which was decorated with triumphal arches.

October 19: Banquet in the Salone dei Cinquecento of the Palazzo Vecchio (Figure 66). Musical offerings consisted[2] of a madrigal sung by Gentle Breeze (Aura), the messenger of Venus, brought in on a sea-shell chariot, followed by a song of Cupid, who rode in on a second flying machine. The curtain that concealed the terrace opposite the Udienza was then lowered, disclosing a choir and instrumentalists grouped in tiers, who paid a panegyric tribute to the bridal pair. The soirée concluded with a tilt of the grandducal pages.

October 20: *Calcio* match in the Piazza Santa Croce.

October 22: The "evening entertainment" (*Veglia*), *Notte d'amore*, performed in the Pitti Palace.

1. Primary sources: [Camillo Rinuccini] Descrizione / Delle / Feste Fatte / Nelle reali Nozze / De' Serenissimi Principi / Di Toscana / D. Cosimo De' Medici, / E Maria Maddalena / Arcidvchessa D'Avstria. / In Firenze / 1608.

Cesare Tinghi's *Diario* published in excerpt form in Solerti, *Musica, ballo e drammatica alla Corte Medicea.* Other archive material is also found in this work.

2. Solerti, *Musica*, p. 54.

October 25: Performance of *Il Giudizio di Paride* in the Uffizi Theatre.

October 27: Equestrian ballet of the winds (*Ballo e giostra de' venti*) in the Piazza Santa Croce.

October 28: *Il Giuoco del ponte,* a mock battle fought by Pisan noblemen on the Santa Trinità bridge (Figure 67).

November 3: *Trionfo* of the Argonauts on the Arno.

November 19: Repeat performance of *Il Giudizio di Paride* for the state visit of the Duke of Mantua.[3]

Notte d'amore

This performance took place in a hall of the Pitti Palace.[4] Francesco Cini[5] wrote the libretto. Giulio Parigi, Buontalenti's successor, may have furnished the décors. The evening was essentially devoted to a court ball. Floor space was kept clear for ballroom dancing between the *gradi* which arose on three sides. On the fourth side of the hall a low stage ("vna Scena bassa"), concealed by a curtain, was erected. A few steps connected it to the dancing area. After the entrance of the Grand Duke, the ball began.

Suddenly, the curtain fell ("cadde la tenda della Scena"),[6] a surprise effect that made the dancers pause. Attention was drawn to the stage, where the spectators were offered a picturesque panorama of the hills surrounding Florence: Fiesole, Monteoliveto, and Monte Morello.[7] Hesperus came forth on a cloud as a winged boy with blue veils fluttering from his waist. He turned to face backward and bade Night bring refreshment to men wearied by their daily toil. Dark-winged Night appeared in a cloak spangled with stars, her head crowned with poppies. She carried an iron scepter and held two small children in her arms, one black, the other white; Repose, Silence, Oblivion, and Sleep were in her entourage. Night sang her aria, while Cupid, with Playfulness, Laughter, Dancing, Singing, Contentment, and a host of amoretti gathered about her. She handed her scepter to Love, and the amoretti began to dance, eventually mingling with the spectators, who took this as a cue to resume their ballroom dancing.

Suddenly, the stage transformed itself into a lovely garden with blooming trees,

3. Rinuccini, p. 24. Cf. also the account of the observer from Mantua, Gabriele Bertazzuolo, reprinted in Solerti, *Musica,* p. 55.

4. According to Rinuccini, p. 27: "nella sala della Foresteria"; in Tinghi's account (Solerti, *Musica,* p. 45): "su nella sala di sopra nominata di Don Antonio"; the Mantuan observer mentions the "salone su ad alto di Pitti" (ibid., p. 55).

5. The text is reprinted in Solerti, *Musica,* pp. 261–79.

6. Rinuccini, p. 27.

7. Everything was more heavily wooded than in reality: "tutto piu seluoso del vero" (ibid.).

meadows, fields, and bowers, all calculated to deceive the eyes ("ingannatrici degli occhi").[8] Seven stars, the Hyades, hovered aloft, dressed as nymphs with gold face masks. Dame Luna, attired as a huntress all in silver, with a half moon as headdress, invited the stars to descend. Endymion appeared in shepherd's costume to dance with the moon goddess, while Cupid extolled the hills of Florence on which so many divine beings had settled. He then invited the guests to continue dancing. Many of the couples might have succumbed to fatigue, had not a fresh spectacle brought a much-needed change of pace.

Again the setting changed, this time into a grotesque jumble of rocks, mountains, bodies of water, burning buildings, and castles in the air—the whole supported by a rainbow. The manneristic impulses that informed this weird landscape also dictated the selection of figures. The Nocturnal Hours seemingly walked on air, one of them conjuring Dreams and Morpheus, their creator. This scene can probably be traced back to Mantua, where, as indicated in the Appendix, Morpheus and his phantasms had been brought on stage five months previously in the third intermezzo of *L'Idropica*. Grotesque dream figures now appeared: here a cripple, there a figure with his head set on backward, and other figures, male and female, young and old, made up of incompatible elements. The most bizarre apparition had a torso shaped like a tower, with a ship for a head and branches instead of arms. Other phantasms had the appearance of wild animals, birds, or fish. Some of them moved quite slowly, others with extreme rapidity. Withal, it amounted to an extravagant piece of ballet, performed by surrealist dream figures.[9]

The setting then changed back to the garden. Morning Breeze (Aura mattutina) came to summon Aurora, who appeared in her traditional variegated costume, her wings and hair strewn with dewy pearls. Aged Tithonus, regally attired, was, of course, also on hand, cursing Morning Breeze, who had deprived him of his beloved Aurora. Tithonus had to remain behind in the sky, while Aurora, accompanied by the song of the stars and the amoretti, descended to earth. Endymion also took part in the following dance, and Luna regretted that she must quit the field for her radiant brother, Apollo. With the appearance of the Sun, it grew brighter on stage, and the amoretti concluded the performance with a choral hymn to the Day and to the bridal pair.

But the dancers were still not inclined to retire, especially since the host's pages now appeared in shepherd's guise and began to dance with the ladies. Finally, however, the Grand Duke decided that it was time to turn in so that the guests might recover their strength for the festivities to come.

8. Ibid., p. 28.
9. Ibid., p. 30.

Il Giudizio di Paride

This pedestrian pastoral was written by Michelagnolo Buonarroti, who spun out the fable of the judgment of Paris, with circumstantial minuteness, into five acts. It began with the spreading of rumors among the shepherds on Mount Ida that Paris had been elected to serve the judgment. Oenone then stormed in, beside herself with jealousy. A number of nymphs sought to appease her, but had as little success as did Paris. Meanwhile, the three goddesses arrived. While they were disrobing at a fountain, Archilaus, Paris' counselor, spoke his advice to the shepherd prince, and the decision was naturally cast in favor of Aphrodite. After the herdsmen crowned the judge, the shallow pastoral ended with a feast of the nymphs and shepherds.

Since no "miracle machines" were needed for the Paris piece ("non ricercaua marauiglie di machine"), something else was required to make the evening more interesting. Thus, as Rinuccini informs us,[10] intermezzi were introduced. The first, essentially the prelude, was invented by Lorenzo Franceschi; we shall refer to it here as "The Palace of Fame." The second, "The Return of Astraea," was an invention of Alessandro Adimari. The third entr'acte, "Calypso's Garden," was contributed by Giovanni Bardi. Giovambattista Strozzi was the author of the Amerigo Vespucci interlude. "The Forge of Vulcan" and "The Temple of Peace" owed their inspiration to Buonarroti.[11]

The performance took place in the Uffizi Theatre, "nel solito teatro di tali spettacoli, sopra la fabbrica de' magistrati."[12] The auditorium—which, according to Tinghi, held an audience of five thousand—assumed the shape of a Roman amphitheatre, with gradi for the ladies on three sides, and seats for the men in the orchestra. The column-and-niche motif of the hall was extended to the house curtain. "Admission tickets" were issued, white porcelain tokens bearing the ducal arms.[13] The Princely personages sat on a dais erected at the end of the torch-lit hall opposite the stage.

FIRST INTERMEZZO: THE PALACE OF FAME

After the curtain descended,[14] the spectators were presented with a view of majestic buildings, temples, theatres, palaces, and triumphal arches, some of them

10. Ibid., p. 34.
11. The authors are named in ibid., p. 95.
12. Ibid., p. 33.
13. According to Tinghi, quoted by Solerti, *Musica*, p. 46.
14. Rinuccini, p. 34: "allo sparir della Cortina."

in good repair, others in ruins. At center stage arose ("sorgeua") the loveliest palace of them all, "made completely of mirrors" ("tutto fatto à specchi"), not of ashlars, with lofty archways and a high tower. The spectators admired this Palace of Fame as much for its size as for the novelty of the "structural material" ("per la nouità della materia"). The sought-after effect was probably achieved by using simulated mirror glass, possibly tin foil.[15] Winged Fama appeared with her golden trumpet on the parapet of the tower. Wearing a robe appliquéd with eyes, ears, and tongues, she revealed to the newlyweds a long procession of immortal ancestors, whose dress and other attributes designated them as such. The chorus of these heroic forebears predicted a glorious future for the bridal couple and their issue. Then the gate of the palace opened, and the heroes entered to ascend to their well-earned transfiguration in the heavens. After the last progenitor had crossed into the palace, the structure suddenly vanished ("sparue subito il Palazzo"):[16] either it was raised aloft or pulled down into a trap. In any case, the heroes must have retired through a trap after their disappearance into the palace. Dame Fama remained suspended in the air until she was finally drawn up into the clouds.

This setting, as well as the six others used in this performance, was designed by Giulio Parigi. Remigio Cantagallina has preserved it for us in an etching (Figure 68). In contrast to the "edifici magnifici, e superbi, Teatri, Tempij, Logge, Palagi, Archi" mentioned in the official *Descrizione,* which were supposed to be partly in ruins and partly in good condition, the engraving shows us only the remains of buildings that might once have been palaces. The etcher focused his attention on the central Palace of Fame, giving it a massiveness and three-dimensionality which it probably lacked in the performance. Cantagallina, incidentally, made no attempt to emphasize the novel building material that produced the mirror effect in his picture.

After Fama soared away, the scene changed ("la Scena tutta si transformò")[17] into a landscape with forests, hills, meadows, barns, huts, fences, and fountains. This was the Mount Ida countryside that was to serve as background for the Paris story. Cantagallina's etching (Figure 69) gives us an impression of the bucolic quality of the scene, although there is no way to determine which particular moment he captured. Amoretti are the traditional escorts of Venus, but the female figure in the middle garbed as a "nymph" was more likely to have been Oenone taking comfort from the amoretti in her despair.

15. Ibid., p. 35.

16. In the sonnet sung by Dame Fama, the expression "to look at oneself in the mirror" ("specchiarsi") was used.

17. Rinuccini, p. 36.

SECOND INTERMEZZO: THE RETURN OF ASTRAEA

After the first act of the *Giudizio,* the stage was covered with clouds through which the spectators could gaze at the city of Florence in the background ("nel foro della prospettiua"). On one side of the stage the god of the river Arno, crowned with beech leaves and wearing a belt of sedge, arose in a grotto ("sorse sotto una grotta"). Leaning against his urn, he held a cornucopia in his right hand. At his feet crouched a lion, holding a lily in its paws. Six pairs of naiads came forth from the grotto. On the opposite side of the stage a luminous cloud adorned with blossoms descended to the strains of a gentle *sinfonia.* On it sat Flora, patron goddess of Florence, calling upon Arno and his nymphs to be joyful. As soon as it reached the stage floor, the cloud vanished. At the same time, farther upstage, a second cloud appeared which exploded to thunder and lightning. An eagle flew out of the chaos, bearing on its back Astraea, gowned in silver with astral motifs. The fragments of the disintegrated cloud aligned themselves to provide seating places for the allegories of Golden Age, Innocence, Simplicity, Purity, Happiness, and Contentment, all dressed in the most sumptuous fashion and carrying devices to make them easily identifiable to everyone. While the eagle was advancing toward the bridal pair, the allegories sang, raising aloft six balls, the heraldic emblem of the Medici. Finally, after Arno and his nymphs had sung a few verses, the performers disappeared, one after the other, leaving the stage bare for a moment before it was again transformed, "in vn momento," into the Ida landscape for the second act of the *Giudizio.*

We are in possession of Cantagallina's etching for the second intermezzo (Figure 70), which again urges caution in the assessment of pictorial documentation for the reconstruction of performances. Rinuccini expressly states that Astraea's cloud did not appear until Flora's had vanished. However, this did not prevent the etcher from bringing both clouds into the picture at once. It is even possible that in this composite etching Flora is not only shown flying through the air but simultaneously standing on the stage as well; for the *Descrizione* mentions only twelve nymphs, while Cantagallina drew thirteen, one of whom might be Flora. There is no evidence of the grotto described by Rinuccini. The etcher introduced the river god on a rock ledge surrounded by reeds, which either arose through a trap or was pulled in from the side.

THIRD INTERMEZZO: THE GARDEN OF CALYPSO

Now the stage was transformed into a formal garden of trees bearing golden fruit, with trellises, dripping grottoes of spongy rock-stuff, and walls supporting floral urns. This was the kingdom of Calypso on the island of Ogygia. The nymph appeared in a bower in the background, encircled by companions who responded to their mistress' summons to dance and sing. In the meantime, the heavens opened for the appearance of Jupiter and his royal household. The lord of heaven commanded Mercury to work out the liberation of Odysseus. Descending on a small cloud, Mercury remained hovering in the air while he conveyed Jupiter's mandate to the nymph. Then the tone of the music changed, losing its hitherto joyful quality. In a madrigal Calypso lamented the loss of her "caro tesoro amato," and then vanished into one of the trellised walks ("viali coperti"). At the same time, Mercury took off into the clouds, and the setting changed back into the mountain landscape for the Paris fable.

Parigi has caught the spirit of this scene in an etching (Figure 71). On the basis of Rinuccini's description, we might have expected to find a less tame nature than the one we perceive in the engraving, with its predominantly architectural elements. Rinuccini failed, for instance, to mention the niches with their statues. Conversely, the etching does not show the "viali coperti" in which Calypso is said to have disappeared. The "fonti in mezzo de' prati" of the *Descrizione* were, to judge from the etching, water basins with putti. The significance of the letters A–D, respectively assigned to Mercury's cloud, the nymph's seating place, the basins, and the Jupiter cloud, remains a mystery. In any case, they do not indicate the sequence in which these machines appeared.

FOURTH INTERMEZZO: AMERIGO VESPUCCI

Following the third act of the *Giudizio* was a marine scene. Exotic trees bordered the tranquil sea, with huts of reeds and palm fronds visible between them, some on the ground, others set in the trees. In the air one saw parrots and on the shore unclothed natives of a West Indian cast. The ship of Amerigo Vespucci appeared on the sea. In order to distinguish him as a son of Florence, a lion was mounted on the bow, and the mast and sails were decorated with lilies. In full armor on the poop sat the navigator. The helm was shaped like a dolphin in fetters, being directed by the allegory Sea Voyage. Further allegoric figures were Hope, Courage, and Valor. The soldiers and mariners greeted the newly-discovered land with shouts of joy, and sang a song as the vessel drew farther into the cove.

A rocky reef, covered with shells, coral, and moss, rose out of the water on which the ship had been sailing. On top of the rock stood Lady Calm ("la Tranquillità") in an azure robe, a nest of sea gulls in her tresses, and at her side a swan. In a hollow in the rocks the stormy winds lay fettered. The driver of this "chariot" was Zephyrus, holding the reins of two seals harnessed to the rising reef. A host of "gentle" winds surrounded the lowest part of the rock, caressing the water with their wings. As Lady Calm was finishing her madrigal, a cloud appeared in the middle of the heavens, revealing the allegoric figure of Immortality throning over a sphere, her blue costume spangled with stars. Apollo and the Muses stood on one side, and on the other, a chorus of ten poets—Musaeus, Amphion, Linus, Orpheus, Homer, Pindar, Virgil, Horace, Dante, and Petrarch—each clearly distinguished by their costumes and headpieces. After the heavenly beings had offered their encomium to Vespucci, the cloud began to drift away, the reef sank into the waves, and the scene changed to the Ida landscape for the fourth act of the Paris action.

Cantagallina's etching, another montage (Figure 72), shows the three large machines (this time with the letters A, B, C, designating the sequence of their appearance) framed by the rocky cove and its luxuriant flora. The natives are nowhere in evidence, nor are there any parrots whirring aloft. The sea water seems to flow off downstage, a waterfall effect not mentioned in our sources. In his report to the Duke of Mantua,[18] Gabriele Bertazzuolo wrote that the marine scene in Florence had quite failed to come off, since the Florentines had avoided making the sea in Mantuan fashion ("a modo di Mantua") lest they be guilty of plagiarism.[19]

FIFTH INTERMEZZO: THE FORGE OF VULCAN

Thus far the *Descrizione* has given no indication as to the techniques employed to change the settings. But when Rinuccini takes up the scene change after the fourth act of the *Giudizio,* he uses the phrase "girando tutte le parti della prospettiua,"[20] whereby the spectators were transported from Mount Ida to Vulcan's smithy beneath Mount Aetna. The verb *girando* would seem to imply that here Parigi was working with turning prisms. Since it is unlikely that the designer would have set up unwieldy periaktoi for a single scene change, we are perhaps justified in assuming that he also made use of turning prisms for all the other transformations.

Vulcan's smithy consisted of a labyrinth of caverns illuminated by the glow of flames and interpenetrated by clouds of smoke which seemed to move to the rhythm of hammer blows. Mars came driving up in his chariot on a reddish cloud. Victory and Glory stood at his feet, holding the reins. While the car still hung in the air, the god of war and his allegorical escorts sang a madrigal. The vehicle then landed on the stage, and Mars proceeded to knock on a grated gate guarded by

18. Dated Oct. 28, 1608, reprinted in Solerti, *Musica,* pp. 54–57.
19. For a description of the Mantuan sea scene, see below, Appendix.
20. Rinuccini, p. 41.

two large dogs. Vulcan and his three helpers, Brontes, Steropes, and Pyracmon, were visible through the grille. Mars asked the master smith whether the invincible weapons he had promised to the new hero of the House of Tuscany were ready, whereupon Vulcan had his Cyclopes display a model collection, from which Mars selected the most beautiful armor for the future lord of Florence. A turning wheel now appeared in the air with winged Fortuna, whose madrigal concluded the intermezzo, and the fifth act of *Il Giudizio* began.

Cantagallina's etching (Figure 73) shows the scene in which Mars is offered his choice of weapons. Vulcan occupies center stage, while Mars appears to stand next to Vulcan, although he is also visible in his cloud car. Fortuna's appearance was not caught in this picture, nor is there a trace of the grated gate. In other respects, however, the etching conforms to Rinuccini's description. Of particular interest is the view into the trap room. Neither Rinuccini nor Bertazzuolo mention such an effect in the fifth intermezzo, while the observer from Mantua reports a similar surprising *coup de théâtre* in the following intermezzo. The open trap room in the Vulcan workshop of the etching may reflect an original idea which the set designer later discarded in order to surprise the spectators with it in the final tableau.

SIXTH INTERMEZZO: THE TEMPLE OF PEACE

For the last time the setting changed, in this instance from the Ida landscape into a golden temple.[21] Parigi recorded the scene himself for posterity, and we gather from his etching (Figure 74) that it was a temple with composite columns supporting mighty entablatures. The throne of the goddess of peace, which occupies the upstage center of the colonnade setting, arose from a trap ("di sotto terra"), while at the same time a large cloud unfolded in the middle of the heavens. On it sat Peace, surrounded by those blessings which originated through her—namely, Remembrance of Old Friendship, Love of Country, Security, Innocence, Faith, Concord, Abundance, Justice, Reverence, and Natural and Civil Law. On the throne sat fourteen priests, and on the lowest step, Pleasure, Jest, Laughter, Forgetfulness of Wrongs, and Trade. After the goddess of peace had settled on her throne, four clouds appeared. One of them, reddish in color, supported Bellona on her chariot drawn by elephants. A greenish cloud held Cybele and her vehicle pulled by lions. Pluto, managing black horses, cast a murky pall over a third cloud. A fourth, colored aquamarine, bore Neptune's chariot; white horses were

21. Ibid., p. 44. The operation is described as follows: "la Scena nascondendo le selue, e i campi, mostrò vno eccelso, e ricco tempio." We venture the interpretation that the landscape painted on periaktoi was "concealed" by pushing out the flat temple wings.

harnessed to his throne of tufa and coral. The four gods had come to offer their services to the bridal couple, and after a brief musical *débat,* Peace concluded that each of the deities should serve Cosimo and his bride in his own peculiar fashion. Delighted by this decision, the gods slowly descended to the stage, and the heavens parted in three places. A celestial chorus was seen in the central opening. From the side apertures issued two clouds, on each of which Light Breezes ("Aurette e Zeffiri") hovered, dancing an aerial round, which was something new to the eyes of the Florentines.[22] As the singing and dancing came to an end, the four deities reached their predetermined places: Bellona and Cybele the earth—i.e. the stage floor—and Pluto and Neptune one of the two respective grottoes that had emerged at the farthest limits of the stage.[23] One of these grottoes represented the sea, with Amphitrite escorted by several Tritons and Nereids; in the other were the representatives of the underworld—that is, Proserpina and her companions. After Cybele had summoned the *Numi Civili* from Tuscany, and Bellona the *Numi Militari,* both groups sang an antiphonal piece. Pleasure then rose to her feet, and the final epithalamium ensued before the curtain came down.[24]

Gabriele Bertazzuolo found much fault with the performance in his report to the Duke of Mantua. We are already aware of his objection to the Florentine seascape. He also criticized the Vulcan scene, as well as the morris dances, and found the lighting inferior to the Mantuan level. But he was fully satisfied by the final intermezzo, and raved about the nine machines in simultaneous operation and the multitude of performers, which he estimated at approximately three hundred, including the musicians. He then concluded his remarks with the statement: "I have seen how the stage cleaved open in front down to the earth, something which I had never seen until now."[25] There can be no doubt, therefore, that Parigi offered the spectators a glimpse of the trap room, a view which he preserved in his etching.

Alfonso Fontanelli, in a report to the Duke of Modena,[26] recorded his overall impression of the evening's entertainment. Without going into details, he pointed out that the chief interest lay in the interludes, while scant attention was paid to the *Giudizio* ("fu ascoltata con pochissima attention"), a fable with which the audience was only too familiar. He found the singing of Signora Hippolita, an artist in the household of Cardinal Montalto, truly superb. The other guests also

22. Ibid., p. 47: "con gran merauiglia degli spettatori, come di cosa non più tentata in aria."
23. Ibid., p. 48: "che all'improuuiso apparuero ne' due estremi del palco della Scena."
24. Ibid., p. 50: "cadendo la cortina."
25. Quoted in Solerti, *Musica,* p. 56: "In questo ho visto spezzarsi il palco istesso dalla parte dinanzi sino a terra, cosa che non solo ho mai più visto, ma non ho manco inteso che dalli antichi, nè da moderni sia stato fatto."
26. The original Italian text in ibid., p. 47.

seem to have shared this view, since "un esquisito silentio" reigned in the auditorium, but only when Hippolita sang. The musical contribution appears otherwise to have been quite modest, if we are to trust the singer Francesco Campagnolo, who blamed "mal governo" for the "infiniti difetti" and the unabashed malice ("mera perfidia") of the participating virtuosi.[27]

The Argonauts on the Arno

A novel spectacle was scheduled for the third of November: Jason's seizure of the Golden Fleece on the Arno. The desire to produce a great water show in Florence may have been prompted by the nocturnal sea battle which, five months earlier, had been staged in Mantua for the nuptials of Francesco Gonzaga on the Lago di Mezzo.[28] To be sure, the Mantuans saw only one Trionfo that could rival the sumptuous barges of the Florentines, a *carro trionfale della Fortezza*, which plowed through the water on four flaming wheels drawn by six sea horses, guided by six sirens. The allegory of valor sat, "armata all'antica," on a throne at the head of seven steps occupied by musicians. Zuccari did not mention any other chariots; he was primarily interested in the pyrotechnic displays involved in the conquest of a specially constructed Turkish fortress, which was defended by two hundred soldiers uniformed as Turks.

The Florentines, on the other hand, were sparing in the use of fireworks. The spectators on the banks of the Arno were offered a spectacle[29] calculated to appeal to their aesthetic and humanistic sophistication. Each of the ships participating in the naumachy was in itself a work of art, and infinite pains were taken in the costuming. Music and song were further essential elements of the overall artistic conception, for which Francesco Cini took the credit. His choice of heroes for the Florentine expedition was based on a reading of the *Argonautica* of both Apollonius Rhodius and Valerius Flaccus. In all probability, he had also to consider the personal wishes of the participating noblemen. The decorative and scenic components, such as ships, the island with the temple, and the fortress, were the work of Giulio Parigi. Remigio Cantagallina's engravings still give us an impression of the fairy-tale splendor of the stately barges.

The battle over the Golden Fleece was waged on the Arno between the Ponte Santa Trinità to the east and the Ponte alla Carraia to the west (Figure 75). Grand-

27. The Campagnolo letter addressed to Cardinal Ferdinando Gonzaga was published in Emil Vogel, "Marco da Gagliano," *Vierteljahrsschrift für Musikwissenschaft*, 5 (1889), 442, n. 1.

28. A description may be found in Federigo Zuccari, *Il Passaggio per l'Italia con la dimora di Parma* (Bologna, 1608), pp. 16–20. For the Mantuan festival see below, Appendix.

29. Our principal source is Rinuccini's *Descrizione*, where the *festa navale* is described on pp. 56–66.

stands were erected for the spectators on the banks of the rain-swollen river along the Lungarno Corsini and the Lungarno Guicciardini; at the mid-point of the latter a box was set up for the courtiers. A number of onlookers followed the spectacle from the windows of neighboring houses. A gangway, where torches and other incendiary materials were stored for use after nightfall, was built directly over the water. The fortress, conceived as the city of Colchis, and furnished with towers, bulwarks, and parapets, had been erected above the central arch of the Ponte alla Carraia. In the middle of the Arno lay an artificial island with a temple, where the Golden Fleece was safeguarded.

As a prelude to the festival, there appeared a miniature galley, the crew of which evidently consisted of children, skillfully executing all the maneuvers that might have been expected of a full-size craft. The spectacle proper began when an armada, which was protecting the island with the Golden Fleece, sailed forth from the harbor of Colchis. Manned by warriors and lacking outward decoration, the ships cruised in an easterly direction about the island. As they passed the princes' loge in pairs, salutes were fired. They then arrayed themselves before the Ponte alla Carraia—that is, directly in front of Colchis.

Jason's fleet sailed from the east, passing beneath the middle arch of the Ponte Santa Trinità. The Florentine Argonauts did not come on one ship but on sixteen, each decorated in a manner appropriate to its passengers. Opening the *mostra* was the ship of Hercules (Figure 76), the bow of which terminated in a hydra, each of its heads emitting flames. An image of Cerberus served as the rudder. Two columns with an eagle between them rose from the stern. Graphic portrayals of the labors of Hercules embellished the sides of the ship. A sculptured lion adorned one gunwale, a bull the other. The mast recalled the tree with the golden apples in the garden of the Hesperides. Instead of the crow's nest atop the mast was a sphere with a pennant bearing the Hapsburg and Medici escutcheons. Seated on the afterdeck was Guidobaldo Brancadoro as Hercules, his lion skin and club making him easy to identify. Poplar branches provided the crest for his helmet. Hercules' lieutenant, Philoctetes, was portrayed by Senator Niccolò Cimenes, who had financed the construction of the ship. A page bearing Hercules' shield was posted at a somewhat lower level on the deck. Several warriors, musicians, and steersmen were also on board.

The second vessel belonged to the winged twins Calais and Zetes, sons of the North Wind (Figure 77). It was covered with snow and ice, its mast an oak tree with icicles. Above the poop rose a grotto on which sat Boreas and Orithyia, parents of the Boreades. The soldiers were costumed as *Venti Boreali*. Harpies plied the oars—an allusion to the Phineus episode.

Parallel to the Boreades sailed the ship of Peleus and Telamon, on the highest point of which was a statue of Thetis seated on a shell. Algae, sponges, and various kinds of moss adorned the hull. An oak with an eagle on its crest provided the mast. Tritons served as oarsmen.

The silver ship of Atalante was the next to follow. Nero Corsini, in the costume of an Amazon, portrayed the sole female participant in the expedition of the Argonauts. Above him, on a crescent made of mirrors sat Diana, goddess of the chase. The figurehead was the head of a wild boar, a gift of Meleager. The oarsmen were dressed as nymphs. In its wake sailed the golden barge of Meleager and Tydeus, a statue of the god of love adorning the poop, and a boar's head decorating the bowsprit.

The following vessel bore the hereditary Prince Cosimo, who enjoyed himself in the role of Jason. Modeled after the Venetian Bucintoro, the ship was lavishly gilded and embellished with reliefs (Figure 78). Silvio Piccolomini officiated as lieutenant. Towering over the stern was a statue of Pallas Athena, whose head and arms moved and seemed to be steering the ship. The soldiers, musicians, and oarsmen wore uniforms in white and gold.

Iphiclus and Nauplius sailed behind Jason in a vessel that resembled a reef rising from the sea, covered with algae and sponges (Figure 79). Two sea horses served as the driving team. Neptune was the protector of this ship, the wheels of which churned the water.

The next barge may have remained a puzzle for even the most erudite Florentines. It belonged to Asterion, son of Cometes—a rampant confusion of mythology. The hull had the shape of a cloud, from which the poop rose in the form of a triumphal chariot crowned by Jupiter and his eagle. The mast was shaped to resemble a comet. A fire-breathing horse provided the figurehead.

Polyphemus and Palaemonius lorded over the following vessel, in front of whose mountain-shaped stern, conceived as a smoking Aetna, stood Ceres. The bow terminated in a cliff to which Scylla was fettered. Phorcys, a god of the sea and father of the Gorgons who duly labored at the oars, piloted the ship.

Three members of the expedition sailed on a singular vessel. Erytus, Echion, and Aethalides (three sons of Hermes) sat on a swimming peacock which from time to time fanned out its mirror-speckled tail—an invention of the Veronese painter Jacopo Ligozzi (Figure 80).

Prince Peretti (Castor) and Paolo Giordano Orsino (Pollux) had commissioned the construction of the barge of the Dioscuri (Figure 81). On the highest point sat Leda on a swan. The rudder was dolphin-shaped, and the animal seemed to clasp the singer Arion with its tail. Sirens, serpents, Harpies, Medusa heads, and episodes from the Leda legend embellished the ship, on the bow of which stood Fama bridling two white horses.

Agamemnon and Menelaus followed the Dioscuri on a vessel commanded by Vulcan, sitting in his smithy-grotto which formed the afterdeck (Figure 82). The oarsmen were Cyclopes who plowed through the water with instruments of the forge.

Alongside the ship of the Atrides swam a huge lobster (Figure 83), also a creation of Ligozzi. As it approached the grandstand of the princes, it transformed itself into a barge, on which sat Periclymenus, who, endowed by his grandfather, Poseidon, with the gift of metamorphosis, now changed from a lobster into a knight.

Idmon and Mopsus, conceived as priests of Apollo, sailed on a vessel on whose stern the sun god throned in his cloud car (Figure 84). The bow terminated in the figure of the Python serpent. Father Chronos stood at the helm. Atop the mast was the figure of Fortuna, holding a sail to indicate the mutability of the human condition. A smoking altar, encircled by priests, stood on the deck. The pages carried various instruments of divination. The oarsmen wore shepherd's costume and laurel wreaths.

Side by side with Idmon and Mopsus came Amphion (Figure 85). The prow of this barge was shaped like a fish head. On the highest point of the bow stood Mercury on a cloud. The sculptures of two Harpies lay at Amphion's feet. A sea monster "à capriccio dell' Architetto" manned the helm.

On the last ship in the mostra rode Bacchus on a wine cask in front of an arbor mounted on the poop (Figure 86). The mast and yardarm were entwined with tendrils and grapes. Two tigers extended the Dionysian theme to the bow. Orpheus sat beneath Dionysus. The soldiers were attired as bacchantes and the oarsmen as satyrs.

The Greek flotilla sailed in a westerly direction along the Lungarno Corsini past Colchis, from the fortifications of which (on the Ponte alla Carraia) the alarums of the aroused inhabitants resounded. The armada then swerved to the east, coming to rest in front of the bridal loge on the Lungarno Guicciardini. From Jason's ship came voices singing a few lines from the lengthy poem composed by Francesco Cini, which gave a synopsis of the Argonaut legend and its heroes. Copies of the text were distributed among the guests of honor.[30]

In the meantime, a ship appeared drawn by two whales carrying instrumentalists and singers under the command of Glaucus (Figure 87), a god of the sea, who had come to fire the spirits of the Argonauts for the forthcoming battle. Tritons again manned the oars.

30. Text in Rinuccini, pp. 107–08, and the wording of the individual *cartelli,* pp. 108–14.

At length the Argonauts approached the island to make a landing. As the disembarcation proceeded, a small island emerged in the east, on which appeared the god of the Arno in the company of four other Tuscan Rivers (Figure 88). The island pursued a course toward the loge of honor, where Arno presented the bride with six golden apples from the garden of the Hesperides—a meaningful gift from Hercules in view of the six balls on the Medici escutcheon. Further offerings were extended to the bride by Thetis, who arrived with her chorus of Nereids on a shell.

Meanwhile, all the Argonauts had landed on the island, and Jason was advancing on the perilous path to the temple with the Golden Fleece. Two fire-breathing bulls and two warriors blocked his way and were duly overcome by the hereditary prince. Next a hissing dragon came forth vomiting from its maw a third warrior, whom Jason deftly dispatched in a duel. The hero was now free to enter the temple and seize the Golden Fleece.

As the Colchian armada had been alerted by the sentinels of the city that the Golden Fleece was in jeopardy, it now also landed on the island, and a tilt at the barriers ("battaglia à guisa di barriera") developed. When the joust was finished, all the participants took to their ships to prepare for the sea battle. Since additional space was required for this, the island with the temple was shoved aside and pulled in front of the Ponte alla Carraia. In order to bridge the time lapse necessary for this technical maneuver, a small island appeared on which the River Ombrone, accompanied by other Tuscan Rivers, paid their respects to the bride with ingenious gifts. A group of nymphs and shepherds provided the music on their wind instruments.

Since it had now grown dark, all the torches were ignited not only on the ships but also along the banks of the Arno. The ensuing naumachy consisted essentially of the firing of cannon volleys. As the barges had been designed chiefly for display, and the architect had concentrated primarily on those parts which lay above the water line ("fabbricate con molt'opera morta") the vessels were not exactly combatworthy, and collision was avoided to preclude any danger to the crews. Afterward, the Colchian flotilla withdrew to the Carraia Bridge, while the Argonauts stormed and demolished the fortress that had been erected upon it—an assault enacted with considerable realism. The Argonauts then returned to their ships and sailed up to the loge of honor, where, to the strains of a madrigal, they handed the Golden Fleece to the bride. Thus ended the Arno festival, which for many was the climax of the nuptial entertainments—at least for those who were excluded from the palace diversions, in other words, the majority of Florentines.

9. Mascherata in the Pitti Palace

1611

The carnival of 1611 at the Medici court was only a routine affair. There were the usual balls and a number of theatrical performances in the palaces of Giovanni de' Medici and Count Giulio Tassoni, as well as performances given by youthful dilettantes and attended by the grand ducal family. The sole artistic event at court was the presentation of a *mascherata,* a mixture of ballroom dancing and operatic scenes.[1] Ottavio Rinuccini wrote the libretto, Giulio Parigi created the settings, Agniolo Ricci was the choreographer, and Marco da Gagliano, Jacopo Peri, Francesca and Settimia Caccini, and Vittoria Archilei were the appointed composers. The performance took place on February 14 in the "sala detta delle Comedie,"[2] the "sala alta de' Pitti,"[3] which the guests reached by climbing the spiral staircase. The main entrance was locked, and was opened after the performance so that the audience could go home via the *scala grande.* The traditional *gradi* were erected in the auditorium, with an open space left in the middle for dancing. Stage and auditorium were connected by ramps or staircases.

As the curtain rose to the strains of a "dolcissima sinfonia," the spectators were given ample time to admire Parigi's setting. The scene represented the port of

1. Our primary source for reconstructing the performance is the letter of Jacopo Cicognini, who witnessed the première. Solerti reprinted it in the second volume of his *Gli Albori del melodramma,* pp. 283–94. This account is referred to here as Cicognini-Solerti. We are indebted to Tinghi's *Diario* for a number of details.
2. Tinghi, in Solerti, *Musica,* p. 61.
3. Cicognini-Solerti, p. 283.

Livorno, the Porto Vecchio, which owed its importance to the Medici. Clearly identifiable were the fortress and lighthouse. Jacopo Cicognini raved about the naturalness of the simulated billows of the sea,[4] and the realistic rocks, touched up with silver and set with coral and shells, helped to deceive the senses. The entire setting was brilliantly illuminated by concealed light sources.[5] Cicognini's admiration was shared by the other spectators who, "attoniti e stupefatti," applauded Parigi's "stupenda invenzione e nobile artifizio."

Neptune rose slowly from the depths, wearing a crown of pearls in his blue hair and carrying the trident. He was portrayed by the singer Jacopo Peri, who also composed the music for his madrigal "nel suo nobilissimo stile recitativo."[6] The Tuscans were flattered by Neptune's aria in which he praised the charms of the rural landscape they inhabited. Meanwhile, sirens and Tritons emerged from the sea, forming a chorus to sing a *canzone* in honor of Cosimo and Maria Magdalena. The sea soon became populated with other creatures of the deep, some of which rode on dolphins and others tossed about on shells. Finally the chariot of Thetis appeared, apparently made of silvered tufa and decorated with shells and marine flora. A nymph bridled the two dolphins which pulled the vehicle, and which presently raised their heads and tails from the water, all with the utmost verisimilitude ("come se vivi fossero").[7] Thetis then alighted, "con misurato tempo e grazioso movimento," from her chariot. Striding from reef to reef with her companions, she entered the auditorium to dance a ballet which, in the inventiveness of its choreography, surpassed everything that our observer had ever seen. This intricate dance was performed by noblemen and ladies of the court who eventually formed into groups of letters, so that the spectators could spell out the names of Cosimo and Magdalena.[8] In the meantime, three nymphs had encamped on the reefs downstage in order to sing a series of madrigals, each of which was composed by its singer. The first was written by Vittoria Archilei, who sang "con la sua grazia e voce angelica." Settimia Caccini delivered her piece "con ogni suprema esquisitezza." The third was sung by Francesca Caccini. At last, the three voices joined in an ottava that Francesca had composed "con stile graziosissimo e vago."[9] While the nymphs were singing, the sea became alive with ships, some of them with

4. "Parebbe a chi non l'ha visto quasi incredibile che l'arte arrivasse a tanta perfezione" (ibid. p. 284).
5. "L'innumerabile quantità di lumi, che, senza vedersi, solo reflettendo rendevano splendidissima la prospettiva" (ibid., p. 283).
6. Ibid., p. 285.
7. Ibid., p. 286.
8. Tinghi, in Solerti, *Musica,* p. 61.
9. Cicognini-Solerti, p. 288.

hoisted sails, others manned by oarsmen, and as they passed the fortress, chambers were fired. At the end of their song, the three nymphs descended into the auditorium, where they distributed gifts in silver shells to the ladies. The curtain was then lowered.[10]

Once dinner had been served and the ball had begun, everyone imagined that the performance was over. But Rinuccini had still another surprise in store. As the curtain again rose on Parigi's seascape, Cupid appeared on the beach and declared in an aria that he had renounced his mother, Venus. A seafarer came along in a bark, singing a French canzone. Cupid bade the sailor take him in his ship, but was refused, and had therefore to make his exit on foot. A second vessel then heaved into view. From this one came sounds of a duet sung between the spokesman of the several passengers and the first mariner, Antonio Brandi and Domenico Poggi taking the parts to Marco da Gagliano's music. The two ships tossed to the rhythm of the waves, from which some of the passengers hauled living fish. A sorrowful Venus appeared seated on a dolphin, lamenting to the winds and waves the loss of her Cupid. Proteus then rose from the deep, and taking pity on her, revealed that Cupid had moved his abode to the court of the Medici. This was the cue for a joyful chorus of *Dei Marini* who appeared in Proteus' retinue, concluding the "maraviglioso festino . . . con applauso e satisfazione infinita."[11]

For the wedding of Count Mario Sforza and Arnea of Lorraine the mascherata was repeated on the sixth of May in expanded and slightly altered form under the title, *Mascherata di Ninfe di Senna.*[12] To honor the bride who came from France, the Nymph of the Seine was introduced in place of Thetis. She rode into the harbor of Livorno on a float, accompanied by eight additional nymphs of the Seine. Since Arnea had landed in Livorno, Parigi's setting gained particular significance. Moreover, no one was surprised when Neptune made his appearance, since he reigned equally over the mouth of the Seine and the port of Leghorn.

10. "La tela caduta al basso" (ibid., p. 289).
11. Ibid., p. 293.
12. Rinuccini's text was published for this occasion; reprinted in Solerti, *Albori, 2,* 266–82.

10. Eros and Anteros

1613

The highlight of the carnival season of 1613 was the *barriera* that took place on February 17 in the Uffizi Theatre, to honor Giovan Carlo, the son of Cosimo II, who had been baptized the previous day at the age of nearly two. Rehearsals for the elaborate tourney had been in progress since December.[1] The theme had been worked out by Giovanni Villifranchi, who probably wrote the anonymous description of the festival as well.[2]

Opening the festivities on the third of February was a court ball in the Pitti Palace, attended by the Florentine nobility. Toward three o'clock in the morning by Florentine reckoning, the dance was interrupted by drum rolls and trumpet blasts. A herald made his way into the hall, escorted by trumpeters, torchbearers, and a dwarf. He announced to the assembled company that the knight Fidamante and the Cavalier of Immortal Passion, two warriors of all-powerful Cupid, would defend, with lance, axe, and rapier, the thesis that the ways of Cupid were just ("che givsta e d'Amore ogni operazione"). Soon after the challenge ("disfida") and the rules of the joust were distributed among the guests by the dwarf, the names of the two challengers, Francesco de' Medici and Paolo Orlando Orsino, began to be whispered about.

The tilt was based on the following *concetto*. Cupid (Eros) resolved to renounce his mother, Venus, and establish his own kingdom, not on Cyprus or in Greece but

1. See the excerpts from Tinghi's diary in Solerti, *Musica,* p. 68.
2. Descrizzione / della barriera, / e della mascherata, / Fatte in Firenze a'XVII. et a'XIX. di Febbraio / MDCXII. / Al Serenissimo Signor / Principe d'Vrbino. / In Firenze, / 1613.

in Florence. He justified his secession in that he desired to help mankind, and above all the Florentines, to enjoy the delights of love, without suffering the attendant emotional ills for which the realm of Venus was to blame. Hence his was to be a new kingdom of love without care and torment, without hatred, jealousy, scorn, ire, dissension, madness, deception, ingratitude, and despair. The two knights, Fidamante and Immortale Ardore, were prepared to fight for this new empire and its governing principle.

Briefly mentioned in the *Descrizione* is the beauty of the Uffizi Theatre, the auditorium of which provided space for six thousand spectators. Six rows of *gradi* were erected for them on each of the three sides. The guests of honor sat on one dais, the judges on another. Giovanni de' Medici was the master of the tilt. Twenty chandeliers hung from the ceiling, which was decorated with lilies. Statues were mounted at various points in the hall—effigies of Tragedy, Old Comedy, New Comedy, the Pastoral, Apollo, and Thalia. Giulio Parigi, who by that time was considered the "Dedalo de' nostri tempi,"[3] was the scene designer and technician. Tickets of admission ("bulletini") had to be shown by the guests.

The festival began at approximately two o'clock Florentine time. To the strains of an orchestral piece the curtain descended, exposing the stage to view.[4] A cloud floated down on which winged Fama was disclosed wearing a blue costume embroidered with tongues and ears. In her right hand she held a golden trumpet, and in her left, three golden balls. Fama reiterated the challenge of the tilt in a madrigal written by Villifranchi. Then appeared Parigi's first setting, the Tyrrhenian Sea, the waves of which surged so convincingly that the onlookers imagined them to be real.[5] Simultaneously, the car of Venus, drawn by two swans flapping their wings with considerable realism, came up between the waves. The chariot was gilded and decorated with paintings from the legend of Venus and Adonis, a love that had begun in joy but ended in pain. Cupid, who had stolen the vehicle from his mother, sat on the highest point, his blond hair wreathed in laurel, his golden arrows sheathed in a silver quiver; jewels were set in his loincloth, and his pale blue wings were edged in gold. Cupid's eyes were evidently blindfolded, since reference is made to his blindness in two passages of the *Descrizione*. In contrast, the sublimated forms of love, Amore Divino and Anterote, were scheduled to appear later, their eyes uncovered. With arms charmingly intertwined, just as the painters of antiquity had portrayed them, the three Graces stood at the love god's feet, wear-

3. Ibid., p. 9.
4. "Calandosi la tenda della Scena" (ibid., p. 11).
5. "Cosi al viuo ondeggiante, che ingannaua la vista de'riguardanti" (ibid., p. 15).

ing body tights to feign nudity.[6] Beneath them sat the knight Fidamante and the Cavalier of Immortal Passion—that is, Francesco de' Medici and Paolo Giordano Orsino. Fidamante wore six lilies as a crest, while from the other knight's helmet sprouted a blooming rose bush. Also adorning both pieces of headgear was a bird of paradise with a star-shaped diamond on its breast. The plumage towered three ells above each helmet—a "superbissima mostra con disegni nuoui."[7] Embroidered on the knights' costumes were golden flowers, fruits, and animals. Somewhat below them sat two of Cupid's priests in antique raiment. At their feet were twelve putti (Riso, Giuoco, Contento, Canto, Diletto, Gaudio, Giubilo, Godimento, Riposo, Ballo, Sperare, and Piacere), each holding a torch and characterized by an appropriate emblem. Thus, Song wore a nightingale for a headpiece, Repose a stork's nest, Laughter a garland of roses with ostrich feathers, and Hope a silver anchor.

In a madrigal, Cupid declared his intention of establishing his realm in Tuscany. Appealing to the "chaste souls" ("pudiche alme") of the ladies, he condemned the "lasciuie" of his mother, Venus.[8] Here the audience heard a faint echo of Neoplatonic thought. As Cupid sang the words "Ergasi Tempio sacro," an octagonal temple appeared on stage between two boulders,[9] with a terrace encircled by a balustrade stretched out before it. Access was provided by two staircases. To the right was a statue of Perseus, to the left a portrait of Hercules. Beneath these were images of Fortuna and Abondanza, and still farther below, reliefs from the legend of Cupid and Psyche. After Cupid concluded his madrigal, trumpets blared, and the herald who had announced the challenge in the Pitti Palace entered. Six pages then appeared with the weapons for Cupid's knights, who now strode into the auditorium with their seconds and pages to present themselves to the spectators, and proceeded to take up positions by the temple. The priests of Cupid and the twelve *amoretti* also posted themselves near the sanctuary, from which instrumental music resounded. Meanwhile, Cupid's car had vanished with the Graces.

A trap now opened, through which the head of a dragon was visible, belching flames and smoke. Nemesis, with her snaky locks, ascended from the monster's chasm. Her appearance in connection with Cupid was probably derived from the *Periegesis* of Pausanias, who spoke of a winged Nemesis, for the Goddess of Retribution appeared most often in the entourage of winged Cupid. In one

6. "Vestite in guisa che pareuano ignude" (ibid., p. 16).
7. Ibid., p. 17.
8. For the metamorphoses of Cupid, see Erwin Panofsky, *Studies in Iconology* (New York, 1939), pp. 95–128.
9. "Ottogono bellissimo in mezzo à due Rocche" (*Descrizzione*, p. 21).

hand Nemesis carried two chains, and in the other a vessel filled with water. Twelve sooty Furies bearing torches emerged from two openings near the dragon's ears, their wild dance[10] followed by Nemesis' madrigal, calling upon Disdain of Love (Sdegno Amoroso) to assist her in the struggle against Cupid and his new empire.

While Nemesis and her Furies were disappearing through the trap, the hell-mouth ejected Disdain of Love and his five "Egyptian" knights, fully armed for the tilt. Sdegno Amoroso, his feet sheathed in lion's skin, wore a red costume and, on his head, the head of a bear. The knight's helmets were shaped like the heads of dragons with enormous red crests. Escorted by their seconds and pages, they paced off the lists. Facing the guests of honor and the judges, Disdain of Love then sang his riposte to the challenge of Cupid's two cavaliers—a madrigal in which he evinced nothing but scorn for the "Cieco fanciul." The first joust then began between the party of Fidamante and Immortale Ardore, on the one hand, and the five Egyptian knights of Sdegno Amoroso, on the other. Four of the Egyptians were defeated, but the fifth emerged victorious. The contest had still not come to a decision, when, to the strains of a sinfonia, Iris appeared on a multi-colored cloud as Jupiter's messenger. She sang her madrigal, thus preparing for the entrance of the Cyclopes and the Knights of the Medicean Stars.

In front of Mount Aetna, which was evidently part of the setting, emerged the one-eyed Cyclops Pyracmon, having been summoned by Iris. With his rosy body tights simulating nudity, this grimy fellow wore, draped across his shoulders, a silver cloak appliquéd with streaks of lightning. Wielding a hammer, he called forth eight more Cyclopes from the volcano in a brief song. Each cyclops carried in one hand a lightning bolt that seemed to burn at both ends, and in the other, a shield that gleamed as though it were made of burnished gold. Depicted on the shields were those of Jupiter's amorous escapades in which he had used trickery to attain the objects of his desire—those with Leda, Danae, and Europa. The spectators were not surprised, therefore, when Jupiter himself appeared on a shimmering cloud, escorted by the personification of Amorous Intrigue (Inganno Amoroso). Somewhat lower down between the clouds shone the satellites of Jupiter which had been discovered by Galileo, "the mathematician of His Highness, that rare and unique genius of our time, the inventor of the extraordinary telescope."[11] Jupiter was able to sing his aria in the vicinity of the Grand Duchess, and have his costume admired by all, as his cloud machine moved forward without revealing its apparatus

10. "Vn ballo assai strauagante" (ibid., p. 25).
11. Ibid., p. 32.

of propulsion.[12] Dressed in a red satin doublet under a cloak embroidered with flowers and streaks of lightning, he carried a bolt of lightning and wore a crown over flowing blond hair. Whether the figure of Amorous Intrigue, who displayed a costume of iridescent fabric, was that of a young man or a young woman, it was impossible to say. The cloud machine, which changed its appearance as it advanced, at length vanished into the gridiron, while the four Jupiter satellites were being transformed into four knights—Ardente, Immutabile, Fedele, and Costante—and were presented with lances by the Cyclopes. Again the arena of the auditorium was enlivened by a tilt.

Now the setting changed to a seascape which differed from the initial marine scene. In the distance one saw the island of Elba "al naturale," with the bay of Portoferraio and its fortifications erected by Cosimo I. On the other side lay the Etruscan city of Populonia. Further downstage stood two towers. Ships plowed through the waves. The spectators were transported by the "raro spettacolo" that Parigi had created.[13] Amazement grew as under booming cannon a galley heaved into view bearing Love's Torment (Dolore Amoroso), with his seven Thracian knights and a band of musicians. The most notable of the seven was the Grand Duke, playing the role of the cavalier Ardenti Sospiri. Without going into the details of his costuming, it should be noted that he wore fourteen diamonds and had a headpiece consisting of fifteen hundred aigrettes. After the ship had dropped anchor, the disembarcation began, accompanied by music *"alla barbaresca"* played by the instrumentalists on the galley. Led by Dolore Amoroso, the Grand Duke and his knights marched from the stage into the auditorium, halting before the Grand Duchess, so that Love's Torment could sing his rejoinder to the original *disfida*. Meanwhile, the seamen on the galley weighed anchor, and the ship vanished from the scene. Then began the tilt between the partisans of Eros and the cavaliers led by Cosimo II.

The jousting ended, as in the further part of the stage a fissure opened,[14] giving a view of hell. The flaming walls of the city of Dis appeared, and before it, the fiery floods of Phlegeton, "di viue fiamme." Megaera emerged from the sea of flames pursued by Jealousy, who rode on Cerberus. Following were seven knights

12. "Senza vedersi come" (ibid., p. 33).

13. "Quando si vide la Scena tutta conuersa in Mare, e se cosa alcuna può apportar merauiglia all'intelletto humano, e se dall'arte può esser imitata marauigliosamente la Natura, ben si poteua scorgere all'ora al viuo, poi che non v'era niuno riguardatore, che non restasse più confuso, che ammirato" (ibid., p. 48).

14. "S'aperse all'ora la Scena" (ibid., p. 64).

conceived as Persians, the first on the back of Hydra, the second on Scylla, the third on Chimera, the fourth on the Sphinx, the fifth on the Python, the sixth on Geryoneous, and the seventh and last on the fiery wheel of Ixion. This group also paraded in front of the Grand Duchess so that Jealousy could sing her madrigal before the tilt began.

After the heavens opened, revealing a congregation of *Numi Celesti* extolling their happy life in chorus, Pallas Athena appeared with six *Eroi Celesti*—Hercules, Achilles, Godfrey of Bouillon, Charles V, Henri IV, and Cosimo Medici—who turned about in a circle, although they hardly seemed to be moving at all. Each historic personality could be identified by his special mask.[15] Having sung a duet with Hercules, the goddess summoned Vulcan from his cave in Aetna and commissioned the naked, bearded god of smiths to forge weapons for the heroes, whereupon the latter proceeded into the cave and reappeared in full panoply.[16] Joined by their seconds and pages, they paraded through the arena as a prelude to the tilt. Verses for this scene with the Eroi Celesti were contributed by Ottavio Rinuccini.

For the following episode, contrived by Andrea Salvadori, the stage transformed itself into "vn Mare Tirreno al naturale,"[17] the same sea which had previously served as background for the appearance of Love's Torment. But this time a colorful garden framed the shore, the abode of Flora and her nymphs. Some of the flowers were real, others were made of silk. The air was filled with the song of birds. A chorus of Nereids stood in the water, singing a *canzonet*. A chariot then appeared bearing the god of war, who had come in a gallant effort to defend Venus against the onslaughts of her impertinent son. At the same time, the god Tirreno, who could have been mistaken for Neptune, emerged from the waves. After Mars and Tirreno had each sung an aria, Mars landed on the shore, leading a host of Persian warriors.

Cybele now entered on a chariot drawn by two lions. Aeneas and his halfbrother Eryx, as well as a throng of Corybants, comprised the entourage of the Great Mother. Once more a tilt began, only to be interrupted briefly by Venus, who, emerging from the sea on a shell, had come to put an end to the senseless combat. However, the tilting was resumed as the so-called *fola*, or melee, developed, and was terminated by the descent of Divine Love, a naked, winged boy without blindfold ("non cieco"). His aria prepared for the appearance of Anteros, who resembled his brother Eros to the point of confusion. Flying in on a white cloud,

15. "Maschera al viso rappresentate al viuo ciascuno de gli Eroi" (ibid., p. 88).
16. Their costume was "simile all'abito militare antico romano" (ibid., p. 87).
17. Ibid., p. 90.

he sang his canzone, in which he revealed himself as the god of reciprocal love, thereby settling the entire conflict. Anteros stepped down into the auditorium and led the ladies to their knights, whereupon the couples danced a short pavan.

Accounts of this extraordinary tourney appear to have spread swiftly to England. For it can hardly be regarded as coincidence that to honor the wedding of the Earl of Somerset and Lady Frances Howard in December 1613, Ben Jonson mounted his masque *A Challenge at Tilt,* the theme of which was a quarrel between Eros and Anteros, the symbol of "reciprocal affection." The moral of this story was the same in Florence as in Westminster. Cartari had formulated it succinctly in his *Imagini* (1556): "Chi è amato dee parimente amare."

In order to give the people of Florence a chance to see at least a reflection of the ornate spectacle, it was decided that a nocturnal cavalcade of the participants in the tourney should be held in the streets of the city. The performers gathered two days after the tilt in the Piazza San Marco. Leading the torchlight procession was the golden car of Fame, drawn by six horses, and bearing the musicians who had played the "barbaric" music on the galley in the Uffizi. Flora followed in the midst of a throng of seconds, drummers, trumpeters, and torch-bearing pages. The next troupe to enter the procession were the Eroi Celesti, followed in turn by Jealousy and Dolore Amoroso with his retinue. The Stelle Medicee and Sdegno Amoroso, with Nemesis and the Furies, preceded the knights on their horses. Eros, Amore Divino, Anteros, Venus, the three Graces, and the amoretti rode on a gilded chariot. The last pageant was reserved for the musicians. A grotesque rounded off the cavalcade: the personification of Carnival. The parade moved across the Ponte Vecchio to the Pitti Palace and thence over the Ponte Santa Trinità back to the Piazza San Marco. A running at the quintain (in the likeness of a Saracen) was staged at two points, in the Via Maggio and in the Via Larga. Thus as Shrove Tuesday of the year 1613 came to an end, the gaping crowds finally dissolved in the grey dawn of Ash Wednesday.

11. Tilts and Equestrian Ballets

1616

The highlight of the carnival of 1616 was the tilt and equestrian ballet, a *Guerra d'Amore* which took place on February 11 or 12 in the Piazza Santa Croce.[1] Grandstand décor, floats, and costumes were designed by Giulio Parigi.[2] Agniolo Ricci worked out the choreography of both the tourney and the ballet. Jacopo Peri, Paolo Grazi, and Giovan Battista Signorini composed the solo and choral pieces. Giovanni del Turco supervised the musicians. The verses were a contribution of Andrea Salvadori, who also invented the meager underlying conceit—that is, the quarrel over the possession of the beautiful Indian queen Lucinda, between two exotic cavaliers, the Asiatic Indamoro, King of Narsinga, and the African Gradameto, King of Melinda. Cosimo II took the role of Indamoro, while his younger brother, Don Lorenzo, portrayed the African King. The spectacle was intended as a compliment to the Grand Duchess Maria Magdalena. Salvadori was cognizant of the fact that with his equestrian ballet he was renewing an ancient tradition.[3]

Parigi erected a wooden, oval-shaped amphitheatre, with *gradi* for the spectators, in the Piazza Santa Croce (Figure 89). At the farthest points of the principal axis to

1. [Andrea Salvadori], Gverra d'Amore / Festa del / Serenissimo Gran Dvca / di Toscana / Cosimo Secondo, / Fatta in Firenze il Carneuale del 1615. / In Firenze / MDC.XV. A supplementary source is the Lettera / al Sig. Alberico Cybo / Principe di Massa / sopra il Giuoco fatto / dal Granduca / intitolato Guerra d'Amore / il dì 12 febbraio 1615, in Firenze. In Pisa, 1615. The *Lettera* gives February 12 as the date, while Cesare Tinghi in his *Diario* (in Solerti, *Musica*, p. 102), regards the event under the date February 11.

2. The names of the artistic collaborators are listed by Salvadori on p. 52.

3. "Rinnouellarsi gli antichi spettacoli di Roma, e di Atene" (ibid., p. 52). Cf. also the reference to Virgil on p. 5.

the east and west were the entrances, decorated with statues, through which the participants in the tourney moved into the arena. The princes' loge was in the south, in front of the Palazzo dell'Antella at one end of the secondary axis.

The *mostra* opened to musical accompaniment with the chariot of the Indian queen Lucinda, who appeared as a statue on a golden chair. Of the sixty-four people who rode on the pageant, some were disguised as maidservants, others as Brahmins, the latter providing the music. The car was followed by one hundred Indian riflemen on foot, "vestiti d'abito ricco insieme capriccioso." Winged Aurora, amidst frolicking *amoretti,* hovered above the Indian queen on a multicolored cloud. Dawn's costume was in three colors—red, white, and yellow. She held a glowing torch in one hand, and scattered flowers with the other. Parigi's design, which shows the goddess in this pose, is preserved in the Biblioteca Nazionale (Figure 91). Aurora sang a number of stanzas in front of the tribune of honor, alluding to the awaited spectacle and flattering the Grand Duchess. The float then made the rounds, while the chorus of Indians extolled the greatness of the House of Hapsburg, and finally came to a halt on the side opposite the princes' loge.

Now the performers began to parade into the auditorium (Figure 90). The Grand Duke, disguised as Indamoro, rode through one entrance, while Don Lorenzo, as Gradameto, advanced through the other. Each of them led four squadrons of cavalrymen and several contingents of foot soldiers. Terminating the grand ducal procession was the car of Asia, while behind Don Lorenzo's warriors rumbled the chariot of Africa.

The Asian vehicle was drawn by two camels from the Medici menagerie. Thanks to certain concealed machines,[4] the camels were able to pull their burden. The highest point of the car was covered with a small meadow on which grew a tree with golden leaves and branches. In the top of this tree was the flaming nest of the phoenix, which flapped its golden wings. A fountain babbled in the meadow. On a crouching camel stood a statue portraying Asia, holding in one hand a scepter, and in the other a golden vessel from which incense was wafted upward. In rocky niches at the foot of the statue were depicted the rivers of Asia—the Meander, Volga, Tigris, and Ganges. Eight giants who strode in alongside the car intrigued the spectators with "infinita merauiglia."

Bringing up the rear of Don Lorenzo's procession was the African float pulled by two elephants, artificial animals which moved, thanks to an "ingegnoso Artefice," with the utmost verisimilitude. Two obelisks with Egyptian symbols were

---

4. "Con l'aiuto di alcune ingegnose macchine non vedute dal popolo" (ibid., p. 30).

mounted on the car. The statue portraying Africa, who held a spear in one hand, and in the other several chains connected to the necks of similar effigies, was flanked by two lions. An elephant's head served as a helmet. River gods were encamped below the statue. The vehicle itself was richly embellished with paintings which referred to African events, such as the wedding of Perseus and Andromeda, the triumphs of Hannibal, and the Labors of Hercules. Also depicted were the cataracts of the Nile, the lighthouse of Pharos, the sacrifices in honor of Isis, and the figures of Anubis and Osiris with the heads of dogs. The car was followed by twelve cannibals, who, according to Pliny, dwelt in the area where the Nile takes its rise.

After these groups had made their rounds in the arena, the warriors took up their positions for the tilt, and the various combats on foot and on horseback, with lance, sword, and mace, could begin. Trained personnel had been selected for the jousting so that the expectations of the audience would be gratified. As the battle reached its climax, a thunderous din resounded from the Via di Fogna. Across from the loge of honor in the northern opening of the wooden amphitheatre, four horses appeared pulling a *trionfo* on which were Mars and Venus. This is the moment captured by Callot in his etching (Figure 92). The chariot drove into the warring hosts, dividing them into two groups. At the same time, the vehicle itself split into two segments, one for the god of war, the other for the goddess of love. Brandishing his lance, Mars sang, "con alta voce," a madrigal in which he commanded the warriors to cease fighting so that Venus could deliver her message. Venus then proceeded on her half-chariot to the grand ducal loge and demanded in a madrigal that joyfulness and the dance now come into their own. This was the cue for the equestrian ballet to begin. Accompanied by music, the Grand Duke and his brother led the rounds of the horses, "con diletto e stupore di ciaschuno." At length, the pageant of the Indian queen left the arena, followed by the knights and foot soldiers and the remaining floats. The spectators then dispersed, assembling once more in the evening to gaze at the horsemen, costumes, and chariots in a torchlight procession of all the participants through the streets of Florence. The cavalcade halted at the most important points, and madrigals were sung.

On October 16 of that same year, the Florentines were again given an opportunity to see an equestrian ballet. On the occasion of the state visit of Federigo di Urbino, the bridegroom of Claudia de' Medici, balls and *mascherate* were given, and on three occasions a "commedia di zanni" was performed.[5] As a climax, there

5. Tinghi, in Solerti, *Musica,* pp. 114–15.

was a tournament on the Piazza Santa Croce. Once again Parigi erected grandstands for the spectators about an oval arena (Figure 93), Agniolo Ricci created the choreography, and Jacopo Peri and Paolo Francesino were the appointed composers. The author of this *Guerra di Bellezza* was Andrea Salvadori,[6] who received a stipend of 16 scudi for his efforts. Tinghi estimated that upward of 25,000 spectators crowded the grandstands as well as the roofs and windows of adjacent houses.[7]

Mount Parnassus was the first trionfo to appear in the arena (Figure 94). The mountain of the Muses had two rocky peaks overgrown with laurel. On the higher summit stood an oak, the heraldic emblem of the Rovere family. Its acorns and branches, hung with trophies, were gilded, and in its shadow sat the Muses, with oak leaves in their hair, playing instruments. Close by were Pallas Athena and Pegasus, who, with a hoof beat, caused a fountain to start flowing. A somewhat lower level revealed those *famosi letterati* who had found a home at the art-loving court of Urbino.[8] On the lower peak stood Fama (Figure 95), with Truth at her feet, holding a mirror in one hand and a whip in the other. The Parnassian float was escorted by 170 personified Lies who were being chastised by Truth. Wearing double-faced masks, and black wings sprouting from their shoulders, they formed a chorus, singing a *canzonet* as they marched in. In front of the princes' loge Fama gave an account of the forthcoming tilt between King Ussimano of Media and King Idaspe of Armenia.

No sooner had she finished than the two kings made their entrance, each leading four squadrons of horsemen and five contingents of foot soldiers. The opulent costumes differed from one another chiefly in color. Behind the Medians rolled the chariot of the sun god in the figure of a youth astride a golden globe, which in turn rested on the shoulders of Atlas, a statue twelve braccia in height (Figure 96). Signs of the Zodiac, the Months (winged youths), and Horae (winged girls), the four Seasons, and the Serpent, the Egyptian symbol for the year, were visible on the float. The vehicle was escorted by eight giants, each one approximately twelve feet tall. The procession of the Armenians was brought up by the gilded car of Thetis, decorated with coral, shells, and sea sponges, and also escorted by giants, each carrying a trident (Figure 97). Sirens, Nereids, and Tritons comprised the sea goddess' retinue.

6. [Andrea Salvadori], Gverra / di Bellezza / Festa a cavallo / fatta in Firenze / per la venvta del Serenissimo / Principe d'Vrbino / L'Ottobre del 1616. In Firenze, 1616. The text of this *descrizione* is printed in Solerti, *Musica*, pp. 115–19.

7. Tinghi, in Solerti, *Musica*, p. 115.

8. Salvadori refers here to *Il Cortegiano*.

The tilt now began, first engaging forty-two horsemen and later the foot soldiers. As the struggle reached fever pitch, a white cloud floated out from a hitherto concealed point in the amphitheatre, and driving into the combattants, separated them. The cloud itself then divided, disclosing Cupid, the three Graces, and the personifications of Laughter, Play, and Pleasure, and other amoretti within (Figure 98). Cupid rose from his seat and sang several stanzas, thus concluding the tourney and providing a transition to the equestrian ballet. When the Lies struck up music for a dance, the riders guided their horses through intricate maneuvers. Fama vowed to promulgate through all the cities of Europe the perfection which the *feste a cavallo* had attained at the court of the Grand Duke of Tuscany.

12. A Vigil in the Uffizi

1617

The occasion for the festivities during the Carnival of 1617 was the wedding of Ferdinando Gonzaga, Duke of Mantua, and Caterina de' Medici, sister of the Grand Duke Cosimo II. A performance of the *veglia*, or vigil, *La Liberazione di Tirreno e d'Arnea, autori del sangue toscano* was the artistic highlight of the carnival season. It took place on February 6 "nella sala della Galleria"—that is, in the Uffizi Theatre.[1] Court poet Andrea Salvadori provided the libretto,[2] Marco da Gagliano the music, and Giulio Parigi the décors.[3] No official description was published, but we have the libretto, three etchings by Jacques Callot, and a letter written by an eyewitness.

A strange assortment of episodes from classical mythology and from Ariosto's *Orlando furioso* make up the libretto. The dramatis personae include Hercules, Circe and her confidante, Mars, Jupiter, Pluto, Minos, Rhadamanthus, "a Lady from Tuscany now enclosed in a Tree," and the allegorical character of Inconstancy personifying fickleness in love. There were several choruses, one of hamadryads, one of witches and sorcerers, one of celestial beings, one of infernal spirits, and one accompanying the god of love. Tirreno and Arnea, the two persons whose "liberation" is promised in the title, do not appear at all, and are merely talked about, as is the monster Typhon.

1. Tinghi, in Solerti, *Musica,* p. 121.
2. The libretto was not published separately. The text is available in Andrea Salvadori, *Poesie, 1* (Rome, 1668), 301–15.
3. Tinghi, in Solerti, *Musica,* p. 124.

Hesiod relates how Zeus drove the Titans from heaven, and how, in revenge for their defeat, the earth goddess lay with Tartarus and bore him a child, the hundred-headed Typhon, who threatened the universe. Zeus, however, attacked the monster with his thunderbolts and buried him underground. According to Pindar, he was buried under Mount Aetna, but other mythographers claim that Zeus trapped him under the island of Ischia, whose volcanic properties troubled many settlers in the past.

Another legend, if not historic fact, that Salvadori borrowed from Herodotus concerns the story of the coming of the Tyrseni or Tyrrheni—i.e. the Etruscans— to Italy. According to the historian, the Tyrseni had lived in Lydia, in Asia Minor, and were forced by a famine to migrate under the leadership of Prince Tyrsenus. Eventually these Etruscans settled in the regions over which Cosimo II was ruling in 1617.

Salvadori had to bring Circe, the island of Ischia, Hercules, and Tyrsenus together. He made Circe the villainess of the story by giving her some of the magic powers of Alcina, the *maga* of Ariosto's epic, who transforms Astolfo into a myrtle tree. According to Salvadori's story, when Tyrsenus landed on Ischia, Circe was attracted by him. As the warrior spurned her, she enclosed him in the volcanic rocks of Ischia and held him captive there. Arnea, in love with Tyrsenus, had followed him to Ischia with her women companions, and also fell under the spell of Circe, who transformed them all into hamadryads. The two Etruscans, Tyrsenus and Arnea, are the legendary ancestors of the people of Tuscany. To make their union possible, the lovers must be liberated. The hero who is to accomplish this liberation is Hercules, helped by his father Jupiter.

The veglia begins with the arrival of Hercules on the island. In the background is seen the smoking volcano, under which lies Typhon. In an aria the hero asks the implacable Juno what labor she now has in store for him. A voice answers from a tree—the voice of "a lady from Tuscany enclosed in a plant,"[4] who tells Hercules of the sad fate of Tyrsenus and Arnea. Hercules is willing to help, provided his celestial father assists him. Next, Circe enters, expressing her desire for Tyrsenus, whom she has imprisoned in the volcano. Now Mars and Jupiter appear in a cloud machine, and while Typhon threateningly belches forth fire and smoke against the Olympians, Jupiter, on the advice of Mars, hurls thunderbolts at the mountain, which evidently breaks into pieces.[5] Out of these emerge what the libretto calls "i Cavalieri del balletto." After the gentlemen have danced for a

4. Salvadori, *Poesie, 1,* 301.

5. "Quì Gioue saetta il Monte, & escono i Caualieri del balletto, e doppo che hanno ballato alquanto esce il Coro dell'Amadriadi con Ercole" (ibid., p. 307).

while, they are joined by the ladies, a "Coro dell' Amadriadi," and by Hercules. Tyrsenus and Arnea are then liberated, and the knights and their ladies dance merrily.

But now (by what we might call the Medici law of contrast) the scene changes to an inferno (Figure 99), and Circe reappears in a machine drawn by dragons, calling on Pluto to assist her in her fight against the forces of love. Pluto arrives with Minos and Rhadamanthus, and they decide to send their warriors to help Circe. Next comes Incostanza on a wheel,[6] symbolizing the opposite of true love, which is pledged to constancy. With Pluto and two infernal judges shouting "a l'armi, a l'armi," the warriors of both parties come forward for a combat at the barriers. When the tilting is at its height, the god of love appears, and the scene changes (again for the sake of contrast) to what the libretto calls the "Regno d'Amore," and which in Callot's etching is a *cortile* (Figure 100). Amor and his chorus chant "Non più guerra, non più furore!" This separates the fighters, and after the three Graces have sung their madrigal in praise of constant love, the evening's entertainment closes with a ballet. Actually, the libretto was nothing but a pretext for the execution of ballets and jousts, both directed by the choreographer, Agniolo Ricci.

Solerti[7] quotes a report written by one Gioseffo Casato, who witnessed this performance, and whose over-all impression is summed up in the words: "una bellissima festa." According to the information he gives concerning the dances, there was, after the defeat of Typhoeus, "a most beautiful ballet danced by twelve gentlemen, first on the stage and then by the same twelve dancers and by twelve richly apparelled ladies in the center of the auditorium. The Grand Duke danced among the gentlemen, and the Archduchess among the ladies." This is the moment that Callot's etching immortalized (see Frontispiece). The report continues: "Then the second intermezzo was sung, and two squadrons of gentlemen, twelve in each, carried out various forms of combat, some with swords, others with the pike. The whole business was over in about forty minutes, and done with such gusto and beauty that everybody applauded, because one is all too well aware of the horror which the length of such combats may entail. In the last intermezzo the fighting was halted by Cupid. This was beautifully staged, and several machines were set in motion which made the intermezzo a delight to behold." This was the tournament at the conclusion of the inferno scene. The report ends: "Finally, there was a ballet of forty ladies and forty gentlemen, and to these were added the jousters." Once again the dancers moved from the stage over the ramps into the hall.

6. "Incostanza si fà innanzi sopra vna ruota" (ibid., p. 310).
7. *Musica,* p. 121, n. 1.

13. Sacred and Profane Love

1624–25

When Cosimo II died in 1621 the hereditary Prince Ferdinando was only ten years old. The Grand Duchesses Christine of Lorraine and Maria Magdalena ruled as joint Regents until, in 1628, Ferdinando II became old enough to take over the responsibilities of government. During the Regency the theatrical repertory acquired a thoroughly religious flavor, and preference was given to *sacre rappresentazione*.[1] For the state visit of Archduke Karl in 1624, it was decided that an opera with a religious subject should be presented, and the choice fell on the martyrdom of St. Ursula. The printed *Argomento*[2] pointed with pride to the edifying aspects of this Christian opera, which clearly manifested "that our souls obtain much more delight and amazement from the true and glorious Christian actions than from the empty fables of the pagans."[3]

The libretto for *La Regina Sant'Orsola* was written by Andrea Salvadori, the music by Marco da Gagliano. According to Tinghi,[4] Giulio Parigi created the settings; the engravings, however, show that Parigi's son, Alfonso, claimed credit for them. The libretto, with Alfonso's illustrations, was published for a revival of

1. On this subject see Giuseppe Baccini, *Notizie di alcuni commedie sacre a Firenze* (Florence, 1889).
2. Argomento / della Regina / Sant'Orsola / Rappresentazione / D'Andrea Salvadori / In Firenze / Per Pietro Cecconcelli. 1624.
3. Ibid., A2 v.
4. In Solerti, *Musica*, p. 174.

the opera in 1625.[5] Agniolo Ricci staged the battle scenes and was choreographer for the ballets. The premiere took place on October 6, 1624, in the Uffizi Theatre, which Tinghi[6] described as follows: "nella sala grande, dove altre volte s'è recitato le comedie regie, sotto alla galleria di Loro Alt. S. me." The auditorium was "graduata atorno atorno"—that is, surrounded on three sides by degrees of benches. Christine sat with the Duchess of Urbino at a place "sopra la porta," where they could not be seen. Two cardinals and several ambassadors followed the spectacle from special windows in the art gallery above.[7]

Preceding the opera was a Prologue in which river nymphs sang a paean to Florence and the Archduke. Having emerged from the Arno, each nymph carried a gilded rebec on which she seemed to be playing her own accompaniment. Father Arno was likewise present with his urn and scepter. The scene showed a view of Florence from a point outside the Porta San Niccolò. At the conclusion of the madrigal, the nymphs and the river god sank back into the Arno. Suddenly the

5. La Regina / Sant'Orsola / del S.r Andrea Saluadori / Rappres.ta nel Teatro del Sereniss. / Gran Dvca di Toscana / Al Sereniss. Principe / Vladislao Sigismondo / Principe di Polonia e di Suetia. Fiorenza 1625.

6. In Solerti, *Musica*, p. 174.

7. In his *Newes Itinerarium Italiae* (Ulm, 1627), the German architect Joseph Furttenbach (1591–1667), who studied the art of perspective scene painting under Giulio Parigi in Florence, mentions "peculiar windows" through which one could "see down" from the grand ducal art gallery into the Uffizi Theatre. Furttenbach's prolix baroque style is inimitable; hence the following passage relating to the Uffizi Theatre, quoted in the original German: "Man kan auch von da an in den Theatro warinnen die Fürstliche Comedien gehalten werden / durch sonderbare Fenster hinab sehen / da dann noch die Sciena di Comedia Scoprirt / vnnd sehr schöne Arteficie, wie etwan selbige / nach dem es die acti Inhaltung der Comedien mitbringt / das Werck in grosser Behendigkeit / vnd in ein andere Gestalt verwandlen / gesehen werden / ist auch darfür zu halten / dass zu vnsern Zeiten dergleichen zierliche Comedien nirgends in opera gericht worden / Vnterschiedliche Manier vnd Abwechslungen werden observirt. Damit aber der Liebhaber derselbigen auch ein wenig geniesse / so wird ein erste Praesentirung (Figure 101) zu erkennen geben / da man dann gar in die ferrne vñ in etliche Gassen Prospectivischer weiss hinein sehen thut / auss welchen die Comedianten sich erzeigen / vnd nach Gelegenheit dess vor ihnen habenden actus agieren, wañ selbiger sein Endschafft erreicht / thut sich das gantze Werck in einen Lustgarten / Meer / Wald / oder anders in solcher Behendigkeit verwandeln / dass dess Menschen Aug dessen in Achtung zu nehmen nicht wol vermag / sondern vil mehr also darüber bestürtzt wird / dass die Persohnen gleichsam die Gedancken verendern / als obs verzuckt weren; Ob aber einige andere Ergötzlichkeit diesem herrlichen Werck vorzuziehen / lasse ich den verständigen hierüber giudiciren; Vnd seyn dergleichen Verwandlungē in vnterschiedlichen Gestalten offt.6.biss in 7. mal in einer Comedien gesehen worden / die Wolckē theten sich auff / mit Erscheinung lieblicher Musici, vnd nach Poetischer weiss erzeigten sich Dij oder Götter / die fuhrē auff die Erden / in mancherley Gestalt." (*Newes Itinerarium Italiae*, pp. 87–88.) On Furttenbach, cf. my "The Furttenbach Theatre in Ulm," *The Theatre Annual*, *II* (1953), 45–69.

Florentine backdrop vanished into the gridiron ("a un tratto sparì al cielo la prospettiva") and a hell scene was "unveiled" ("si scoperse"). Lucifer, conceived as the symbol of hybris, stood on the seven-headed Hydra in the middle of a fiery sea (Figure 102). Twelve devils were gathered there to deliberate, and decided that Ursula, daughter of the King of Cornwall, and her eleven thousand virgins had to be undone. Ursula had undertaken a sea voyage along the English coast. A tempest had driven her and her virgins to German soil, from which they attempted to reach Cologne by sailing up the Rhine. A Furia Infernale, worshiped as a deity of war by the Huns who were besieging the city, was commanded to reveal to the barbarians that they could conquer the city only after they had first violated and killed Ursula and her virgins. A heavenly defender appeared with a choir of angels in the clouds. Announcing himself as the Archangel Michael, he presented a menace to the devils.

The setting changed, perhaps with the help of turning wings (not necessarily periaktoi, for Tinghi mentions the sudden turning about of the "prospettiva" which "si voltò a un tratto."[8] The walls of the city of Cologne occupied the background of the next scene. In front of them flowed the Rhine, spanned by bridges. In the right foreground was the Temple of the Furia Infernale with the Mars idol and downstage left, a bastion. Gauno, King of the Huns, appeared, "superbamente vestito," with twenty of his cohorts, also "vestiti riccamente," and swore that he would not rest until Cologne was leveled to the ground. A prisoner, the English Prince Ireo who was in love with Ursula, was then brought in with his fellow warriors. A choral piece sung by the Christian captives ended the first act.

At the beginning of Act II, six priests of Mars came forth from the temple and were commanded by Gauno's messenger to offer sacrifice to the god of war. Ursula then appeared, "vestita da regina con la corona in testa," escorted by twelve virgins preparing for their martyrdom. Ursula urged them, and above all Cordula, the fainthearted maid, not to lose courage. In the following scene the Huns attempted to take the bastions by storm (Figure 103). Interlocking their shields above their heads, they formed a Roman *testudo,* but the Roman defenders managed to repulse them.[9]

In the third act the priests of Mars reported to the King of the Huns that Ursula had landed with her virgins. The Furia Infernale proclaimed through her mouth-

8. In Solerti, *Musica,* p. 175.

9. Tinghi describes the battle in greater detail: "Poi venne l'esercito del Re delli Unni a dare l'assalto alle mura della città di Colonia et ferocemente combattendo quelli di drento si difesero alla galliarda, a poi fatto una sortita di uomini armati contro a sei altri armati del Re delli Unni e fecero un abatimento galliardo, con spade e rotella armati d'arme bianca, e se n'andorno" (in Solerti, *Musica,* p. 175).

piece, the Mars idol, that Cologne would be invincible as long as Ursula and her companions remained alive. Lucifer and his demons then ascended through traps ("S'apre la Terra") in order to goad the Huns against the Christian virgins. As soon as the Archangel Michael appeared with his heavenly hosts, however, the devils had to take flight (Figure 104). A messenger informed Ireo that the virgins had been slain, all but Ursula, with whom the King of the Huns had fallen in love. The third act ended with a hymn extolling the martyrs.

In the fourth act Ursula recoiled at Gauno's advances. And although Ireo then protested his love to her, she already felt herself a bride of heaven and spurned his importunings as well. The chorus of Huns sang a hymn in praise of sensual love, and when the King made one last effort to bend the virgin to his will, Ireo threw himself at Gauno's feet and revealed that he was Ursula's bridegroom (Figure 105). Finally, the tyrant led the virgin into the Temple of Venus, where he slew her with an arrow. In despair, Ireo rushed after her, intending to kill the King, and in a *lamento* the chorus weighed the perils to which the English prince was exposed.

The fifth act brought the news of Ursula's death and Ireo's conversion to Christianity. But when Ireo confessed his new faith, the King promptly murdered him. A bolt of lightning then struck Gauno from on high, and the earth swallowed him up. The Huns fled before the Romans; the heathen idol crumbled (Figure 106). The Romans then began to celebrate a victory feast, with a "ballo tutto in aria et in caprioli."[10] For this ballet, in which twelve Tuscan nobles took part, the stage was transformed into a colonnaded courtyard. Finally, the heavens opened: Ursula and her virgins floated on clouds, and a choir of angels and saints extolled the joys of Paradise (Figure 107). The curtain then came down ("casca dal cielo una tela").[11]

The opera was given a repeat performance, with minor changes in the sequence of scenes, for the state visit of Prince Ladislaus Sigismund of Poland on January 28, 1625.[12] On the second of February the Polish guest was driven to the Villa Poggio Imperiale, where the following day he attended the performance of the operatic ballet *La Liberazione di Ruggiero dall'isola d'Alcina*. Ferdinando Saracinelli wrote the libretto,[13] for which Francesca Caccini composed the music. If we may rely on Tinghi,[14] the settings and machinery were furnished by Giulio Parigi,

10. Ibid., p. 176.
11. Ibid.
12. Ibid., p. 178.
13. La Liberazione / Di Rvggiero / Dall' Isola D'Alcina / Balletto / Rapp. to in Musica al Ser.mo / Ladislao Sigismondo / Principe di Polonia / e di Svezia / Nella Villa Imp. della Sereniss.ma / Arcid. ssa d'Austria Gran Duch.sa / di Toscana / Del sig. Ferdinando / Saracinelli Balì di Volterra / Per Pietro Cecconcelli 1625.
14. In Solerti, *Musica*, p. 183.

137

although his son Alfonso again claimed credit as "inventore" on the etchings of the libretto.

In the Prologue, Neptune made an appearance on his chariot (Figure 108), which seemed to be tossed by the billows of the sea ("con vaghissima vista di mare"),[15] the entire pageant pulled by sea horses. Neptune paid homage, in his aria, to the Polish visitor, while the god of the river Vistula also appeared just to make Ladislaus Sigismund a bit nostalgic. The scene then changed to the island of Alcina (Figure 109). In the foreground to the right and left were the elements of a French garden, and in the background a view of the sea and the castle of the witch Alcina. The good sorceress Melissa rode in on the back of a dolphin, resolved to take on the appearance of Atlas in order to warn Ruggiero, who was caught in the web of Alcina's charms. Ruggiero himself then entered with Alcina and a chorus of ladies, and a lengthy duet ensued. Alcina withdrew, while Ruggiero, lulled by a siren's song, fell asleep. Melissa, disguised as Atlas ("Huom di canuto aspetto"),[16] awakened him to warn him of Alcina. His chivalrous instincts immediately aroused, the hero called for his weapons. At that moment, he heard the singing of Alcina's bewitched lovers: weary of her admirers, she had transformed them into trees. Meanwhile, a messenger informed Alcina that Ruggiero had resolved to flee. Failing to restrain the hero, she called on the demons of the underworld for help. The sea and the garden landscape were suddenly enveloped in flames. (Figure 110.) The libretto[17] contains the following stage direction: "Qui si trasforma la Scena, & il Mare in fuoco." Tinghi[18] describes the scene change thus: "voltata la prospettiva in fiamme et fuoco." Alcina appeared on a monstrous bark ("vna mostruosa barca contesta di ossi di Balena"),[19] surrounded by her nymphs, who had now assumed demonic shapes. She herself was transformed into a winged monster, and after singing an aria of revenge, she plunged into the inferno. The setting changed into a rocky landscape ("et voltato la prospettiva in scolli di mare").[20] Eight nymphs emerged from grottoes ("aprendosi la scena per il mezzo"),[21] followed by eight liberated knights (Figure 112). In a ballet they expressed their joy at the defeat of the evil sorceress. There ensued an equestrian ballet (Figure 111), momentarily interrupted by a madrigal of Melissa, who arrived in a car drawn by centaurs.

15. Ibid.
16. Libretto, p. 22.
17. Ibid., p. 29.
18. In Solerti, *Musica,* p. 181.
19. Libretto, p. 29.
20. Tinghi, in Solerti, *Musica,* p. 182.
21. Ibid.

14. The Medici-Farnese Wedding

1628

To unite through marriage the houses of the Medici and Farnese had long been the dream of the Farnese Duke, Ranuccio I. His ambition was to marry his son, Odoardo, the hereditary prince, to a daughter—virtually any daughter—of Cosimo II. For years negotiations dragged out. Finally, in 1628, after the death of Cosimo II (1621) and Ranuccio (1622), the long-awaited union of Odoardo Farnese and Margherita de' Medici, both sixteen, was realized.

Nuptial celebrations began in Florence, continued in Parma, and were there brought to a climax. On October 11, 1628, the wedding took place in the Duomo in Florence, followed in the evening by a ball in the Sala delle Guardie (Salone delle Statue) of the Pitti Palace. On the fourteenth there was a performance of a new opera, *La Flora,* in the Uffizi Theatre. The libretto was written by Andrea Salvadori, and the music composed by Marco da Gagliano. Jacopo Peri contributed the score for the role of Chloris, and the settings were designed by Alfonso Parigi, who also made the five etchings attached to the libretto.[1] On the seventeenth a rustic ball, or *contadina,* was given in the Villa Poggio Imperiale. This *fête champêtre* was followed by a tourney, after which the court returned to Florence to dance in the Salone de' Forestieri of the Pitti Palace.[2] There, a course of refreshments was suddenly interrupted by the appearance of the sorcerer Ismeno,

1. Parigi's original designs for the costumes of *La Flora* are preserved in the Biblioteca Nazionale in Florence. They may be found attached to pp. 79–90 of Vol. 2 of the *Disegni di vestiture per deità.*

2. Solerti, *Musica,* p. 192.

dressed as a barbarian. Escorted by a swarm of Furies, Ismeno proclaimed in a ghastly voice that the knights of the Orient had challenged the heroes of the Occident to combat. The Furies shrieked, "Alle armi!" whereupon the guests left the hall and proceeded to the area in front of Buontalenti's grotto, where, by the light of torches, they watched the tilt, *La Disfida d'Ismeno*,[3] which Andrea Salvadori had contrived. Stefano della Bella designed the costumes for the four squadrons of ten noblemen each who took part in the joust. Finally, Gildippe and Odoardo, the couple whom Tasso had extolled for their valor and devotion, appeared on a *trionfo*. Gildippe handed a garland which she had received from Immortality to the bride, Margherita, and Odoardo gave his namesake his shield and rapier. Everyone understood the allusion and rejoiced in the fact that a new Odoardo had found a new Gildippe.

For this celebration the Medici did not greatly exert themselves. The sole artistic event was the performance of *La Flora*[4] in the Uffizi Theatre. Actually, Andrea Salvadori's effort turned out to be rather tedious, and for the most part he merely relied on the established tricks of the set designer. Originally he had written another libretto, *Iole ed Ercole,* for the wedding, but the intrigues of the singer, Francesca Caccini,[5] prevented its execution.

The first act of *La Flora* was played in a forest setting designed by Alfonso Parigi. Center stage was a mountain which opened to disclose Berecyntia seated on a throne within. A chorus of mountain nymphs and fauns (Figure 113) stood at the sides. Hermes then appeared as a messenger of Jupiter to announce to the Great Mother, goddess of fertility and mistress of nature, that the father of the gods had decided to endow the earth with a counterpart to the stars—that is, flowers. Parigi captured this scene in an etching (Figure 114). The set designer also contributed an illustration of the following scene, which would seem to show that the side elements of the second décor were nearly identical to those of the first: Berecyntia's mountain had evidently disappeared into a trap, disclosing a sea scene in the background (Figure 115). Here the libretto called for a landscape in which Venus, escorted by Cupid, Zephyrus, and a company of Nereids and Tritons, was to land on the Tyrrhenian shore. Zephyrus confessed to the goddess that he had fallen in love with a Tyrrhenian nymph by the name of Chloris; at the same time he paid the Tuscans a compliment by referring to the littoral where the

3. La Disfida / D'Ismeno, / Abbattimento à Cauallo con Pistola, e Stocco . . . / Inuenzione d'Andrea Salvadori / . . . Firenze, 1628.

4. La Flora / D'Andrea Salvadori / . . . Firenze, 1628.

5. A. Ademollo, *La Bell'Adriana* (Città di Castello, 1880) p. 147.

nymph abided as the "seat of earthly gods." Venus promised him the girl, without of course considering the caprices of Cupid, who not only refused to shoot his golden arrow at Chloris but swore that he would contrive to set the nymph's heart against Zephyrus.

A duet between Zephyrus and Chloris opened the second act of the opera. The chaste nymph spurned all protestations of love. "Io nemica d'Amore" she declared to her suitor and withdrew. Hermes then appeared with Cupid, but as even he could not convince Cupid, he realized that he must resort to more drastic measures. Putting Cupid to sleep, he stole his bow and arrows. A throng of satyrs then awakened the love god, who, as he discovered the loss of his weapons, was mocked by the wood sprites. It is not clear from the text in which décor the second act was played. The second setting, however, was entirely suited for it and probably also served effectively in scenes 1–5 of the third act.

In the fifth scene of Act III, Venus derided the unarmed Cupid, whereupon he called on the underworld gods for help. Here the libretto bears the marginal notation: "S'apre l'Inferno."[6] A third etching by Parigi (Figure 116) shows us the stage after its transformation, the kingdom of Pluto with smoking, ruined towers inhabited by demons. The caption reads: "Cupid demands Jealousy from Pluto." The three figures seen escorting Cupid are Rhadamanthus, Minos, and Aeacus, who, after some hesitation, deliver Jealousy to him. The libretto then remarks: "Torna la Scena al suo solito,"[7] which probably indicates a return to the second décor—that is, the Tyrrhenian littoral. Be that as it may, Jealousy promised Cupid that she would take root in the heart of Chloris.

In Act IV complications developed. Cupid persuaded Pan to tell Chloris that Zephyrus had a mistress, promising to repay the Forest God with a nymph. Pan duly carried out his task of awakening jealousy in Chloris, and here a stage direction points to the following symbolic action: "Jealousy, unseen by Chloris, flings a serpent at the nymph's breast."[8] With the appearance of Zephyrus, Chloris gave vent to her jealousy. The West Wind could not grasp this reversal of emotions. When Pan then explained to him that Chloris had a lover, Zephyrus vowed to renounce the Tuscan countryside and abandon it to Auster and Boreas. The stage direction, "La Scena di verdi si cangia in orrida,"[9] provides, with its almost Latin conciseness, a link to the following storm scene. Once again an etching by Parigi assists our

6. *La Flora*, p. 52.
7. Ibid., p. 56.
8. Ibid., p. 69.
9. Ibid., p. 79.

imagination: with rain, hail, thunder, and lightning everywhere, the nymphs of the streams and meadows are shown running for cover (Figure 117). A *ballo strepitoso* danced by the Chorus of the Storms ended the fourth act.

Act V opened with Neptune taming the winds from his pageant. After Cupid had implored the sea god to return the leaden arrow that Venus had stolen from him and cast into the sea, Neptune commanded a Triton to fish it out of the waves. The love god, however, still lacked the golden arrow, the bow, and the torch. Jupiter therefore appeared in a rift in the heavens ("S'apre il Cielo"),[10] in order to return the golden bow and the arrow to their rightful owner. An eagle, commanded by Jupiter, swooped down with Cupid's implements. To complete the reconciliation of her son—for without his good will, Chloris and Zephyrus could still not be mated—Venus brought him the torch of love, whereupon Cupid cleared up the misunderstanding. Jealousy now withdrew from Chloris, and the nymph was united with Zephyrus, who began to weep for joy. From his tears sprang the flowers, or *fiori,* evoking an obvious connection with Fiorenza. The stage direction also stated: "Here the entire stage is to be filled with flowers, particularly with the lilies of Florence and Parma."[11] The significance of "tutta la Scena" may be deduced from Parigi's fifth etching (Figure 118). Here we find a colonnaded courtyard, in which lilies are placed in ornamental urns. Twelve dancers portray the *Aure,* or Gentle Breezes, which were indispensable to the thriving new vegetation. Venus and Cupid, now in full panoply, appeared on a cloud machine. On the opposite side sits the erstwhile Chloris, now called Flora, in accordance with V, 195 of Ovid's *Fasti:* "Chloris eram, quae Flora vocor." With her is Zephyrus, weeping flowery tears that are clearly visible in the print. At center stage hangs a gushing fountain borne aloft by the Muses, and on it, an effigy of Apollo astride Pegasus.

On October 22 the young Duke of Parma left Florence in order to supervise preparations for the reception of the bride at his residence. On the sixth of December, Margherita arrived in Parma, where Odoardo Farnese was eager to show the Medici and other rival courts how a wedding ought to be celebrated. Our principal source for the festivities in Parma is the description of Marcello Buttigli,[12] the literary adviser of the two leading Farnese architects, Giovanbattista Magnani and Girolamo Rainaldi, who were commissioned to build the triumphal arches and ornamental façades. Supplementary descriptions may be found in the letters

10. Ibid., p. 85.

11. Ibid., p. 96.

12. *Descrittione dell'apparato fatto per honorare la prima e solenne entrata in Parma della serenissima principessa Margherita di Toscana, duchessa di Parma, Piacenza* (Parma, 1629).

of Luigi Inghirami,[13] Gian Carlo Medici's secretary, who sent reports to the bride's mother, Maria Magdalena, as she did not accompany her daughter on the journey to Parma.

The theatre historian is naturally drawn to two selections of unusual interest from the rich festival program at Parma: the performance of Tasso's *Aminta* (with intermezzi) on the thirteenth of December, and the great tourney spectacle with which the Teatro Farnese was opened eight days later.

Aminta was given in a specially constructed theatre in the courtyard of San Pietro Martire, adjoining the Palazzo della Pilotta. Since the fable was widely familiar,[14] the pastoral play was only tepidly received, the audience showing far more interest in Claudio Achillini's Prologue[15] and in the five interludes of Ascanio Pio di Savoia,[16] for which Claudio Monteverdi had composed the music.

Giovanbattista Magnani (1571–1653) was the architect of the cortile theatre, which was so laid out that it occupied only half the courtyard. The stage was situated to the north and the auditorium to the south, the latter appearing as an hexagonal semi-oval ("Giraua il Teatro in sembiante di mez'ouato essagono").[17] A neutral strip eighteen braccia in depth stretched in front of the proscenium, an area in which there were no seating facilities. At either end of the strip, to the east and west, was an entrance to the auditorium in the shape of a triumphal arch. The auditorium itself was 54 braccia broad and 48 deep, not including the neutral space.[18] It was divided into two clearly demarcated sections: an area with ascending scaffolding, as in an amphitheatre, with gradi surmounted by two loggias; and a parterre noble, embraced by gradi on three sides. In the middle of the arena rose a dais for princely personages, and to the right and left extended benches for the ladies. The wooden gradi rested on a substructure three braccia high, framed in front by a balustrade; from this point the degrees rose to the two loggias in the

---

13. Paolo Minucci del Rosso, "Le nozze di Margherita de' Medici con Odoardo Farnese Duca di Parma e Piacenza," *La Rassegna nazionale, 21* (1885), 551–71; *22* (1885), 550–70; *23* (1885), 19–45. Letters from Luigi Inghirami may be found in Vol. 22 and will be referred to below as Inghirami, with page number.

14. Inghirami, p. 562.

15. Teti, e Flora / Prologo / Della gran Pastorale recitata in Parma / Nel maraviglioso Teatro fabricato quest'anno / Dal Serenissimo Signor Duca . . . . Composto dal Sig. / Clavdio Achillini . . . Parma, 1628.

16. Intermedii / Recitati / In Musica . . . / Opera dell' Ill.mo Sig.re Don / Ascanio Pio di Savoia. Parma 1629. The text of the intermezzi and the Prologue are in Solerti, *Musica,* pp. 409–79, and also in Buttigli, passim.

17. Buttigli, p. 148.

18. The braccio of Parma was equal to 54 cm.

background, one of which was finished in Ionic style, the other in Corinthian. Additional seats for the spectators were located within these loggias. Buttigli estimates the total capacity of the theatre at nearly six thousand; Inghirami counts "trenta gradini" and mentions a kind of terrace situated behind the princely dais, from which certain chosen spectators enjoyed a distortion-free view of the décors and their central perspective ("stettero molti che godevano per linea retta della prospettiva").[19] The proscenium[20] extended across the entire width of 54 braccia. The stage opening in the middle was 27 braccia wide. To the right and left, 13½ braccia on either side, stood the decorative elements, providing a massive picture frame with its niches, statues, pilasters, trophies, columns, escutcheons, garlands of fruit and festoons of blossoms, all made of gilded, silvered, or bronzed wood and stucco. An awning, what the Imperial Romans would have called a *velarium*, was stretched over the auditorium from the upper edge of the proscenium to the topmost loggia. Inghirami[21] remarked that as this enormous linen roof did not cover the stage, blasts of cold December night air rushed from there into the auditorium, making the spectators shiver during the performance.

According to Buttigli, the curtain rose at two o'clock, or by Inghirami's reckoning, at three[22]—that is, at seven or eight in the evening. Our two commentators also make contradictory statements as to the tempo with which the curtain was raised out of sight. If we are to believe Buttigli, this took place "in vn balleno d'occhi"; Inghirami, however, saw it ascend "adagissimo."

The evening began with a madrigal sung by Hymen, standing in front of the gate of his temple, which occupied center stage. This was a rectangular structure built in Corinthian style, twelve braccia wide and eighteen high. The columns seemed to have been made of lapis lazuli, and the architraves of gold. Buttigli[23] filled two pages of print in describing this temple, which stood in a landscape, a "scena boschareccia," composed of hills, gardens, rivers, and copses, "so deceptive to the eye that the painting was taken for reality."[24] Here we have once again a triumph of illusionistic scene painting producing a plastic three-dimensional depth effect on flat surfaces. Even the clouds in the heavens were so convincingly imitated "that it was difficult to decide whether art or nature could make them

19. Inghirami, p. 562.
20. The following description is based on Buttigli, pp. 151–53.
21. Inghirami, p. 562. Buttigli states, p. 154, that 3600 braccia of cloth were used to make the velarium.
22. Buttigli, p. 154; Inghirami, p. 562.
23. Pp. 155–57.
24. Ibid., p. 154.

better."[25] In the watercourses one saw navigators and fishermen "al natural ritratti," which again testified to the "eccellenza del pennello."

At the end of his madrigal, Hymen and the temple ascended into the heavens, and the stage transformed itself into a coastal landscape for the Prologue. To the left extended an arm of the sea, while to the right was a flowering meadow with blossoming trees. It was a glowing spring day. The waves surged against the beach, now from east to west, now in a backward direction. From the left appeared the sea goddess, Thetis, singing the praises of Tuscany; from the right, Flora came forth to extol the House of Farnese. Both goddesses then made their exit, and the setting changed back to the *scena boschareccia* for the first act of *Aminta*.

FIRST INTERMEZZO: BRADAMANTE AND RUGGIERO

At the conclusion of Act I, the rustic setting was succeeded by a wild Alpine landscape with steep escarpments, between which were scudded clouds of various sizes and colors. Center stage stood the stronghold of the sorcerer Atlante, who held Ruggiero captive along with other nobles. The fortress gleamed as though made of steel. To achieve this effect, tin foil was employed ("finto col talco quasi d'acciaio").[26] The rectangular, many-towered citadel rose from sheer sandstone cliffs. It consisted of an outer and an inner central part, and was evidently quite a complex structure, for Buttigli devoted almost two printed pages to it.[27]

The action began with the appearance of an extraordinary horse—a black beast with bat wings, spewing flames from its eyes, ears, and nostrils—which flew in from the left. Astride it were Bradamante and the sorceress Melissa. Bradamante hurled her challenge at the lord of the castle, and Atlante, carrying a blinding shield on his left arm and fetters on his saddle, then appeared on his hippogriff, a creature half horse and half griffin. Since Bradamante's magic ring made her immune to the shield, she outwitted Atlante, forcing him to open the way to the fortress. But as the sorcerer removed a stone from the entrance gate, the citadel vanished (not disintegrating into rectilinear segments, but rather falling into irregular components which were then torn away left and right as by a gale) with its master, and the setting was transformed into a garden.

In this next scene[28] Bradamante and Ruggiero sang a love duet, as knights

---

25. Ibid.: "che non era facile il giudicare, se più belle, e gratiose le facesse l'Arte, o la Natura."
26. Ibid., p. 167.
27. Ibid., pp. 167–68.
28. For the garden scenery, see ibid., pp. 173–76.

strolled about the garden with their ladies. At the vanishing point in the background ("all vnione del punto in prospettiua") stood an octagonal pavilion, a kind of bower, from which pergolas ran out from the sides to smaller rectangular arbors. Other trellised walks extended laterally to the foreground, leaving an open space in the middle for a charming fountain. The garden itself was a mixture of floral and architectural elements. A statue of Venus stood on a shell; from her breasts gushed two small jets of water, an effect which appeared to have been borrowed from Giovanni da Bologna's Harpies on the mannerist Neptune fountain in Bologna. Adjacent to it was a statue portraying Cupid with drawn bow; water jetted from the arrow, emptying into the Venus shell.

After the love duet, a cloud appeared in the heavens and took on the most diverse shapes, changing from a pyramid to a rhomboid to a bird to a human figure with incongruous anatomical features—in short, a fantastic, mannerist creation. Finally, the cloud opened, revealing Atlante seated within and surrounded by a throng of satanic imps, some of whom had human bodies but the heads and tails of serpents, others resembling eagles above and certain quadrupeds below—again, a typical mannerist phenomenon. The sorcerer commanded his demons to transport the magic garden to another place, whereupon the entire landscape rose into the heavens. Buttigli raved over this ascent as a "cosa miracolosa,"[29] and Inghirami concurred: "This forward and upward movement of the garden prior to its disappearance was a marvelous thing."[30] Then followed the second act of *Aminta*.

SECOND INTERMEZZO: AENEAS TAKES LEAVE OF DIDO

Center stage was an inlet, with the city of Carthage to the left, a pine grove with hills to the right, and in the foreground a lovely plain on which the singers acted. Carthage was still in the process of construction, as evidenced by cranes, windlasses, blocks and tackles, and unhewn stones. As far as the Byrsa had been completed, its towers evinced a warlike character. Ships could be seen in the harbor, eleven of which later hoisted sail and moved out to sea.[31] Inghirami found, however, that the sea lacked the "esquisitezza di Toscana," and that the storm failed to measure up to Florentine standards; he nevertheless marveled at Fama's flight, considering it a "cosa mirabile."[32]

Flapping her wings, Fama flew downstage to the proscenium, traversed the stage, and finally pursued a diagonal course. All of this was accomplished "senza

29. Ibid., p. 178.
30. Inghirami, p. 563.
31. For the maneuvers of the fleet, cf. Buttigli, p. 188.
32. Inghirami, p. 563.

carro" and "con ingegno non veduto."[33] Mercury, who had to remind Aeneas of his mission, appeared on a magnificent chariot. Juno also arrived on a cloud machine, surrounded by fourteen nymphs, while other clouds began to move in from all points of the compass. In a madrigal the goddess lamented the fate of the disconsolate Dido. She then flew away over Carthage, while the clouds about her chariot first expanded and then contracted, to the considerable delight of the spectators.

Clutching her sword, Dido rushed forth from the city in search of the vanished Aeneas, who was now soaring aloft on a dragon six braccia in length, bridling it as though it were a horse. The monster had glistening scales which dazzled the spectators, and the fact that no one could see how it was held in flight caused an even greater sensation.[34] Next, Dido hastened back to the city to kill herself, having prepared for her suicide in a long aria. A rainbow appeared in the heavens, spanning the stage from the hills on the right to the city on the left. Then came a cloud bearing Iris, Juno's messenger, who sang a final madrigal, after which she crossed over the rainbow to the dying Dido.

The third act of *Aminta* won scant notice, for by this time the spectators were freezing and vainly trying to keep their feet warm by moving about. The guests of honor had spent that time indulging in a repast. Sweets and beverages were offered to the ladies, but at this point a little warmth would have been more welcome than refreshments.[35]

THIRD INTERMEZZO: DISPUTE OF THE OLYMPIANS

The rustic landscape of *Aminta* suddenly changed, "subito con incredibile velocità,"[36] into a sea scene. This time the stage floor was also removed in order to make room for the waves, which in all probability consisted of a series of undulate cylinders dyed blue. At first the sea gave the impression of being altogether serene, with dolphins frolicking in the waves. Flowered meadows formed a shore line to the right and left, above which, on the right side, rose hills, woods, and vineyards. Imposing villas stood on the slopes. Fields, interlaced with canals, were visible on the left, along with some peasant houses. An early morning sky vaulted over the scene. Between the waves three sirens emerged to sing a madrigal in honor of

33. The assumption that Giacomo Torelli was the first to show these complicated flights in Venice is thus incorrect. Parma witnessed "Torelli flights" as early as 1628. For more on the flights, see Buttigli, p. 183.
34. Ibid., p. 192.
35. Inghirami, p. 563.
36. Buttigli, p. 197.

Venus, who forthwith appeared on her silver shell-car. Diana came on a cloud, riding a trionfo pulled by white stags.[37] In a brief *débat* the two goddesses lauded the respective merits of love and chastity. Meanwhile, a cloud unfolded in the upper part of the heavens, expanding as it neared center stage. Within it sat Minerva on an ornamental chariot, the gold and silver wheels of which turned in a most realistic fashion. Two owls pulled her trionfo.[38] Entering the debate, Minerva took Diana's point of view. Then Mars, as a champion of Venus, appeared on another cloud, in a pageant drawn by two white horses. Finally, even Pluto engaged in the dispute, appearing in a fissure of one of the lateral mountains, which, as it opened, revealed the City of Dis.

Pluto's kingdom resembled a fortress enveloped in flames. Its populace consisted of the traditional allegories and creatures of myth: Cerberus, the Gorgons, the Harpies, War, Discord, Death, Necessity, Age, Hunger, and Fear. Proserpina sat on a throne encircled by the Parcae. Although the details of this scene could not be made out because of the thickness of the smoke, Buttigli[39] maintained that people who knew their Virgil had no difficulty identifying these figures. Escorted by his three judges, Pluto emerged from the central tower, guarded over by Alecto, Tisiphone, and Megaera. Having reached center stage, he sang his aria. On Pluto's advice, Minerva and Mars withdrew, as Venus and her sirens sank into the waves. Pluto then retired to his realm, but not until he had pointed out that even Diana might fall in love some day. In the following scene with a shepherd, however, she remained steadfast. Minerva appeared once more to sing a brief hymn to the chaste goddess. Venus, escorted by Cupid, also reappeared: the god of love had lost his weapons, for which his mother upbraided him.

Inghirami found the third intermezzo "mirabilissimo." He was impressed by the fact that five machines were simultaneously in motion; he also found it extraordinary that the clouds not only traveled parallel to the footlights but could also be maneuvered downstage ("che le nuvole, oltre ad avere un movimento trasversale ne avevano un altro di voltarsi tutte in faccia").[40]

Like Act III, Act IV of the pastoral piece was ignored. Everyone was delighted when the "scena boscareccia" disappeared, "con incredibile velocità,"[41] in order to make room for a sea scene.

37. Description in ibid., pp. 199–200.
38. Ibid., pp. 201–02.
39. Ibid., p. 205.
40. Inghirami, p. 563.
41. Buttigli, p. 215.

FOURTH INTERMEZZO: THE ARGONAUTS

In the center lay a creek. To the left rose a high mountain with a deep cavern against which the surf was pounding; to the right was the palace of Neptune, a "capriciosa compositione" with a "bizara facciata."[42] In a certain measure the set designer had worked marine fauna and mythical sea creatures into the architecture of the palace. For example, the heads of two dolphins formed the base of a column, the shaft of which consisted of the intertwined bodies of whales, whose tail fins formed the capital. Sea horses, Tritons, sirens, crabs, mussels, and fish, partly silvered or gilded, were similarly incorporated into the décor.[43] The spectators were thus confronted with one of the most transitory manifestations of the mannerist style.

To begin with, an island emerged from the waves, revealing Neptune seated on his throne composed of sea animals. Tritons gathered round him as he sang his aria, after which he sank back into the deep, leaving behind a solitary Triton blowing his conch. This was the signal for four sea creatures to rise to the surface—a dolphin, a swordfish, a seal, and a whale, all "ben condotti al naturale."[44] At the same time, Aeolus became visible in the grotto on the left side, singing a madrigal by which the winds were unleashed. The waves pounded higher and higher, the heavens darkened, cloud piled on cloud, thunder could be heard. Just then, the gilded ship of the Argonauts heaved into view, the details of which do not warrant investigation here. Hercules, Mopsus, Jason, and Tiphys the helmsman could be seen on deck. Because of the sudden tempest, Tiphys ordered the crew to strike the shimmering, bluish-golden sail and man the oars. With that, the four sea monsters proceeded to attack, but were fended off with clubs and lances by Hercules, Jason, and the other Argonauts. The helmsman, however, soon discovered that his rudder no longer functioned. Mopsus the seer then suggested that the arts of Orpheus be put into action. Accompanying himself on a lyre, Orpheus sang a madrigal by means of which he appeased the elements. Tiphys praised this fortunate turn of events in an aria which the chorus of Argonauts accompanied with echo effects. The heavens cleared, and sunbeams shone forth as harbingers of Apollo, whose luminous chariot, drawn by four horses, ascended from the left. Phoebus sang his madrigal, after which Neptune again emerged from the deep on a shell-car pulled by sea horses. In a duet between Neptune and Apollo, the Argo-

---

42. Ibid., pp. 215, 217.
43. See Buttigli's detailed description, pp. 215-17.
44. Ibid., p. 218.

nauts were granted free passage to conquer the Golden Fleece. The Argo now weighed anchor, and the interlude ended with a choral piece sung by the crew.

Buttigli's semiofficial description creates the impression that everything ran like clockwork. Inghirami, however, was less enthusiastic. He remarked that, "the ship, the sea, and the storm did not come off as they should have."[45] On the other hand, he had nothing but praise for Apollo's sun chariot and Neptune's shell-car. As for the actors, no one paid much attention to them, and they hastened[46] to have done with the fifth act of *Aminta*.

FIFTH INTERMEZZO: ASSEMBLY OF THE PAGAN GODS

The scene was now transported to a barren mountain landscape, with peaks of steep and rugged cliffs reaching up into the clouds. From the left appeared Europa and Asia, and from the right, Africa and America. Europa sat on a white bull dappled reddish-brown, with gilded hoofs and garlands of flowers hanging on its horns. Asia rode on the back of a crocodile, Africa on a lion, and America on a gigantic silver tortoise. Inghirami considered the animals "ottimamente fabbricati,"[47] and found their movements altogether convincing. The quartet of the continents summoned Pluto. In a startling scene change, flames darted from the crags, and in the farthest part of the stage a great fiery cavern gaped open, from which Pluto's chariot drove forth. Buttigli[48] was proud of the fact that the pitch-black trionfo did not have three wheels, as Boccaccio had assumed, nor was it drawn by four horses, as Claudian had maintained, but ran on just two wheels and was pulled by Cerberus. The Sphinx stood on the right side of the car, the Chimera on the left. On the pageant sat Charon, the judges of the underworld, and the Furies. On the highest point of the vehicle, which rose up toward the rear, stood Pluto. The Furies later alighted from the car and flew up into the heavens. Here Inghirami[49] noticed a technical flaw, since "un pezzo della trave che le conduceva" was plainly visible.

As the earth began to quake, a trap opened in the farther cavern, within which the inferno could be glimpsed. Flames leapt toward the heavens. On a neighing horse sat a knight in armor, the Marchese Cornelio Bentivogli, accompanied by several monsters. Riding down a ramp which suddenly unfolded from the stage into the auditorium, he assumed the stance of "mantenitore"—that is, the chal-

45. Pp. 563–64: "a me però non parve che la nave, la tempesta, andassero come dovevano."
46. Ibid., p. 564: "presto, presto!"
47. Ibid.
48. P. 234.
49. P. 564.

lenger of the tilt—at the east entrance gate. Mercury now flew down to the stage to announce the coming of Jupiter, whereupon the heavens parted, revealing an assembly of the gods with Jupiter in their midst on a golden throne, flanked by Juno and Minerva. Sixty putti (children in flesh-colored tights) hovered above him. The other Olympians were also present. Expanding until it filled the entire width of the stage, the celestial machine moved forward on a horizontal plane, then descended vertically. Buttigli[50] mentions hidden iron clamps ("occulte staffe di ferro") that turned about on axes ("che girauano sulli poli"). The entire conveyance of the gods rested on these brackets in such a way that whenever the clouds sank, the gods soared aloft, and vice versa. So skillfully was this Olympus illuminated that the spectators could not tell where the light was coming from. Inghirami[51] refers to the "lontananza stupenda" of the heavens, which were formed of circles.

The dramatic climax came when Pluto and the "party of the earth," represented by the knight Bentivogli, challenged the celestial inhabitants to a joust. Jupiter immediately responded by dispatching three Cavalieri Celesti as his deputies. A cloud-borne "città celeste" now unfolded, on the central square of which the three celestial knights sat mounted on live horses ("sù caualli reali, e vivi").[52] Unaware that the steeds and their riders were held fast to each other by iron girdles which prevented them from making any false moves,[53] the audience was afraid that the animals might shy and throw their mounts. As soon as the heavenly city reached the stage floor, the three horsemen made their obeisances to the princely personages, then took up positions by the west entrance gate—that is, directly across from the challenger. Inghirami[54] observed that Count Troilo Sansecondo's horse became too skittish but that the rider managed to control it.

The central plaza of the heavenly city from which the three horsemen had come was contained by four galleries on either side, while in the background there arose "vn Teatro" composed of loggias. The set designer had used painted gems for building material: lapis lazuli, chrysolite, rock crystal, turquoise, alabaster, as well as agates, beryls, rubies, sapphires, emeralds, and amethysts.[55] Nevertheless, the chief attraction was the descent of living horses from the heavens. Camillo Giordano, an observer from Urbino, may thus have spoken for all the spectators:

50. P. 240.
51. P. 564.
52. Buttigli, p. 242.
53. "Non vedendosi alcuni gran perni di ferro, che cingendo d'ogni intorno i caualli, impediuano loro il mouersi, non che il precipitarsi," ibid.
54. P. 564.
55. Description in Buttigli, pp. 242–43.

"Finally, there descended from the heavens three knights on horseback, verily the climax of the evening."[56]

After the final chorus of celestial beings had rendered homage to the bridal couple, the jousting began, evidently taking place in the neutral strip between the proscenium and the first gradi. For want of space, the tilt was not concluded with a grand melee. At about ten o'clock Florentine time the spectacle finally ended, having lasted seven hours.

Who, in the final analysis, won the laurels for this evening? Certainly not Tasso, nor the librettist of the intermezzi. Even the opinions on Monteverdi's music were rather cursory. Yet if we put all the eyewitness accounts together, we find unanimous praise for the settings and, above all, the machines. Although Buttigli fails to mention the names of the set designer or the machinist, we find, with the help of other documents, that the machines and décors for the *Aminta* intermezzi were designed by Francesco Guitti (c. 1605–45) and Alfonso Rivarolo, called Il Chenda (1591– or 1607–40).[57]

The guests for the winter festival in Parma were left in the dark as to the opening date of the Teatro Farnese. Originally scheduled for Sunday, December 17, the date of the nineteenth was later considered. On the eighteenth, Camillo Giordano still didn't know whether or not the performance was to take place the following day. He was, however, armed with a program of sorts, "ristretti de gl' intermedij," which he sent off to his wife.[58] Finally, on December 21, the opening of the Teatro Farnese took place. No one in Parma, incidentally, used this modern expression; they referred simply to the Teatro nel Salone.

The theatre had been completed for ten years. Ranuccio I had wanted to inaugurate it in 1618 in honor of Cosimo II, when the Grand Duke was considering a stop in Parma on his planned pilgrimage to Milan. But as nothing came of the journey, due to the poor health of the Tuscan prince, the opening was called off. Giovanni Battista Aleotti, called l'Argento, had finished the construction on time. Even

56. Giordano's letter was published in A. Saviotti, "Feste e spettacoli nel seicento," *Giornale storico della letteratura italiana, 41* (1903), 49.

57. Cf. Guitti's letter published by Giuseppe Campori, *Lettere artistiche inedite* (Modena, 1866), p. 106. Campori maintains that Chenda's collaboration was "probable." It is evident from Guitti's statements that he relied chiefly on artists and craftsmen drawn from Bologna and Ferrara, since the "Parmeggiani" were "inesperti." At the International Colloquium at Royaumont in March 1963, Irving Lavin submitted letters from the Archives of Ferrara, in which Guitti and his assistant, Francesco Mazzi, informed the Marchese Bentivoglio of the progress of the technical work for the performances of 1628.

58. The text of the *Argomento, e ristretto del torneo* is reprinted in Glauco Lombardi, "Il Teatro Farnesiano di Parma," *Archivio storico per le Province Parmensi pubblicato dalla R. Deputazione di Storia Patria,* N.S. *9* (1909), 13–16.

work on the scene designs and machines for the projected premiere of the spectacle-tourney *La Difesa della Bellezza*[59] was so far advanced that by March 1618, Aleotti was able to quit Parma and go to Ferrara on a private mission. In his final report to Ranuccio,[60] he pointed out that the model of Mercury's flying machine achieved the desired effect, that Aurora's machine was in working order, and that certain "tellari" had also been tried out—that is, wing-carriages "which make the side scenes go forward and backward ("che dovranno fare le scene che dovran' andare inanti e in dietro"). There was also a central drum for moving the wings forth and back ("un mangano per tirarli, e spingerli inanti e in dietro"), as well as an undulate cylinder ("una dell' onde a vite") for imitating waves of the sea. Finally, the machine for the appearance of Venus, Virtue, and Neptune (one mechanism for three uses) worked to everyone's satisfaction.

When Aleotti received his permission to depart, the Marchese Enzo Bentivoglio, supported by artists and craftsmen from Bologna, Ferrara, Parma, and Piacenza, assumed supervision of the still unfinished tasks. Bentivoglio's principal alteration was to extend Aleotti's semicircular auditorium into its present U-shape (Figure 128).[61]

And yet, as we have said, Cosimo II had to call off his trip, and the Teatro Farnese remained dark for ten years. Not until December 21, 1628, did it finally open with the "torneo regale" *Mercurio e Marte,* which Claudio Achillini[62] had contrived (Figure 129). When at about two o'clock (approximately seven in the evening) Odoardo Farnese and his wife, escorted by two Cardinals, Giovan Carlo de' Medici and Francesco Maria Farnese, appeared and gave the signal for the performance to begin, the auditorium was filled down to the last seat.[63]

Monteverdi's symphonic prelude was played by five orchestras, the first of which was stationed in front of the proscenium, the second and third above the side entrance doors, and the fourth and fifth to the right and left behind the proscenium. The curtain, decorated with the golden emblems of the Farnese and the Medici, then rose.

High mountains framed an inlet of the sea, which occupied center stage. It was

59. An invention of Count Alfonso Pozzo. Lombardi published the projected sequence of scenes in ibid., pp. 45–50.

60. Text in ibid., pp. 29–31. The following Italian quotations are taken from Aleotti's letter.

61. "Signor Marchese Entio Bentiuoglij, ch'ampliò il Theatro, e le loggie, riducendole dal semicircolo al mez'ouato, prolungando il campo del Theatro, e rendendo ambedue più capacci di spettatori," Buttigli, p. 267.

62. The text is reprinted in Solerti, *Musica,* pp. 481–518.

63. The 10,000 spectators mentioned by Buttigli, p. 271, are an exaggeration. The seating capacity of the Teatro Farnese was probably 5,000.

shortly before dawn, and the stage grew bright with the appearance of Aurora on a silver chariot drawn by Pegasus.[64] Rising from the sea, the trionfo cast light on the rocks and waves. Aurora was portrayed by Settimia Caccini, the daughter of Giulio Romano. She sang her aria "con angelica voce," while sirens listened attentively in the waves. At this point Buttigli reveals[65] that Settimia, who had already sung Dido in the second intermezzo of *Aminta*, would appear as Juno in the present performance.

After the Aurora scene, the farther part of the stage was filled with clouds that finally covered even the rock wings. For a few moments the clouds played, as it were, drifting up and down. Then a zodiac appeared, twelve braccia in diameter. On it were the twelve months, portrayed by living persons. Within the zodiac the spectators distinguished eleven circles segmented by straight lines, thus forming the twelve celestial houses, each with its appropriate sign. The four months related to the changing of the seasons—March, June, September, and December— sang madrigals composed by Monteverdi as they rose in turn toward the zenith of the zodiac, which finally vanished with its performers behind gathering clouds.

Golden Age entered from the right on a *carro trionfale*.[66] The allegory was portrayed by a young man who sang a lengthy aria as his car, drawn by two white doves, moved from right to left. Flames shot up in the background, signaling the appearance of three underworld figures, Discordia and two Eumenides. Although independent of one another, the three Furies, as Buttigli called them, executed the same movements: they first rose slowly upward, as though in flight, and then moved horizontally toward the front, halting at center stage. All of this was accomplished with "occulte machine."[67] Following a trio, Discord ascended into the heavens "per retta linea," while the two Eumenides flew off "per obliqua," one to the right, the other to the left.

Mercury then rushed in from an opening in the "finto Cielo." So artful was the device which sustained him in flight that the spectators fancied he kept himself aloft merely by beating the wings on his sandals. (Figure 130.)[68] Flying in from the left, he first appeared in profile. He then described a circle, coming to rest in the middle of the stage. There Mercury expressed his displeasure that the Duke of Parma, a young man with artistic inclinations, had become so intrigued by warfare that he desired to pay homage to Mars. In order to spoil the war god's pleasure

64. Description in Buttigli, pp. 269–70.
65. Ibid., p. 272.
66. Ibid., p. 277.
67. Ibid., p. 279.
68. Ibid., p. 281.

and prevent the scheduled tourney from taking place, Mercury bewitched the would-be jousters, transporting them to inaccessible regions. For example, he concealed the *Mantenitore*, or Challenger, Duke Odoardo Farnese, in a stronghold at the bottom of the sea, and hid the first squadron within certain boulders, the second in an infernal swamp, the third beneath Aetna, and the fourth in the bellies of sea monsters. We can imagine, even now, the scenic possibilities that were to be involved in their liberation, which was to take up the remainder of the evening.

Mars himself next appeared concealed in a red cloud that took on various shapes —rhomboid, rectangular, and irregularly polygonal, in turn. To the crash of thunder and lightning, the cloud opened, revealing Mars and his cohorts within (Figure 131). Gathered at the war god's feet in a semicircle were Castor, Pollux, two Vittorie, Good Name, Bad Reputation, Glory, and Triumph. Rage, Madness, Terror, Fear, Revenge, Cruelty, Conquest, and Plunder comprised a second semicircle. Eight Roman warriors also stood on the cloud car. The costumes and signs of the allegories[69] followed the traditional prescriptions of iconographic compendiums. In this respect, nothing had changed since the days of Vasari's *Geneologia*. Provoked by Mercury's attempted sabotage of the tourney, Mars disclosed his plans to liberate the warriors with the help of other deities. He first turned to Venus, since the Challenger had to be freed before the others. Borne aloft on a radiant cloud, Venus decreed that Odoardo Farnese be released from the depths of the sea where he lay banished. One part of her cloud then transformed itself into a shell, while the other half, on which stood the Graces, floated away. The metamorphosis of the cloud segment was a technical *coup de théâtre* that verged on the magical. But the spectators scarcely had time to admire the decorative details of this shell, since a new spectacle was already demanding their attention.

Now, from the sea, began to rise the fortress in which the Mantenitore had been spellbound. This complex machine exhibited all the elements of a citadel, from the scarp to a donjon, on which fluttered the Farnese standard. The structure glittered, as though made of diamonds. Suspended by golden chains, the silver drawbridge opened, and out stepped Odoardo Farnese, whom Venus welcomed and bade climb onto her shell. A chorus of *amoretti* in her retinue celebrated the happy outcome in a *canzone*. To offer her hero a spectacle, Venus commanded the city of Cnidus to appear. Suddenly, the boulder side wings vanished ("in vn tratto suanirono") so that the sea now extended across the entire breadth of the stage.

69. Detailed description in ibid., pp. 286–87.

From the waves, at points nearest to the proscenium on either side, there emerged towers ("cominciarono a sorgere fuori delle onde marine, che di già s'erano dilatate per tutta la Scena, nella parte più prossima al Proscenio, sì dall'vno, come dall'altro lato di quello, vaghe velette [i.e. vedette], coperte di cupolette").[70] Center stage arose the façades of magnificent palaces ("al mezzo della Scena, vedeuasi sorgere lunghe facciate di superbi Palagi"). Behind these, on the right side, a monumental column could be seen, on which the convolutions of a spiral relief told of Cupid's triumphs ("una colonna rappresentante in macchie, che la raggirauano a chiocciola, il Trionfo d'Amore"). The column was surmounted by a statue of the love god. Toward the background were two pyramids and a Gothic tower ("una torre d'ordine Gottico, ornata di molte torricelle"). For the first time in his description, Buttigli here mentions the set designer responsible for the city of Cnidus (and presumably for the other settings as well), the architect Carlo Rainaldi. Praise was due him, because he "con singolar puntualità rappresentò al viuo" the details of this scene.[71] Far off in the left background ("nella più remota parte della Scena"), between the monument and the Gothic tower, rose a flight of three colonnades. On the right side of the background, between the two pyramids, stood a temple with a statue of Venus. Facing the temple, a fountain of Neptune could be seen. On the left side a fortress provided a symmetrical counterpart to the temple. At the vanishing point ("al punto della prospettiua") the spectators saw the open gateway of a palace, beyond which a cortile enclosed by loggias could be distinguished.

Carlo Rainaldi (1611–91) was only seventeen years old when he designed these settings. At the time he was working in Parma as an assistant to his father, Girolamo Rainaldi—a role he had to play until the latter's death in 1655. Girolamo was the "primo Architetto de' Serenissimi Farnese." To the art historian he appears as a typical exponent of mannerism. It is interesting to note in this regard that his project for the façade of S. Petroni in Bologna (1626) revealed a bizarre mixture of mannerist and Gothic styles. It is not surprising then that the Cnidus scene featured a Gothic tower in the midst of mannerist palace architecture.

The Challenger, who had been observing the rising city from the Venus shell, now learned from the goddess' lips that this was none other than her beloved Cnidus. Venus commanded the seconds, pages, and drummers to appear, and out they marched from the various streets of the city between the colonnades. Between the shell and the downstage beach two Tritons laid a golden bridge, over which the jousting parties now crossed into the proscenium and proceeded, via flights of

70. Ibid., p. 296.
71. Ibid.

steps, into the U-shaped arena. The entire troupe then took seats on special gradi to the right of the balcony of the princely personages. All eyes were turned to the parade, so that the spectators scarcely noticed the sudden submersion of Cnidus and Venus with her shell ("il subito sommergersi nel Mare, che fecere la Conca di Venere e la bella Città di Gnido"). The change of scenery was accomplished "in vn atomo di tempo," and in place of Cnidus there appeared the Elysian fields. So rapidly did this transformation take place that the spectators could not ascertain whether the scenic elements of which Elysium was composed rose from the earth, descended from the heavens, or had been pushed in from the sides.[72]

Here Buttigli mentions the three types of scenic changes that were then standard procedure. According to his description,[73] four flat wings on either side and a back scene had been installed. Each side wing represented a range of hills, and each hill had a special shape and particular architectural features with respect to its landscaping. In one place gardens were connected by flights of steps stretching out in front of a palace; in another a bridge spanned a stream, leading to a villa. A third range of mountains was crowned by a citadel, and on a fourth stood a casino, built in a most peculiar hybrid style: "La fabrica hauena del Gottico, con torricelle piene di aguglie . . . Il più alto era parte Gottico, parte Rustico, fatta vna mescolanza di membra regolari, ed irregolari, in modo, che pareua, che l'ultimo ordine correggesse il primo."[74] Again we are confronted with the characteristic Rainaldi mixture of the Gothic and mannerist styles. Various and most lifelike animals enlivened the landscape. Painted on the back scene was a "rotondo Tempietto," surrounded by "fabriche antiche" and statues representing the forebears of the Farnese and Medici families. Whether Rainaldi the elder or the younger—who, at the age of seventeen, was not likely to have developed a style of his own—conceived the Elysian décor is of little importance. The setting unmistakably bore the Rainaldi stamp, as did all the others of the tourney-spectacle.

Apollo appeared on his chariot drawn by four white horses. His mission was to move Orpheus, who was in Elysium, to song. Mercury had imprisoned certain knights within boulders, and only the singing of Orpheus could set the rocks in motion. A simple appearance of the singer, however, would not have satisfied the planners of the festival: Parnassus had to be invoked; so the entire width of the

---

72. "Se sorgessero da terra, se discendessero dal Cielo, o pure se da' fianchi s'auanzassero otto tratti di colline, a quattro per parte, distinti da vna bella pianura, terminata da deliciosissima Prospettiua," ibid., p. 302.

73. Buttigli uses seven printed pages to describe the Elysium setting; cf. pp. 303–09.

74. Ibid., p. 307.

stage was soon filled by "vna bella machina." On the summit stood Pegasus under a laurel tree. Down the slopes, on which sat the Muses and a group of poets and figures from the early history of Florence, trickled the Castalian spring. After a short piece by the Muses, Orpheus appeared and sang, accompanying himself on the lyre. The right entrance gate into the arena then opened, through which three boulders propelled themselves in slow motion, coming to rest in front of the proscenium. Trumpets blared, drums rolled, the rocks cleaved open, and out jumped a squadron of knights, released from Mercury's spell by the song of Orpheus. A brief tilt ensued in the arena. Apollo and the muses looked on from the stage.

New animation was brought to the scene by the entrance of Juno on her peacock pageant. The goddess (Settimia Caccini) implored Berecyntia to intervene with Proserpina on behalf of the knights whom Mercury had bewitched in the Stygian swamps. Berecyntia's chariot, pulled by two lions, rumbled forth from one of the chains of hills. Thanks to an appeal to the Great Mother, Proserpina was also brought on stage in her car, while a change of scenery took place simultaneously. A great chasm yawned in the background; and on the sides, where the eight wings showing hills had been, there rose from the substage flaming ruined towers.[75] The schematic arrangement of the setting remained the same: "eight elevations of buildings, four to the right, four to the left" ("otto alzati di fabriche, quattro alla destra, e quattro alla sinistra"); behind these appeared the "ultimo prospetto" on which the fortress of Pluto was depicted, "vn horribile prospettiua." A drawbridge led into the citadel, in front of which crouched Cerberus. Colonnades extended to the right and left, behind which the burning kingdom of Dis could be seen. The eight flat wings were painted with essentially architectural motifs—that is, towers, loggias, and columns, all in a state of dilapidation.[76]

From the left appeared the chariot of Pluto, drawn by four black fire-breathing steeds. Pluto heeded the pleas of his mother-in-law and spouse, and promised to set free the knights that were held prisoner under Mercury's spell. Once the three Parcae and Necessity had given their assent, the right entrance into the arena opened, and flames leapt through the gate. Demons pushed in a mountain on which sat knights, drummers, seconds, and pages, who descended and presented themselves to the prefects of the tourney. The demons then hauled the mountain out again, and the tilt began in the arena, with Pluto looking on.

75. "Alle parti cominciarono a sorgere varij, e belli edificij, nella sommità rotti, e fiammeggianti," ibid., 323.

76. Ibid., pp. 323–26.

At the end of the Sbarra the setting was transformed into a pastoral landscape,[77] consisting of a back scene and eight wooden hills ("otto compartimenti di boschi, e di colline"). Each of the eight wings was decorated in a different manner. Predominant on one were fig and peach trees, on another orange trees and cedars, and on a third grapevines. In the background was a palace with a pond and statues spouting water. Above the palace hovered Cupid's cloud, which soared aloft and then moved on a horizontal plane until it reached the proscenium, where it divided itself into the six spheres of the Medici coat of arms, on each of which sat a little Cupid. A short sextet sung by the amoretti followed the love god's aria. A pageant drawn by two hippogriffs brought Bellona (Pallas Athena) into the scene, and no sooner did she proclaim that the captive heroes beneath Aetna had now been released, than the right entrance into the arena again opened to admit a horse-drawn carro trionfale bringing in yet other participants in the tourney.

Still missing were the knights spellbound by Mercury in the bellies of sea monsters. With the appearance of Saturn's cloud, the pastoral landscape was transformed into a sea scene, for which the stage floor was now removed ("videsi il pauimento del palco in vn'istante transformato in vn gran golfo di Mare").[78] Cliffs framed the sides of the stage. The background was occupied by a palace. Saturn implored Neptune to free the captives. A chorus of eight Tritons, who rose out of the waves and sang in a semicircle, prepared for the appearance of the sea god. From his shell car Neptune decreed that the billows of the sea should surge into the arena, whereupon water rushed in through the side gates of the auditorium, turning the tiltyard into a lake. Buttigli indicates[79] that the waves lapped up to the "secondo grado esteriore del Theatro." Abbé Folchi, a visitor from Florence, grew apprehensive, as he confessed in a letter:[80] "I was afraid to sit in such a large hall overloaded with thousands of spectators and many machines. Moreover, the same hall later had to sustain the weight of the water which rose to a height of more than half a braccia,"—that is, approximately twelve inches. And his anxiety seemed justified, for the engineers themselves had felt some misgivings even on the eve of the performance. But the Teatro Farnese passed its load test: it was not, in all events, destined for destruction by water. Although in 1589 a Medici had had already transformed the courtyard of the Pitti Palace into an aquatic arena, the venture of the Farnese prince in 1628 was far more risky, since he flooded a gigantic arena situated on the second story.

77. Ibid., pp. 330–36.
78. Ibid., p. 340.
79. Ibid., p. 345.
80. Published by Lombardi, in *Archivio, 9, 10.*

Seven sea creatures[81] swam through the door on the right side, six of the smaller ones conceived as dolphins and the largest a whale fifteen braccia long, five wide, and seven high (at the top point of the spinal column). From its nostrils the beast spouted great quantities of water. Eight of the knights liberated from Mercury's enchantment sat on its back, while drummers and pages riding the dolphins navigated into the Salone. The creatures and their riders were born into the arena by the initial torrents, but after the water had risen to the prescribed level, the waves subsided and a procession could be formed. Suddenly, the whale was given to pranks and sprayed the pages with its spouts. After this, it swam up to the central balcony and rendered homage to the new Duchess of Parma. Meanwhile, the Tritons on stage were still singing in chorus between the artificial waves.

Two floating islands now entered through the right gate. On one of them stood Galatea, and on the other, two nymphs. The island with Galatea sailed up to the princely balcony, whereupon the goddess in a madrigal bade the knights take up their places on her island. The second island also received its number of cavaliers. Then the two islands came together, a barrier was set up, and a tilt unfolded in this unusual floating arena. The jousting was finally put to a stop by the appearance of Celeste Gloria, and all eyes turned back to the stage, where an assembly of the gods was discovered, with Jupiter astride his eagle in the center (Figure 132). Juno rode a peacock, Venus a ram, Diana a deer, Bacchus a panther, Pallas a hippogriff, Apollo a lion, and Ceres a dragon, all of them arranged in a semicircle. Somewhat below the gods, almost concealed in a grotto, sat the Father of the Golden Age. At the lowest point a mournful Discord and the two Furies lay in fetters. Altogether, upward of a hundred people were borne aloft by the great machine which advanced to the proscenium opening. There, Jupiter concluded the combat with his madrigal of arbitration. The coming of these celestial beings caused "gran marauiglie a gli osseruatori,"[82] who could not see the "arteficij mecanici" and so were unable to overcome their stupefaction. Jupiter banished Discord and the Furies to Tartarus, whereupon the three plunged into the storm-tossed sea on stage. There followed a concert of the heavenly musicians, as the gods formed a full circle

81. The swimming animals were mounted on small barks, and were animated by stage hands concealed within; see Francesco Guitti's letter to the Marchese Bentivoglio published by Campori, *Lettere,* pp. 106–07. "Si fa lavorare da terazeri veneziani il pavimento del salone e de' vasi dove va l'acqua . . . Feci fare certi burchielli per i pesci che vanno nell'acqua . . . e sono fatti nella presente maniera. La cassetta posta nel mezzo segnata A [the pertinent drawing has evidently been lost] va nel fondo della nave, la quale è bugiata, et è tanto alta che l'acqua per ogni sforzo non può entrare molto sù: nel detto bugio entra un uomo il quale governa tanto facilmente la barca che per la detta prova si vede essere di buona riuscita."

82. Buttigli, p. 351.

and seemed to embrace one another. Peace now reigned in the heavens, hence also on earth. The jousters in the arena began to cry, "Pace, Pace!" Celestial Glory vanished, and the water was drained out of the arena, leaving the islands and sea monsters stranded on the "pauimento del Salone." Great applause from the audience rewarded the performers. The following day, Camillo Giordani summed up his final impression as follows: "There has never been a grander tournament, one employing a greater number of ingenious machines."[83]

83. Quoted by Saviotti, in *Giornale storico, 41,* 49.

15. Le Nozze degli dei

1637

At the time of her engagement to Ferdinando II, Vittoria della Rovere, Princess of Urbino, was just thirteen years old and still in a convent. Her fate was linked to the Duchy of Urbino, itself a bone of contention between the Pope and the Medici, and source of a discordant counterpoint to the marriage negotiations. Suffice it to say that the papal lawyers reduced Vittoria's inheritance to a distinctly meager dowry. It also soon became apparent that Vittoria could not adapt herself to Florentine ways, and still less to those of her husband: theirs was a misalliance, on the human as well as the dynastic level. But this did not impair the festive mood of the audience which gathered in the Pitti Cortile for the beginning of the nuptial celebrations, a memorable performance of the opera *Le Nozze degli dei* on July 8, 1637.[1] The libretto was written by Giovanni Carlo Coppola,[2] and five

1. Primary sources: [Francesco Raffaello Rondinelli] Relazione / delle Nozze / degli Dei / Favola / dell' Abate / Gio: Carlo Coppola / Rappresentata nelle reali Nozze de' Sereniss. / Gran Duchi di Toscana / Ferdinando II. / e Vittoria / Principessa d'Vrbino. / Alla Medesima / Gran Dvchessa / di Toscana. / In Firenze / Nella nuoua Stamperia del Massi, e' Landi. 1637. (In the following, referred to as *Rel.*)

[Anon.] Descrizione / delle feste fatte / in Firenze / per le reali nozze de Serenissimi sposi / Ferdinando II. / Gran Dvca di Toscana, e Vittoria / Principessa d'Vrbino. / In Fiorenza, Per Zanobi Pignoni. 1637. (In the following, referred to as *Descr.*)

2. Le Nozze / degli Dei / Favola / dell' Ab. Gio Carlo Coppola / Rappresentata in Musica in Firenze / Nelle Reali Nozze / De' Serenis. Gran Duchi di Toschana / Ferdinando II e Vittoria / Principessa d'Vrbino / In Firenze per Amadore Massi, e Lorenzo Landi, 1637 (libretto, with etchings by Stefano della Bella).

unknown composers contributed the score.[3] Alfonso Parigi created the settings and Agniolo Ricci the choreography. Ferdinando Saracinelli was in charge of the overall direction.

Coppola states in the Foreword to his text that at the behest of the Grand Duke he had completed the work in seven days. The printed version was in any case longer than the one used in the performance, since the music and time-consuming machinery had to be taken into consideration. The basic conceit of the libretto was as follows: To shower the earth with happiness, Jupiter decided to celebrate four celestial weddings on the same day. He himself would marry Juno, Venus was to become the bride of Vulcan, Pallas Athena was intended for Pluto, and the chaste Diana was meant for Neptune. However, Jupiter's plan ran into difficulties. He dispatched Mercury to earth to invite Diana to the wedding, but she politely declined, desiring to remain a virgin. Pallas too conveyed her regrets to the messenger of the gods: she just happened to be visiting Parnassus, where she heard the Muses sing of Ferdinando and Vittoria. Venus was beside herself on learning that Jupiter intended her for Vulcan. Neptune, for his part, infatuated with Amphitrite, wanted none of Diana. Pluto, still unaware that Jupiter had chosen him a bride, summoned the underworld to armed rebellion against the heavens. Jealousy overcame Mars when he heard that Venus was promised to Vulcan. Thus prospects for an Olympian feast of joy were anything but bright. Clearly, Coppola showed no lack of skill in planting his dramatic effects. Armed with his mythological omniscience, the librettist shifted his celestial alliances until everything was resolved in an atmosphere of good feeling. Of course, the deities also had to help and could not leave everything to Jupiter. Venus bade Cupid shoot his golden arrows at the frigid Amphitrite, so that she could fall in love with Neptune, and enticed Proserpina from the palace, where she was being carefully guarded by her mother, so that Pluto could abduct her in his chariot. This satisfied Diana, Neptune, Pallas Athena, and Pluto. Mars and Vulcan, however, still posed a problem. A struggle broke out between them over Venus, the victor's prize. Mercury, sent down by Jupiter, separated the pugnacious fellows, and Juno succeeded in pacifying Mars. A fourfold wedding could now be performed. Neptune and Amphitrite were wedded in the sea, Pluto and Proserpina in the underworld. Jupiter brought Juno home to the heavens as his bride, and Venus became the spouse of Vulcan.

As Vittoria had enjoyed a very pious Christian upbringing, Coppola had a bad conscience because of the large number of pagan deities. He thus took pains to point out to the readers of his libretto that the concepts of Fato, Destino, and

3. According to *Rel.*, p. 7, the Grand Duke commissioned five leading composers of the city to write the score; he expected the "varietà di stile" to provide greater pleasure for the listeners.

Fortuna mentioned in his opera should merely be taken "fauolosamente"—that is, as a form of poetic license which could not conflict with Christian piety.

The idea of staging the performance in the courtyard of the Pitti Palace evidently originated with the Grand Duke.[4] Ferdinando was eager to give the many foreign guests who were expected every opportunity to attend the opera, and there was no adequate auditorium available. Moreover, he was afraid that the July weather would be unbearable to visitors packed together in a crowded hall. The acoustics of the cortile were therefore tested, and it was found that a singer could be clearly heard in all parts of it. Yet another question had to be considered: How would the painted scenery and machines turn out under an open sky? But these were problems for Alfonso Parigi to solve. Every contingency was anticipated, and it was only hoped that there would be no rain. Since the Grand Duke was visiting in Pisa, he appointed his brother Giovanni Carlo chief supervisor of the preparations.

Parigi set up his stage on the garden side of the courtyard—that is, in front of the grotto. The ladies were seated on gradini arranged in a crescent. Facing the stage a dais for princely personages was erected, with fifteen seats upholstered in gold fabric. From the roof of this portico, Ferdinando could easily reach his apartments on the second story. Male spectators sat or stood in the courtyard itself.

It is evident from the title page of the libretto (Figure 119) that the stage occupied the entire width of the cortile, although Parigi exploited only about three fifths of the total width for his décors, up to and including the penultimate scene. For the final tableau, the designer removed the side screens visible on the frontispiece, thus widening the stage opening to a breadth of approximately 120 feet. The depth of the stage is not known, nor is there any information as to the height of the stage platform. Evidently the stage, including the gridiron, rose up to floor level of the third story—an imposing height of a little over seventy feet. Since Parigi needed an operable grid for his flying machines, we may assume that his stage opening did not rise above the floor level of the second story, at least not until the transformation into the final cloud scene. We gather from the frontispiece that the third story lay open to the night sky.

The Prelude

After the curtain had disappeared,[5] the spectators beheld a charming landscape with hills giving a view of Florence and the Arno in the center. The anonymous

---

4. The following section is based on *Descr.*, pp. 23–25.
5. *Descr.*, p. 27: "sparì in vn momento la tenda"; *Rel.*, p. 8: "s'alzò la Cortina."

chronicler was entranced by the depth of this setting and its excellent illumination ("bene illuminato"). When the heavens parted, out floated a small white cloud with golden reflections. Fair-haired Hymen appeared in flight, holding a torch in his right hand and a golden noose in his left. His white velvet costume with silver tassles reached to the knees. From his shoulders hung a cloak of gold brocade, which billowed in the wind as the cloud descended. The God of Nuptials came with two escorts: Honesty, completely wrapped in white veils, and Fertility, in a yellow damask undergarment and a cape of green satin embroidered with gold sequins, holding in her right hand a cornucopia with blossoms and fruits. As the cloud was lowered, the three sang a *canzonet* in which they wished happiness and contentment to the couple. Hymen had come in order to spark the fires of inextinguishable love in the hearts of the newlyweds. During the song three nymphs, gorgeously attired in bright blue silk interwoven with silver, emerged from the waters of the Arno. They had risen on a small, mobile island on which a mother-of-pearl shell was set. The nymphs also brought their blessings, especially for the descendants of the new couple.

Stefano della Bella's etching (Figure 120) shows the setting essentially as Rondinelli had described it. Hymen and his two companions are portrayed twice, once on the cloud and again on the stage. The three Arno nymphs stand in the foreground, while twelve additional nymphs form a semicircle in the background. Mercury appears in flight, although he had no function in this prologue and Jupiter did not send him to earth until the following scene.

ACT I: *Scena di Diana*

At the end of the Prelude the heavens parted again and Jupiter appeared on a dazzling throne, the bolt of lightning in his left hand, the scepter in his right, and the eagle at his feet. Dressed in gold brocade, he was encircled by a celestial choir which sang his praises and waited on his commands. Jupiter declared that he had resolved to take Juno for a wife and bring about three other marriages of the gods. He commissioned Mercury to assemble the individual couples, whereupon the gods voiced their joy in a chorus. This gathering of the gods evidently took place in the heavens above the Florentine setting of the Prelude.

Now the heavens closed ("Serrato il Cielo"),[6] and the scene was changed into a "Boscaglia,"[7] a forest landscape, which, to judge from the etching (Figure 121), included pine trees, whereas the hills surrounding Florence were planted with

6. *Descr.*, p. 28.
7. *Rel.*, p. 12.

deciduous growth. Diana appeared in this meadow wearing a dress of thin white taffeta embellished with gold lace. Her hair was contained by a golden net and adorned by the moon. The six nymphs of her train, robed in white sendal bordered with dark blue, carried hunting gear with them and pondered where the wounded stag might have fled. Six other nymphs now came with the news that the animal had died of its wounds. Diana invited the nymphs to crown the triumphant huntress Nerine with flowers, after which they ran off to gather blossoms. Mercury appeared aloft in a cloak of iridescent material (an allusion to the powers of metamorphosis attributed by astronomers to the planet). Diana's vehement rejection of the marriage proposal followed. In a canzonet the chorus of nymphs extolled the virtue of chastity. Simultaneously, a throne-shaped cloud rose from a trap ("sorgere del Palco")[8] and slowly ascended into the heavens after Diana and her nymphs had seated themselves on it. When the cloud had reached the highest point, it was seized by a strong wind and driven upstage—a sharp, right-angle change of direction. The *Descrizione* maintains that Hymen's cloud was used for the ascent of Diana, whereas Stefano della Bella's etching shows Diana and her nymphs at once on stage and on the cloud.

ACT II: *1. Scena di Vulcano*

Directly after the conclusion of Act I, the scene changed ("si mutarono le Scene")[9] to a mountain landscape on the island of Lemnos. In the background ("nella parte più lontana della Prospettiua")[10] rose Vulcan's smithy, a gloomy cavern filled with smoke and implements of the forge. Here and there lay suits of armor, some of them rusted, others half finished. In the middle stood naked Vulcan with a hammer in his right hand and a pair of tongs in his left, surrounded by a number of Cyclopes,[11] among whom towered Steropes, Brontes, and Arges,[12] also naked. Jupiter's eagle was also present. The whole scene was in imitation of Virgil's *Aeneid*, 8.424 ff. The three assistants beat in time on their anvils, on which they forged arrows for Jupiter. As soon as an arrow had been finished, the great bird snatched it up in its claws and carried it off to Olympus. Vulcan, a god of grotesque beauty, commanded his Cyclopes to produce a shield to be destined for a great hero. He even indicated the blazonry: an aged oak (Rovere) with a young offshoot from which hung six golden apples.

8. *Rel.*, p. 14.
9. Ibid.
10. Ibid.
11. Coppola called for seventeen in his libretto.
12. *Rel.*, p. 15, calls the third Cyclops Pyracmon.

Winged Iris, robed in green, white, red, and yellow sendal, now appeared as an envoy from Jupiter. Standing on an extremely realistic rainbow at mid-elevation, she informed Vulcan that he had been elected Venus' bridegroom and must present himself for the heavenly nuptials as quickly as possible. Thereupon he ordered his helpers to beautify the grotto so that Venus might feel at home in it. Rondinelli remarked that Vulcan ascended to Olympus in a burning globe; Coppola's libretto called for a fiery chariot.[13] The scene ended with a choral piece sung by the Cyclopes.

ACT II: 2. *Scena di Parnaso*

The next scene took place on Mount Parnassus,[14] where Athena joined the gaily singing Muses. With the Medusa shield on her arm, a lance in her right hand, and a Sphinx adorning her helmet, she extolled Tuscany and its civilization in a song with the Muses. Polyhymnia, robed in white and wearing a crown of pearls and precious stones, paid homage to Cosimo the Great. Clio, wreathed in laurel and wearing a gold-embroidered white velvet gown and a rather simple headdress, then followed, holding a book in her right hand. Her costume may be interpreted thus: history must tell the shining truth, embellished with the gold of wisdom but without the adornments of poetry. After Clio had sung the praises of Cosimo's grandson Lorenzo, came Urania's turn. Enveloped in blue and gold brocade, the Muse of astronomy wore a constellation for her headpiece and held a celestial globe. She lauded the popes of the Medici line, Leo X and Clement VII, as well as the military triumphs of Lorenzo, the Duke of Urbino, and Giovanni delle Bande Nere. Next appeared Melpomene, for her eulogy of Cosimo I. She wore the cothurnus and a dress of violet velvet with a train. Erato followed her, wearing flesh-colored silver sendal, her curly hair perfumed and crowned with roses and myrtle. The Muse of lyric poetry compared Francesco and Ferdinando I with Castor and Pollux. Sheathed in gold and carrying a flute, Euterpe sang a hymn to Cosimo II. Ferdinando II was the hero of Calliope, her costume consisting of gold brocade, a golden crown, and a pearl necklace. Finally, Thalia appeared on the *soccus*, wreathed in ivy and holding a mask. Wearing a costume of "grossagrana," or grosgrain, she alluded to the wedding of Ferdinando II and Vittoria, for whom she wished a blessed posterity.

Athena was beside herself at the thought of being married to Pluto. Mercury, who had conveyed the proposal, managed to appease her, and the Muses strength-

13. *Descr.*, p. 29, refers to a "nuuola di fuoco."
14. *Rel.*, p. 16: "si muta la Scena."

ened her in her resolve to remain unwed. The scene, which the engraver did not record for us, ended with the ascent of the singing Muses up into the heavens.

ACT II: *3. Scena Giardino di Venere*

Rondinelli merely informs us that the scene changed ("si mutò la Scena"). The anonymous *Descrizione* states: "Si volta doppo la scena," and the libretto has the stage direction: "Si volta la Scena." Judging from the use of the verb "to rotate" (*voltarsi*), Parigi may have been working with turning prisms here.

The Venus garden was enclosed by gilded loggias. In the background gushed a fountain, and an alley of plane trees ran off into the depths. Although Rondinelli[15] mentions a garden encircled by a "mura d'oro," a glance at Stefano della Bella's print (Figure 122) shows patently that it could not have been a golden "wall." The anonymous *Descrizione*, in speaking of the "colonne, & architraui indorati"[16] which surrounded the stage "in forma di Teatro," more closely approximates the actual setting.

Venus' costume was of flowered gold brocade, over which she wore a flesh-colored cloak embroidered in silver. Her hair was adorned with pearls, roses, and myrtle. With her were the three Graces in white silver brocade. Three children personified Jest, Laughter, and Play—Jest in white, Play in yellow, and Laughter in an iridescent costume. Adonis, of course, was also present, garbed as a shepherd. His trousers and jerkin were of a dark blue material interwoven with gold, and his white stockings were adorned with roses and golden bows. Across his breast a sable was slung, and his hat of grey beaver was trimmed with white feathers and a band of diamonds. At his side he wore a rapier, which did not quite suit his effeminate appearance. Six shepherds in green garb edged in white ermine were his escorts.

Venus and her companions sang love's praises. The six then danced a ballet with six *amoretti* invented by Agniolo Ricci. A love scene between Venus and Adonis was interrupted by the untimely entrance of Mercury. Venus indignantly rejected the suggestion that she marry Vulcan, and Mercury diplomatically withdrew. Juno now joined the action, appearing on her cloud car drawn by peacocks, from which she commanded the Winds to upset the idyll of Venus and Adonis. On the highest point of the stage the four winged Winds with puffed cheeks were then revealed. Thunder and lightning struck, and it began to rain and hail. The lovers fled, and the stage filled with clouds as the act approached its

15. Ibid., p. 22.
16. *Descr.*, p. 29.

end. Two successive actions are again captured in the etching, the ballet and the appearance of Juno.

ACT III: *1. Scena di Plutone*

The locale of this scene has not been precisely determined. Rondinelli simply refers to a scene change in which the stage floor opened ("si muta la Scena"; "s'apre il palco"). A "scena boschereccia" is mentioned in the *Descrizione*. Pluto arose from the trap on a fire-spouting scaly dragon, surrounded by Furies, Harpies, Gorgons, and Polyphemus, Geryon and the Chimera, their masks and costumes truly horrifying ("spauentose"). Pluto, furious because Jupiter had still not sent him a bride, threatened to overrun Olympus with his hordes. Twenty *Numi Infernali* promised him their support. At this moment the Parcae entered and reassured Pluto with the news that Athena was promised for him. Ascending into the heavens, the Sisters then sang a hymn to love. No print exists for this scene.

ACT III: *2. Scena di Mare*

Now the stage was transformed into a sea scene on Cyprus. Venus, inconsolable because of her imminent marriage to Vulcan, found distraction in the company of Mars, and scarcely had he taken his leave than she was consoled by Cupid. At the same time, Neptune rose from the deep in his chariot drawn by sea horses. The carro appeared to be made of tufa and rolled on silver wheels. A glowing mother-of-pearl shell formed the rear of the car. Puffing and snorting "aqua falsa," the sea horses plowed through the waves. Neptune, escorted by Tritons and Nereids, appeared with his trident and crown of spruce, naked. Algae were embedded in his hair and beard. In a canzone he lamented Amphitrite's coldness, for his love seemed to go unrequited. Moved to pity, Venus commanded Cupid to mollify the nymph. She then climbed onto her shell-car and sank into the waves. The sea creatures sang a choral piece and Neptune a second canzone. Amphitrite next appeared on a dolphin, wearing a crown of coral and a costume of azure double taffeta. She confessed her inclination to Neptune, thus assuring him of bliss. Venus and Cupid again emerged from the sea as a chorus of amoretti sang a hymn to beauty. So, thus far, runs Rondinelli's account.

The anonymous *Descrizione* gives a different ending to the third act. It claims that Neptune's joy at Amphitrite's change of heart was such that he allowed the sea to flood the shores: "Suddenly the stage floor opened in the center and from certain openings there surged forth a sea which so resembled the true element in movement and coloration that it surpassed everyone's expectation."[17] As Nep-

17. Ibid., p. 31: "apprendosi in vn momento il palco vsci da quelle aperture vn mare tanto simile al vero, e nel colore, e nel moto, che superò l'espettazione d'ognuno."

tune and Amphitrite withdrew to a throne, thirteen Tritons rose out of the water to execute a bizarre dance.[18] Center stage two sea horses emerged from the deep, and the Tritons hopped over their backs and into the waves. According to Rondinelli, this scene took place at the beginning of Act V. The ballet of the Tritons is commemorated in an etching by Della Bella (Figure 123).

ACT IV: *1. Scena di Venere*

Rondinelli has the act begin with a scene between Venus and the Parcae, thus following the printed libretto. The *Descrizione*, however, does not mention this scene, which may have been omitted.[19] In any case, Venus received Jupiter's command from the Parcae to lure Proserpina, until now carefully guarded by her mother, from her hiding place, so that Pluto might easily ravish her.

ACT IV: *2. Scena d'Inferno*

This scene took place in the underworld palace of Pluto, with its flaming iron walls. In the middle of the "funesto Teatro" stood Pluto surrounded by Numi Infernali. Chafing because of Jupiter's silence, he demanded his shades to prepare war against the heavens. The Fates appeared and encouraged him to seize Proserpina. Delighted by this idea, the god then mounted his car and sang an aria on the omnipotence of love.

ACT IV: *3. Scena di Proserpina*

Following a choral piece sung by the infernal spirits, the scene changed to the palace of Ceres. Proserpina, in a costume of gold fabric, with lavender blossoms in her curly hair, was enticed by Venus from her mother's stronghold, and innocently set to picking flowers in a meadow. Pluto then appeared on his cloud car and carried off the shrieking maiden.

ACT IV: *4. Scena di Cielo*

Here Jupiter was shown in the midst of an assembly of the gods. He was delighted at the prospect of the forthcoming nuptials. In fact, everyone was pleased, with the sole exception of Mars. Jupiter therefore arranged for a duel between Mars and Vulcan and promised Venus to the victor.

ACT IV: *5. Scena di Cerere*

In Rondinelli we read the enigmatic remark that the décor rotated, "La Scena si volta," but the setting is not described. In any case, Ceres appeared on a car pulled by two dragons. She was wreathed with ears of corn and wore a dress of yellow

18. Ibid.: *"vn ballo per la novità, e bizzarria marauiglioso."*
19. Coppola pointed out in his Preface that the text had been cut for the performance.

velvet trimmed with silver lace. Holding a burning torch, she lamented the loss of her daughter in an aria. Here we have the situation described in Ovid's *Metamorphoses* 5.438 ff.

ACT IV: *6. Scena di Vulcano*

Vulcan's grotto, which the spectators had already seen in the second act, again opened. Vulcan's helpers handed him his armor, and he chose six of his most stalwart men to wage war with him against Mars. Following a choral piece by the Cyclopes, the heavens parted in two places: on one side appeared the chorus of Venus to give Mars encouragement, and on the other the chorus of Juno to support Vulcan. The struggle now began and was fought in realistic detail by the pages of the Grand Duke. Each of the two contending divinities was aided by six helpers. As the combat reached its climax, Mercury appeared, escorted by Juno and Venus, and called the fighting to a halt. The battle scene is preserved for us in an etching by Della Bella (Figure 124).

ACT V: *1. Scena d'Inferno*[20]

Here Pluto and Proserpina were seated together on their throne. Mercury appeared aloft with Ceres, having come to proclaim a compromise solution: Proserpina would spend half the year in the underworld and the other six months with her mother on earth. Ceres acquiesced in this plan. Hymen now entered with his torch to bring a cheerful light to the gloomy kingdom of the dead. The shades were transported with joy. Even the sinners declared a holiday: the team of vultures ceased picking at the liver of Tityus; Sisyphus was relieved this once from rolling his stone; the Danaïdes could stop drawing water, and Tantalus suffered neither hunger nor thirst. Then the underworld populace paid homage to their new mistress. Coppola's libretto called for a ballet of eight centaurs who crept forth from the jaws of the Chimera, while eight dancing devils popped from the mouth of Cerberus. Della Bella commemorated this grotesque dance in an etching, incidentally showing Ceres in flight, although she had made her exit some time before (Figure 125).

ACT V: *2. Scena di tutto cielo*

At the conclusion of the centaur ballet the entire stage filled up with clouds ("diuenta la scena tutta nuuole").[21] The stage was broadened on either end by side wings painted with clouds ("tutto il Cielo veniua a sporgersi innanzi con due

20. Rondinelli has the act begin with a sea scene and the water games of the Tritons, hence a scene with which, according to the *Descrizione*, the third act would have concluded.
21. *Descr.*, p. 33.

grand' ale coperte di nuuoli"). Here the anonymous chronicler records his impression of the scene that Stefano della Bella captured in his print (Figure 126). A comparison of his rendering of the "Sesta Scena" with the frontispiece shows us just how this lateral extension of the stage was technically achieved. On the frontispiece the central stage opening is framed on either side by ornaments (niches with statues) mounted between columns. On these side frames rested the draperies. For the final scene, Parigi removed the side panels, raising the draperies and lowering cloud strips from the grid in front of the columns, thus creating a tripartite stage.

In the highest part of the heavens stood four empty throne seats. After a chorus of the Muses, which began the act, Apollo entered from the right, escorted by twelve signs of the zodiac, while Diana came from the left with twelve nymphs dressed as stars. Both groups met at center stage; then Apollo and Diana descended with their retinues to the lower stage ("oue si rappresentaua la parte più bassa del Cielo"),[22] crossed to change sides, and finally assumed positions—Diana and her nymphs to the left, Apollo and the zodiac to the right. Hymen now appeared, leading Jupiter's chorus. The brightness increased as Jupiter alighted from his eagle-drawn chariot and mounted to his throne. Juno's chorus, consisting of fourteen nymphs, now made its entrance. Juno left her pageant, drawn by peacocks, and sat upon her throne. Vulcan then appeared with his helpers on his lion car; there was also a throne prepared for him. The fourth throne was claimed by Venus, who entered on a carro pulled by swans.

Jupiter now gave the command for singing and dancing. A bolt of lightning streaked across the stage—the signal for the ballet to begin. Twenty-four cavaliers —the combined retinues of Diana and Apollo—danced at center stage. On a higher cloud level, two knights, Castor and Pollux, performed an equestrian ballet. Coppola's libretto also called for a dance of the amoretti on floating clouds.

Let us now turn to Della Bella's etching of the ballet scene. The twenty-four knights occupy center stage. Somewhat higher, the amoretti are floating on clouds. Still higher are four horsemen, the Dioscuri, accompanied by two additional jousters. At the zenith we see the assembly of the gods and the four thrones in their midst. Two further celestial choruses stand to the right and left, on the level of the amoretti. On the stage floor, in the side wings of the triptych, still other dancers form the letters FO (for Ferdinando) and VA (for Vittoria). The horses, which in the picture seem to be prancing on clouds, actually had solid ground under their hoofs—that is, the flat roof over the grotto. The entrance of the celestial choruses may also have been made over this roof, after which the trains of Diana and Apollo

22. *Rel.*, p. 44.

would have reached the stage floor via staircases concealed behind the clouds. Naturally, the spectators had neither the time nor the inclination to brood about solutions to technical problems, dazzled as they were by the beauty of the scene. When the curtain finally fell on a spectacle which had lasted four hours, the audience was reluctant to leave the cortile. The Florentines were particularly proud of the fact that it had not been necessary to import foreign artists for the performance. Some 150 singers had participated, all of whom resided in the Grand Ducal territory.[23]

Equestrian Ballet in the Boboli Garden

The nuptial festivities ended in a horse ballet staged on the evening of July 15, in the amphitheatre of the Boboli Garden. The task of equipping the theatre and providing pageant cars and machines was assigned to Felice Gamberai, who had much experience in this field.[24] Ferdinando Saracinelli borrowed the idea for the symbolic action from Tasso's *Gerusalemme liberata*.

The guests of honor were seated on a grandstand erected on the palace side. The remaining spectators sat on the stone benches of the amphitheatre, which was illuminated by "stars"—actually torches suspended aloft. Gamberai masked the central opening, which led into the garden proper, with a *scena boschereccia*, a painted continuation of the natural flora of the garden, so that by torchlight it was impossible to distinguish where nature left off and art began.

A carro drawn by four elephants brought Armida into the arena. Gorgeously attired and bejeweled, she sat on the peak of her chariot. Twelve trumpeters on horseback, wearing red and silver, led the van. Following them came a hundred torchbearers and five riders on either side. Armida drove about in a circle, halting in front of the princes. Descending from her high seat to a lower part of the chariot, she sang her boastful address. She then made a test of her magic powers and gave a sign, whereupon the forward, lower part of the vehicle detached itself from the higher part. Armida now sat on the smaller car, which the elephants pulled through the arena. The highest part of the pageant stood in place, transforming itself into a mountain with three caves. A fire-spitting serpent issued from one opening, hitched itself to the pageant, and pulled the mountain out of the arena (Figure 127). The *scena boschereccia* was then transformed into the façade of a palace. From the west came the knight Eustachio, and from the east Eberardo with his retinue, all of whom paid homage to the sorceress and then displayed their talents in

23. Ibid., p. 7. Among the soloists, Signora Paola and Settimia Caccini were highly praised (*Descr.*, p. 34).

24. *Descr.*, p. 37.

an intricate equestrian ballet. Armida praised the valor of the knights and invited them to her palace. After she and the knights had vanished through the gates of the palace façade, the stage remained empty for a moment. The character of the music changed, the trumpets having hitherto been dominant. Gentler tones were now heard, and from the west appeared the pageant of Chaste Love (Amor Pudico) drawn by six white horses. Amor Pudico had come to liberate the noble cavaliers from their captivity and entanglement with sensual delights. Following a canzone to Chaste Love, Amor shot a fiery arrow at the castle. Instantly, the palace disappeared and the grove of the first scene returned, from which the liberated knights poured forth to dance a ballet composed by Agniolo Ricci.

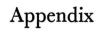

Appendix

Intermezzi in Mantua

1608

For the nuptials of the hereditary Prince Francesco Gonzaga and Margherita di Savoia, Duke Vincenzo I arranged a series of festivals that bore an implicit relationship to theatrical performances at the Medici Court. The Mantuans were anxious to surpass previous Florentine achievements in this field, just as the Florentines, for their part, would try to outshine Mantua a few months later during the wedding festivities of Prince Cosimo. We have already seen evidence of the rivalry between the two courts[1] in the critical comparisons drawn by the Mantuan observer between the Florentine scene designs for *Il Giudizio di Paride* and the technical and artistic accomplishments of his native city.

CALENDAR OF EVENTS

May 28: Première of Claudio Monteverdi's *Arianna* in the Court Theatre of Mantua, which had been recently completed by Antonio Maria Vianini.[2] The libretto was contributed by a Florentine, Ottavio Rinuccini.

May 31: Assault on a specially constructed fortress in the Lago di Mezzo, with

---

1. Cf. above, pp. 110–11.

2. Actually Antonio Maria Viani, also called Il Vianino. Since 1591 Vianini, a native of Cremona, had been "prefetto delle fabbriche dello Stato di Mantova." He probably contrived the brilliant décors and machines for the performance of Giovan Battista Guarini's *Il Pastor fido* in the old castle theatre in Mantua (1598). Cf. Eduard Flechsig, *Die Dekoration der modernen Bühne in Italien von den Anfängen bis zum Schluss des XVI. Jahrhunderts* (Dresden, 1894), pp. 30–32.

elaborate firework displays such as we have previously mentioned with reference to the procession of the Argonauts on the Arno.[3]

June 2: Performance of Giovan Battista Guarini's comedy *L'Idropica,* with intermezzi by Gabriello Chiabrera.

June 4: Conclusion of the festivities with the *Ballo dell'ingrate,* again a text by Rinuccini with music by Claudio Monteverdi.

Federico Follino, to whom we are indebted for the official festival description,[4] estimated the capacity of the new theatre at six thousand spectators. The agent of the Este, however, was more conservative and wrote to Modena that the auditorium could not hold more than four thousand.[5] Duke Vincenzo refused to have native residents of Mantua attend his theatre, since he wanted to give foreign visitors every opportunity to be present at the performances.[6] Actually, the crowd pressing to enter the theatre was such that the ducal bodyguard could not control it, and the presence of the Duke himself was required to restore order. Guests were not admitted until they identified themselves by showing copper tokens.[7]

By Renaissance standards the first night of *L'Arianna* was a brief theatrical evening, lasting but two and a half to three hours.[8] The libretto[9] called for only one setting, a steep rocky reef in the middle of the sea, with billows tossing in the far distance ("alpestre scoglio in mezzo all'onde, le quali nella più lontana parte della prospettiva si videro sempre ondeggiar con molta vaghezza").[10] Apollo entered first, seated on a cloud "piena di lucidissimo splendore," which already floated in the air even as the curtain was being raised. As sweet instrumental music was heard from backstage, the machine began its slow descent. Apollo then alighted on the shore of the rocky island, and the cloud vanished abruptly ("in un momento"). Striding majestically downstage, he began to sing the Prologue. After he

3. Cf. above, p. 111.

4. [Federico Follino], *Compendio / Delle Sontvose / Feste / Fatte l'anno M.DC.VIII. / Nella Città di Mantova, / Per le reali nozze del / Serenissimo Prencipe / D. Francesco Gonzaga, / Con la Serenissima Infante / Margherita di Savoia / In Mantova / M.DC.IIX.* Parts of this *Compendio* are reprinted in Solerti, *Albori,* 2, 145–48, and 3, 207–34. They shall be referred to in the following as Follino-Solerti. After Follino, the next source to be consulted is Zuccari, *Il Passagio per Italia,* pp. 16–30.

5. Solerti, *Albori, 1,* 94. He estimated that approximately 5,000 spectators witnessed the performance of *L'Idropica* (ibid., p. 101).

6. Follino-Solerti, 2, 145.

7. "Medaglie di rame" (Follino-Solerti, *3,* 208).

8. Follino counted 150 minutes, the Mantuan observer "from the Ave Maria until three o'clock."

9. Reprinted in Solerti, *Albori,* 2, 146–87, following the first edition in Follino's *Compendio.*

10. Follino-Solerti, 2, 145.

withdrew, there ensued a duet between Venus and Cupid. The second scene brought Theseus, Ariadne, a chorus of warriors, and another of fishermen onto the stage. Theseus departed, whereupon Ariadne[11] sang her famous *Lamento,* the only piece of music in Monteverdi's opera that has survived, a threnody which brought tears to every eye. Follino wrote: "The lament of Ariadne, abandoned by Theseus on her rocky reef, was sung so movingly that the listeners were deeply touched, and there was not a lady in the house who failed to shed a tear." In his Foreword to *Dafne,* Marco da Gagliano concurred: "The most celebrated Claudio Monteverdi, Master of the Ducal Chapel, composed pieces of such distinction for his *L'Arianna* that one may truly feel assured that the laudable achievements of ancient music had been renewed, for the entire audience was virtually moved to tears."[12] The observer from Modena likewise noted the moist cheeks.[13] At the conclusion of the opera Ariadne found a comforter in Bacchus, who appeared in the final scene with a band of soldiers. Sixteen warriors performed some frisky dances ("balletti in capriole"), whose intricate choreography ("intrecciandosi in mille guise") greatly pleased Follino. Finally, Venus arose from the sea, while Jupiter came on a cloud to bless the new bonds of love.

L'Arianna was essentially a musical experience. Monteverdi, "a man whose excellence is known to all the world, and who on this occasion has surpassed even himself,"[14] was clearly the hero of the evening, for the set designer, probably Antonio Maria Vianini, had only modest tasks to perform.

But Vianini was also to have his great evening on the second of June, when Guarini's comedy *L'Idropica,* with Chiabrera's intermezzi, was performed in the Ducal Theatre. The play tended to be rather dry and mechanical, but when the players of the Fedeli troupe tried to inject some verve into it, the spectator from Modena complained of the "crude and unpolished actors" and their uncouth displays: he was particularly embarrassed by a scene in which a woman searched in the trousers of a young man for a radish, to which therapeutic powers were attributed. Six composers were absorbed in the task of turning out music for the evening. Claudio Monteverdi wrote music only for the Prologue. The composers of the four intermezzi were Salomon Rossi, Giovanni Giacomo Gastoldi, Monco, and Giulio Cesare Monteverdi. The concluding pieces were composed by Paolo Biat.[15] Withal,

11. The singer was Virginia Andreini, a member of the Fedeli troupe who used the stage name Florinda. Cf. Solerti, *Albori, 1,* 94–95, and 2, 69.

12. Follino-Solerti, *2, 145.*

13. Solerti, *Albori, 1,* 94.

14. Follino-Solerti, *2,* 145.

15. Emil Vogel, "Claudio Monteverdi," *Vierteljahrsschrift für Musikwissenschaft, 3* (1887), 350.

the musical significance of the evening was negligible. The chief burden lay on the shoulders of set designer Vianini, and he alone received unanimous praise, having evidently taken considerable pains to prevent ennui from creeping into the almost seven-hour-long performance.

For example, amazement was provoked by the rapidity with which he raised the curtain. After the torches had been lighted and the third trumpet blast from back-stage had given the signal for the beginning, the curtain flew up, as Follino wrote, "in un batter di ciglia."[16] Zuccari also mentioned the "prestezza, velocità," and at once betrayed the technical secret: Vianini had used extremely heavy counter-weights ("grauissimi contrapesi").[17]

The Prologue began in a setting which everybody at once identified as Mantua. At the sides stood palaces, towers ("torri di rilievo"), and arcades. Follino empha-sized the "simiglianza," which he thought worthy of a landscape painted. The city lay in the full glare of the sun, and although the spectators could not recognize the light sources, they did not have the impression that the conventional torches were being used ("di torchi o d'altri fuochi"), but rather that real sunlight was flood-ing the scene. The painter had achieved this effect by the skillful distribution of light and shadow ("bene erano divisate l'ombre e la luce da quei riflessi"). Center stage was a lake. Three clouds floated in the air. Again, they did not resemble the-atrical clouds but rather natural phenomena, "fabricate con tanto artifizio." The water in the middle of the lake began to burble, and soon the figure of Manto, daughter of Tiresias and legendary foundress of the city of Mantua, rose from the waves. Standing on an island overgrown with sedge, she sang a madrigal to the accompaniment of instruments concealed backstage. As she began the final stanza, the three clouds opened. On the center one throned Hymen, holding the torch, his gold costume taking on special brilliance from the lights concealed behind the clouds. On the right cloud were the three Graces, and on the left, the allegories of Fertility and Peace. Each figure carried a burning torch that gave off sweet per-fumes. Manto now sank down, while the clouds slowly descended, masking the city upstage. The island that had risen to the surface bearing Manto did not sink with her, so that the *Numi* were able to gather on it while Hymen sang his madrigal. In a flash the three clouds dissolved into a fog, blanketing the background.[18] The island split into two halves ("l'isola si spezzò dividendosi in due parti uguali"),

16. Follino-Solerti, *3,* 208.

17. Zuccari, *Passaggio,* p. 21.

18. "Le tre nuvole, rimando vuote, mirabilmente si dissolverono ad un batter d'occhi, e di tre ch'erano se ne fece una sola, ma però d'altra forma perciocchè pareva una densa nebbia che ingombrasse tutta la prospettiva del palco dietro all'isoletta" (Follino-Solerti, *3,* 212).

which were pulled away to either side. Then the side wings depicting Mantua disappeared, and the stage was transformed into a Paduan *veduta,* the locale of Guarini's comedy. A first intermezzo followed Act I.

FIRST INTERMEZZO: THE RAPE OF PROSERPINA

Proserpina's abduction was carried out in a garden setting "tutto di rilievo." The garden was full of trees and blooming plants, and was enclosed by hedges. Pergolas could be seen in the background. From the foliage came the twittering of birds. Everywhere there were statues and fountains gushing real water which had been perfumed, so that the scent was wafted deep into the auditorium. Sixteen nymphs appeared in the garden, four of whom struck up music for dancing, while four others sang a madrigal. Eight nymphs danced in order to divert Proserpina, who had retired to a bower. Lured by the dance, she now approached the nymphs. This was the moment for Pluto to act. A flame shot up on the left side of the stage, and a fiery chariot drawn by black horses appeared, followed by monstrous *Ombre*. Pluto, reining the horses himself, alighted from the vehicle, raped Proserpina, and then drove off. The entire action took place with lightning speed. While horror still registered on the faces of the nymphs, as in the painting of Niccolò dell' Abbate, a cloud descended from the heavens with Venus, who in a madrigal conceded that even the underworld had the right to love. Scarcely had the Venus cloud disappeared into the gridiron than the chariot of Ceres entered from the left, drawn by two fire-breathing dragons. The goddess bemoaned the loss of her daughter in a song. Fama then flew into the scene, her appearance causing amazement, since she was not borne on a cloud but seemed to stay aloft merely by flapping her wings. Hovering in perfect equilibrium, she sang her madrigal and from time to time elicited a few notes from her trumpet. Ceres was evidently consoled when Fama told her that Proserpina had become queen of the underworld. Fama then flew away, and Ceres guided her pageant offstage. Instantly ("in un subito"), the scene changed to the city of Padua, where the second act of the comedy was played.

SECOND INTERMEZZO: THE RAPE OF EUROPA

Following Act II, the stage was enveloped with clouds, probably to mask the change of scenery. Finally, there unfolded a view of a tranquil sea with fish darting from the waves. Winged *amoretti* frolicked amidst the clouds. The sea was framed by two mountainous escarpments ("s'alzavano a i fianchi della prospettiva due sommità di monti alpestri che surgevano da una istessa radice").[19] From the

19. Ibid., p. 218.

left a bull appeared in the water, "formato con tanto artificio" that some of the spectators believed they were watching a live bull swimming in the sea. Garlands of flowers hung from its head, and on its back sat Europa firmly holding onto the left horn with her right hand, while with her left she held up the seam of her dress to prevent it from becoming wet. Dazed and sad, she gazed back in the direction whence she had come. The whole composition originated with Ovid, in whose *Metamorphoses* Europa is described grasping one of the horns of the bull with her right hand, while in the *Fasti* she is said to have gathered up her dress with her left. The beast reached center stage, and Europa bewailed her fate, another lamento which brought tears to the eyes of the listeners. On the right side of the stage a cloud was revealed, glittering with trophies and bringing in Cupid. The love god had come to console Europa and confide in her the identity of the bull. As the cloud rose into the heavens, the beast withdrew, carrying off its gentle burden. From the sea a whale emerged, and on its back sat Glaucus, who congratulated Europa on her lover in a brief song with echo effects. He then submerged, and the spectators fixed their attention on the chariot of Juno, which seemed to float freely in the air as the peacocks drawing it fanned their wings. Halting at stage center, the goddess made a signal with her scepter. The left range of peaks now opened to reveal Aeolus sitting in a cave three ells above "sea level." Juno commanded the god of the winds to unleash a tempest, whereupon the right range cleaved open to disclose another cavern, the abode of the Chorus of the Winds. Some of the Winds sang, while others flew howling through the air. Juno's pageant seemed first to sink before it rose again, ascending with a circular movement ("abbassandosi prima e alzandosi poi formasse girando un cerchio"),[20] an effect described as a "cosa mirabile." Then the cave of Aeolus was swallowed up. On the farthest horizon there arose a rainbow on which Iris was seated. Alighting from it, she began to fly, singing a brief madrigal as she flapped her wings "perpendicolarmente," dipping them down into the sea. The spectators followed this novel performance "con molto maraviglia." Finally, the Winds withdrew to their cave, the mountain closed, and the setting transformed itself into the city of Padua.

THIRD INTERMEZZO: THE WEDDING OF JUPITER AND ALCMENE

Since the unifying theme of the intermezzi was that of the nuptials of the gods, Jupiter's "long night" with Alcmene was also given the status of a wedding night. "In un istante" Padua was supplanted by a bleak, forbidding landscape with steep cliffs, chasms, and dark grottoes. Everywhere were sleeping animals: bears, badgers, and dormice. Mercury glided in from the left and remained hovering in place

20. Ibid., p. 221.

with the aid of his *talaria*. In his aria, he conjured the goddess of the night, who drove forth on her star-spangled *trionfo* drawn by a black and a white horse. Mercury circled about in the air, while Night's chariot ascended into the heavens as the stage visibly grew darker. Patches of fog conceived as dream phantasms rose from the abysses. Morpheus, escorted by his sons Phobetor and Phantasus, stood on a cloud in close proximity to Night. The entire scene related to the Protean shapes of mortal dreams. This was, moreover, the long night in which Jupiter was united with Alcmene. The moon sent out its beams, and the firmament was strewn with stars. Highest praise was again given to Vianini, who feigned everything with such verisimilitude that the deception of the senses was complete ("tanto simigli-anti al vero ch'ingannarono la vista di chiunque le vede").[21]

As the three Parcae appeared on a vast cloud, singing a madrigal "con grazioso concerto," the night ended. On the farthest horizon ("dalla più lontana parte e nel mezzo della prospettiva") the golden car of Jupiter could be seen. Borne aloft by two eagles, it turned first to the right, then to the left. Radiant beams shot upward, "nelle più infime parti della prospettiva," a prelude to the dawn. A fiery comet blazed through the heavens, "per artifizio dell'ingegniero," terrifying the spectators with its glowing tail. There were sudden cries of "fire!"[22] some of the onlookers shouting that the flames must be extinguished.[23] But nothing was amiss after all: day came, and the fourth act could begin. Vianini's blazing comet and his realistic sunrise anticipated the illusionist magic which Gianlorenzo Bernini would develop three decades later in his Barberini entertainments.

FOURTH INTERMEZZO: THE NUPTIALS OF HERCULES AND HEBE

Revealed to the spectators was a hilly, wooded landscape. On the slopes stood palaces and castles. Springs and waterfalls flowed down to the valley. A large central cloud brought a throng of dryads on stage. On one side several naiads stood on another cloud facing nymphs of the dell on a third. The three groups began a concert, singing in chorus of the forthcoming nuptials of the gods. The heavens now opened in the far distance, permitting the spectators to witness an Olympian banquet, which Jupiter had arranged in honor of the newly wed Hercules and Hebe. A chorus of celestial beings extolled the hero's Labors. As the three clouds bearing the nymphs rose into the heavens, six men in Greek dress stepped forth from the lanes between the wings ("dalle strade che dividevano quelle colline").

21. Ibid., p. 224.
22. "Si dubitò nel teatro ch'in quella parte si fosse acceso accidentalmente il fuoco e che quella tela ardesse" (ibid., 225).
23. "Onde gridarono molti ad alta voce che si dovesse estinguere" (ibid.).

Gazing with astonishment at the heavenly spectacle, they executed a ballet as the nymphs sang a dance air. Each carrying a silver ball in his right hand and in his left an antique shield, the six dancers thrust forward with their spheres, thus alluding to the Olympic Games which Hercules had revived. Three of them then took up positions to the right, the remaining three to the left, and, as the nymphs began their second dance piece, yet another six men appeared in Greek attire, carrying bows and arrows. In their ballet they feigned skill at archery: the sound of whizzing arrows could be heard, even though their shafts never left the strings. When they had finished, these six also assumed stances at one side, while the next group of dancers appeared with naked swords and shields to perform a morris dance. A fourth detachment followed, carrying silver lances tipped with maces in Turkish fashion. They also danced a *Moresca,* accompanied by a dance song. The twenty-four men then assembled to perform a tilt-ballet.

BALLET FINALE

As the last act of the comedy was ending, thunder and lightning struck in the auditorium. The actors fled from the stage, and the audience was no less taken by surprise. This too was an anticipation of Bernini's effects. In an instant the stage was transformed into a stormy sea. The heavens were veiled with clouds from which lightning streaked. Hail began to fall, which again almost threw the spectators into panic. The end of the world seemed at hand, and only Neptune's intervention could save the situation. The sea god now came forth on his trionfo drawn by two horses. Striking the waves with his trident, he appeased the elements, so that the words of his aria were clearly audible. The tranquil sea was now populated with swimming Nereids. To the right Zephyrus appeared in his flowery costume on a small cloud that dripped dew. The heavens opened to reveal an assembly of the gods. According to Follino's description,[24] a golden sphere glittered in the extreme background, turning steadily about its axis. Simultaneously, from the same part of the stage, the audience heard the gentle harmonies of a celestial chorus singing of the wedding in the House of Gonzaga. Zuccari may have grasped the intention here which was to combine the two Pythagorean concepts of the central fire and the harmonious music of the spheres: he mentions a "ruota grandissima, à guisa di Napamondo, e Sfera celeste"[25]—that is, a gigantic celestial sphere encircled by rings ("altri cerchi"), thus representing the "primo mobile," or the ninth sphere, of the heavens. Vianini succeeded in creating the illusion of an extraordi-

24. Ibid., p. 231.
25. *Passaggio,* pp. 25–26.

nary depth of perspective.[26] The machine bearing the gods moved slowly forward toward the proscenium, coming to rest at center stage. According to Zuccari, more than fifty people were supported on this "machina mouibile."[27] As it advanced, certain segments of the apparatus rotated in opposing circular courses ("si vedeva ogni sua parte girar con moti contrarii in varie guise").[28] Before the spectators could recover from their astonishment, a cloud appeared bearing the personification of Light-Heartedness, escorted by Laughter, Jest, Riches, and Beauty. While her companions played on their instruments, Letizia sang a madrigal, after which her cloud descended. At the same time, there emerged from the waves an island with six nymphs and six shepherds, who danced a ballet, their burning torches emanating sweet perfumes. The evening ended with a chorus of the gods.

Federigo Zuccari, who would not be denied a close look backstage, was impressed by the technical equipment:

> It was delightful to see the windlasses mounted over the machines, the cables of optimum strength, the ropes and lines by which the machines were moved and guided, and the many stagehands who were needed to keep the apparatus in operation. Every man was at his station, and at a signal the machinery could be raised, lowered, moved, or held in a particular position. More than three hundred workers were engaged and had to be directed, which required no less experience and skill than it did foresight and reason; it must be realized that in such a situation anything might go awry and unforeseen incidents must be prevented, since one fiery spark could put an end to everything. It was really amazing that not a mishap occurred. There were special guards with large vessels and buckets, kettles, and pots all filled with water which stood prepared for any contingency.[29]

Zuccari's interest in these matters is all the more noteworthy in that, as a painter and theoretician, he is primarily known to us as a Neoplatonist, whose views on the nature of beauty were exclusively conditioned by the notion of *disegno intorno.*

26. Zuccari mentions "vna vista di sfondato grandissimo, che appariua mezo miglio di prospettiua, e di sfondato."
27. P. 25.
28. Follino-Solerti, *3*, 232.
29. *Passaggio,* p. 27.

Index of Names

ILLUSTRATIONS

1. Federigo Zuccari's design for the front curtain for the performance of *La Cofanaria* (1565) in the Salone dei Cinquecento, Palazzo Vecchio.

2. Stage setting by an unknown artist for Lionardo Salviati's comedy *Il Granchio*, produced by the Accademia Fiorentina in the Sala del Papa in Florence (1566). Published in the first edition of the play, Florence, 1566.

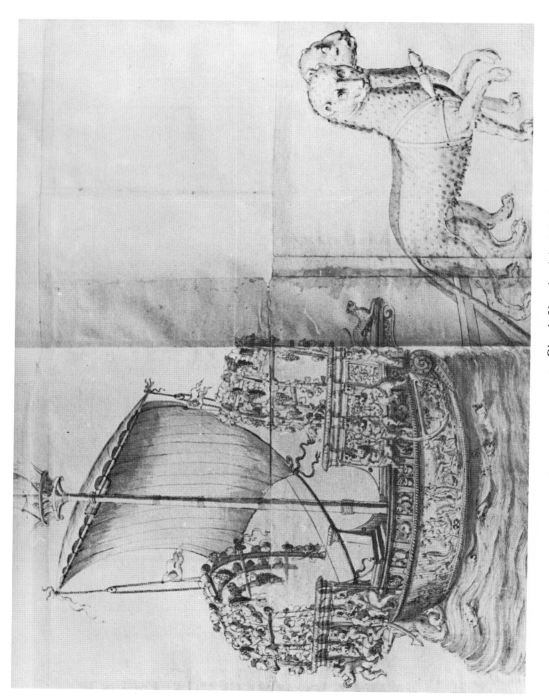

3. Giorgio Vasari, original design for the chariot of Bacchus (1566).

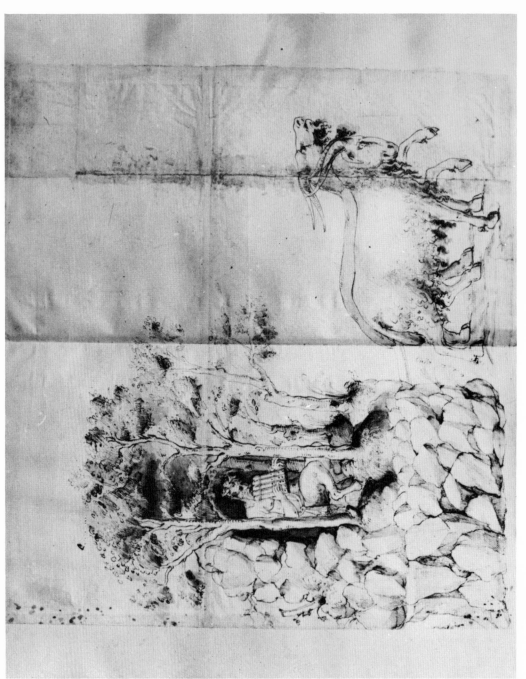

4. Giorgio Vasari, original design for the chariot of Pan (1566).

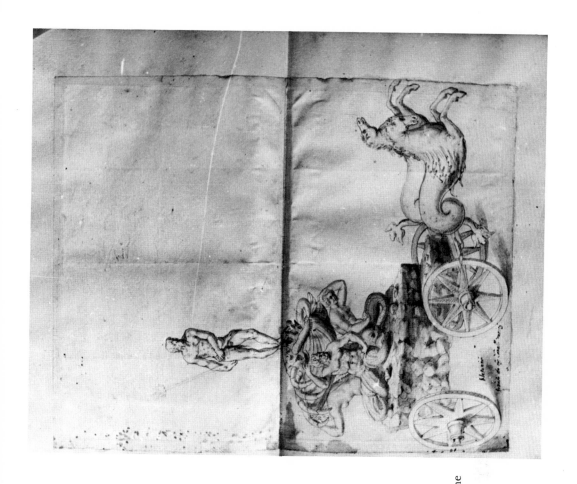

5. Giorgio Vasari, original design for the chariot of Neptune (1566).

6. Giorgio Vasari, original design for the chariot of Mars (1566).

7. Giorgio Vasari, original design for the chariot of Jupiter (1566).

8. Giorgio Vasari, original design for the chariot of Uranus (1566).

9. Copy of Giorgio Vasari's original design for the float of Demogorgone (1566).

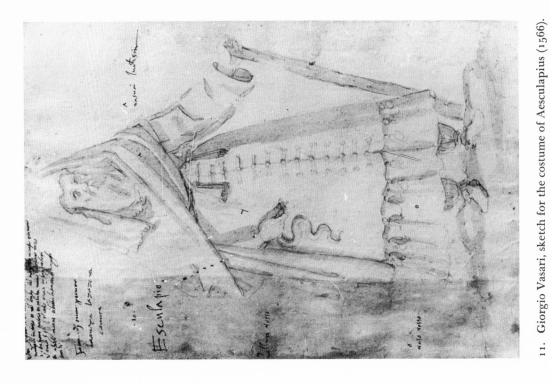

11. Giorgio Vasari, sketch for the costume of Aesculapius (1566).

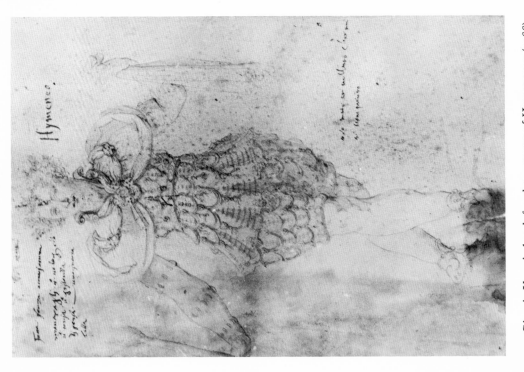

10. Giorgio Vasari, sketch for the costume of Hymenaeus (1566).

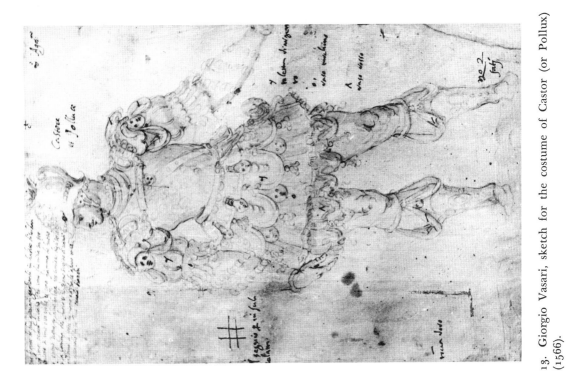

13. Giorgio Vasari, sketch for the costume of Castor (or Pollux) (1566).

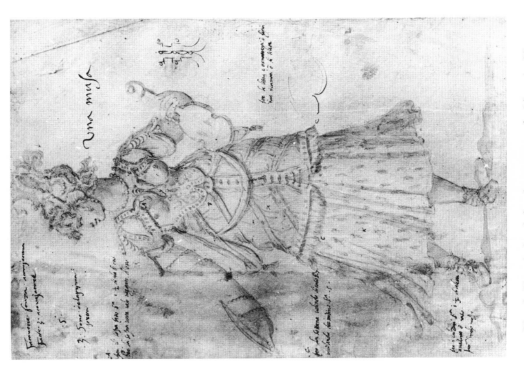

12. Giorgio Vasari, sketch for the costume of a Muse (1566).

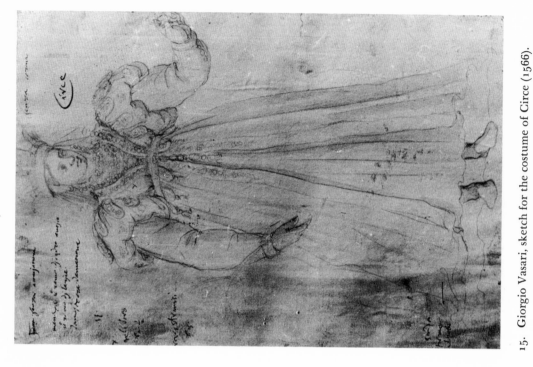

14. Giorgio Vasari, sketch for the costume of Harmonia, wife of Cadmus (1566).

15. Giorgio Vasari, sketch for the costume of Circe (1566).

17. Giorgio Vasari, sketch for the costume for the Hyades (1566).

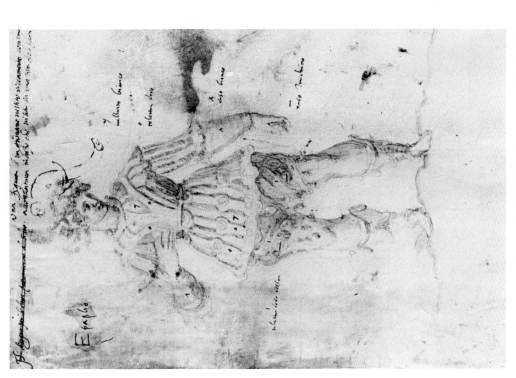

16. Giorgio Vasari, sketch for the costume of Epaphus (Apis) (1566).

18. Giorgio Vasari, sketch for the costume for the Pleiades (1566).

19. Copy of the costume designed by Giorgio Vasari for Erichthonius (1566).

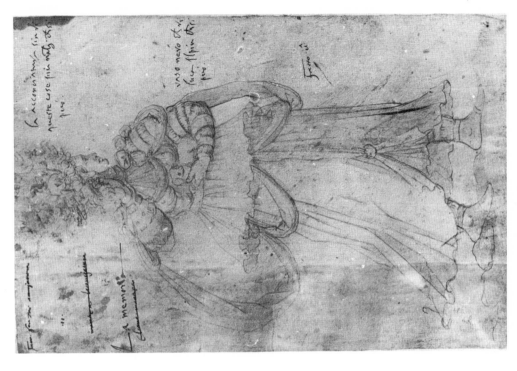

21. Giorgio Vasari, sketch for the costume of the allegorical figure of Memory (1566).

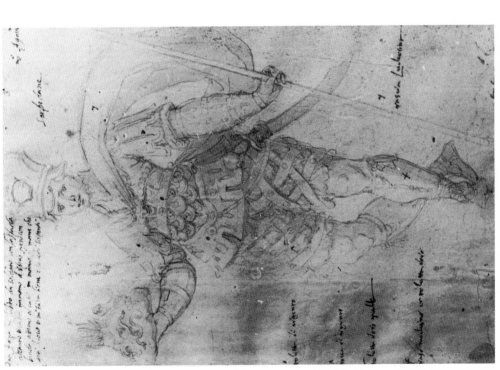

20. Giorgio Vasari, sketch for the costume of Sarpedon (1566).

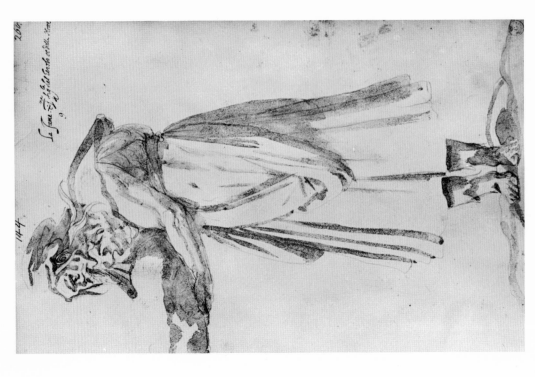

22. Giorgio Vasari, sketch for the costume of the allegorical figure   23. Copy of the costume designed by Giorgio Vasari for the alle-

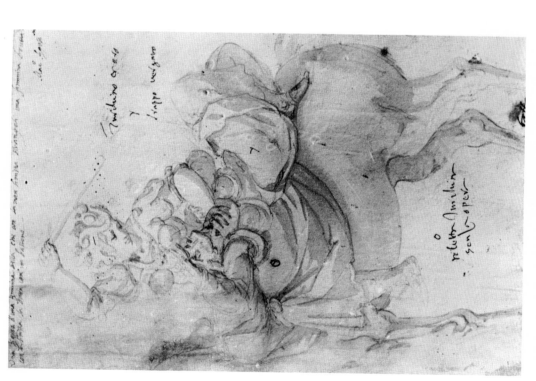

24. Giorgio Vasari, sketch for the costume of the allegory of Justice (1566).

25. Copy of the costume designed by Giorgio Vasari for the allegorical figure of Thought (1566).

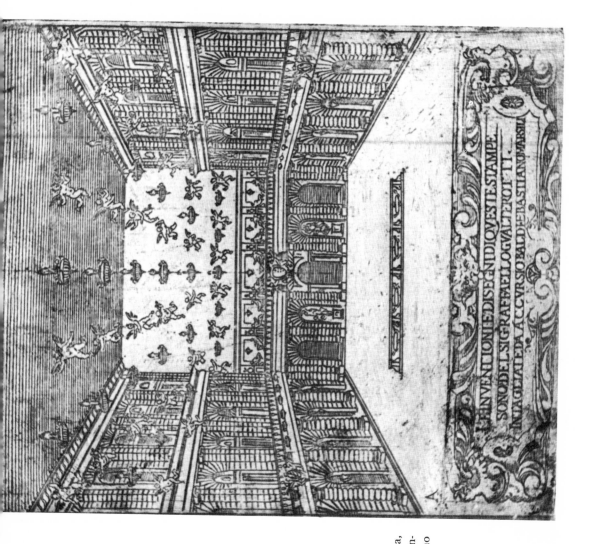

27. The cortile of the Pitti Palace. Sbarra,
1579. Designed by Raffaello Gualterotti, engraving by Accursio Baldi and Bastiano
Marsili.

28. The chariot of the Persian Knights. Sbarra, Pitti courtyard, 1579.

C

30. The Maga and the Dragon. Sbarra, Pitti courtyard, 1579.

31. The chariot of Night. Sbarra, Pitti courtyard, 1579.

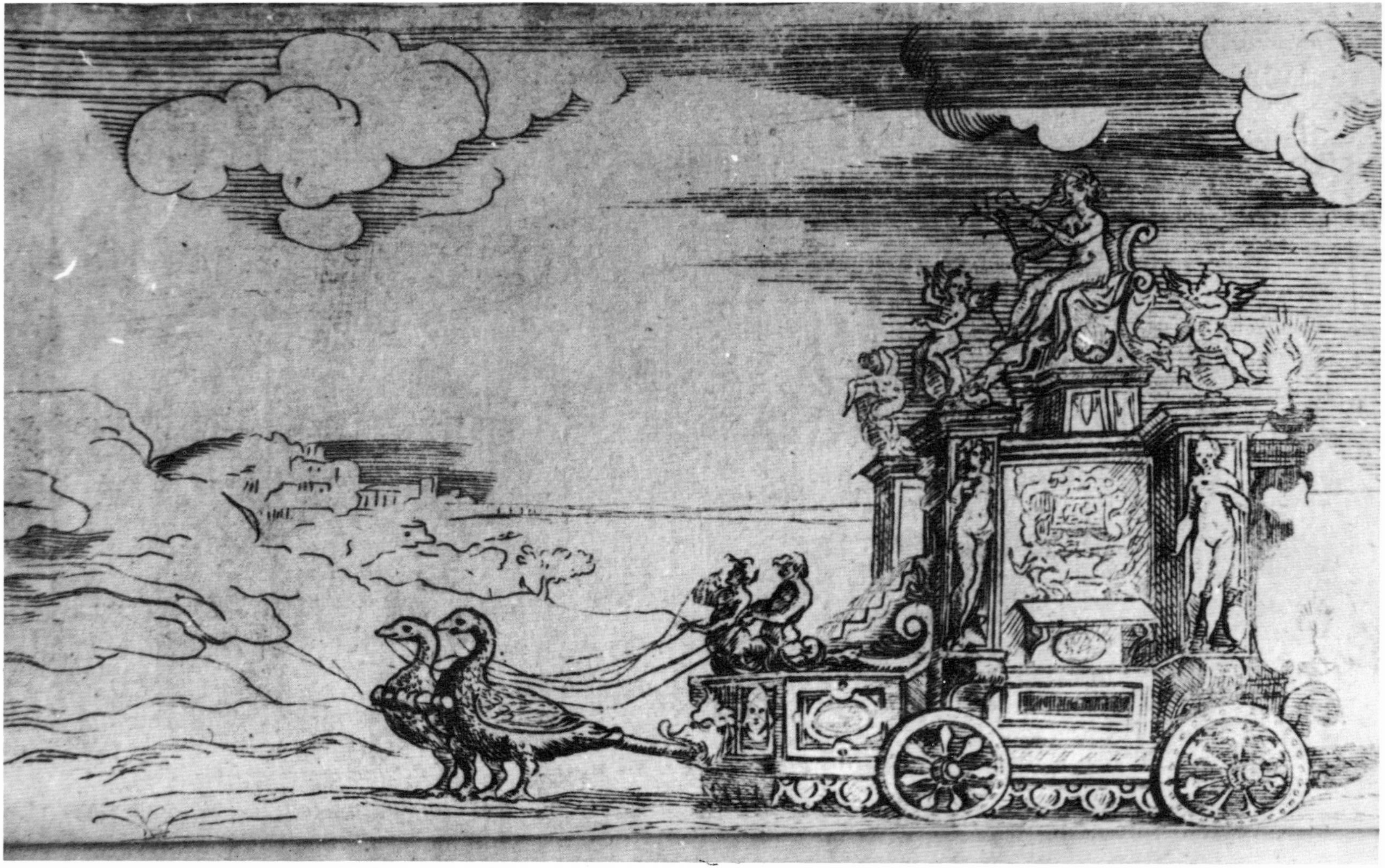

32. The chariot of Venus. Sbarra, Pitti courtyard, 1579.

33. The chariot of Europe and Africa. Sbarra, Pitti courtyard, 1579.

34. The mountain closed. Sbarra, Pitti courtyard, 1579.

35. The mountain open. Sbarra, Pitti courtyard, 1579.

36. Whale with sea gods. Sbarra, Pitti courtyard, 1579.

37. The Triumph of Aphrodite. Sbarra, Pitti courtyard, 1579.

38. The chariot of Mars. Sbarra, Pitti courtyard, 1579.

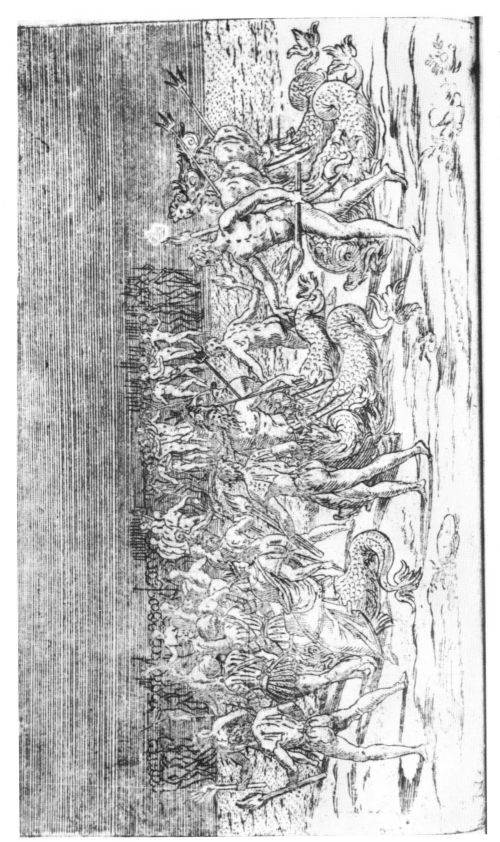

39. The Triumph of Lady Adria. Sbarra, Pitti courtyard, 1579.

40. The Venetian galley Sharra Pitti courtyard, 1570

41. Bernardo Buontalenti's design for an unidentified scene, perhaps a discarded idea for the first intermezzo of 1586.

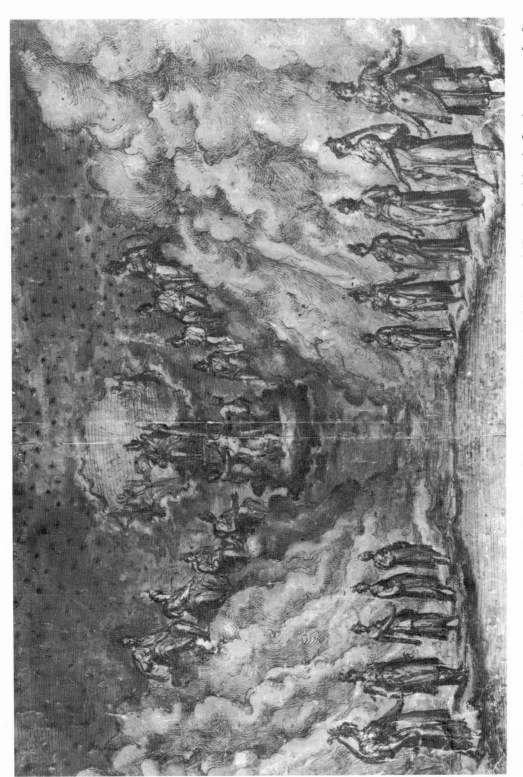

42.   The Harmony of the Spheres, original design by Bernardo Buontalenti for the first intermezzo of 1589.

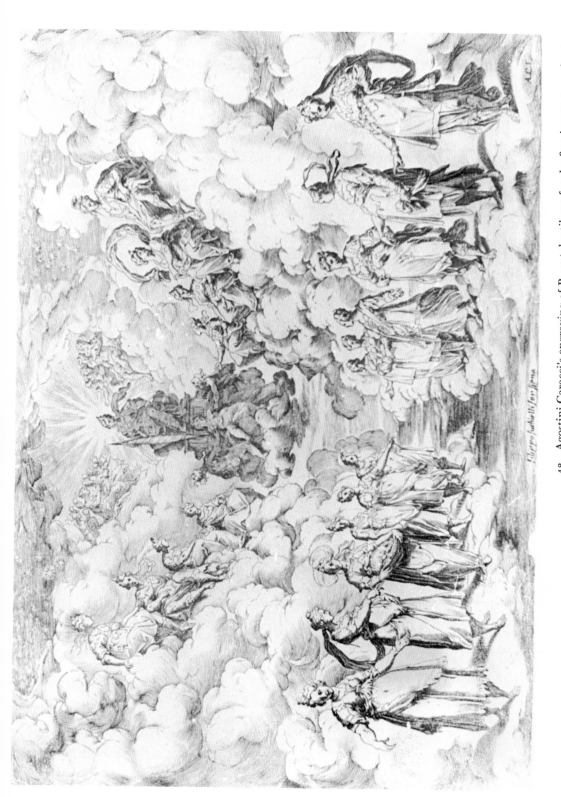

Filippo Suchielli for: fec: Roma

43. Agostini Caracci's engraving of Buontalenti's set for the first intermezzo of 1589.

44. Bernardo Buontalenti's original designs for the costumes of Mercury, Apollo, Jupiter, and Astraea in the first intermezzo of 1589.

45. Bernardo Buontalenti's sketch for Necessitas and the Three Parcae in the first intermezzo of 1589.

47. Bernardo Buontalenti's original design for the costume of Armonia Doria in the first intermezzo of 1589.

46. Bernardo Buontalenti's original design for a Siren's costume in the first intermezzo of 1589.

48. Garden setting by Bernardo Buontalenti for the second intermezzo of 1589.

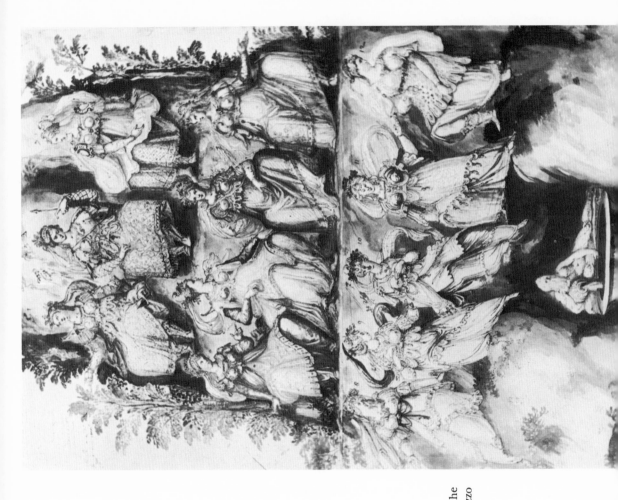

49. Bernardo Buontalenti's original sketch for the mountain of the Hamadryads in the second intermezzo of 1589.

50. Magpie costume designed by Bernardo Buontalenti for the second intermezzo of 1589.

51. Engraving by Epifanio d'Alfiano (1592) of Buontalenti's set for the second intermezzo of 1589.

52. The Parnassian forest scene for the third intermezzo of 1589. Original design by Bernardo Buontalenti.

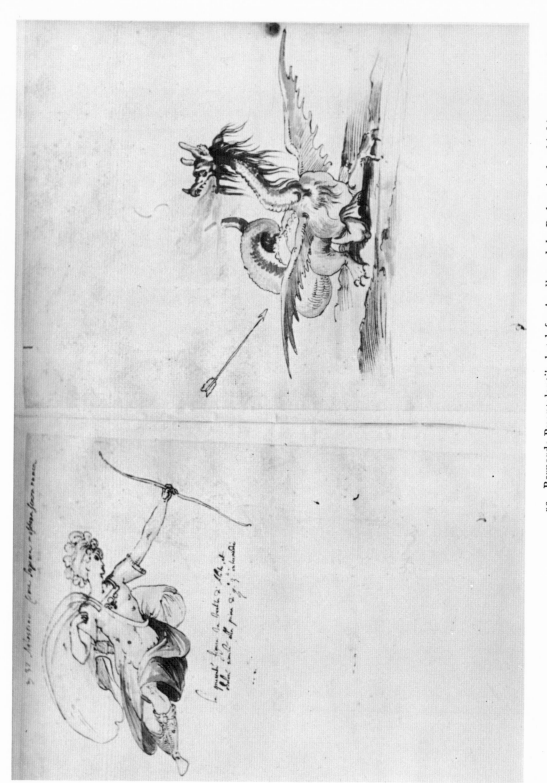

53. Bernardo Buontalenti's sketch for Apollo and the Python in the third intermezzo of 1589.

54. Agostino Caracci's engraving of Buontalenti's setting for the third intermezzo of 1589.

55. Delphic couple. Original costume by Bernardo Buontalenti for the third intermezzo of 1589.

56. Bernardo Buontalenti's Inferno for the fourth intermezzo of 1589. Engraving by Epifanio d'Alfano.

57. Engraving by Epifanio d'Alfano after Buontalenti's seascape for the fifth intermezzo of 1589.

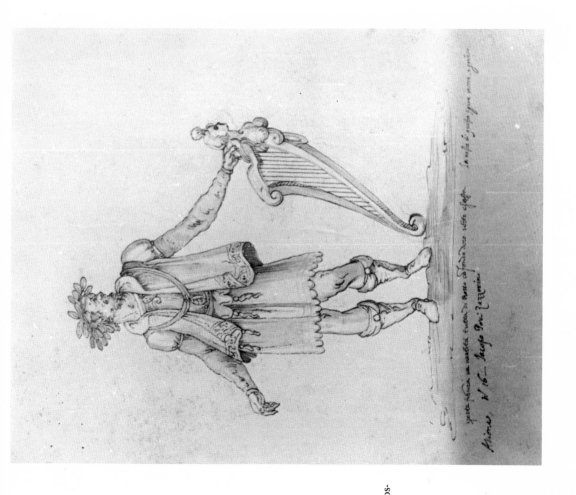

58. Bernardo Buontalenti's original sketch for the costume of Arion in the fifth intermezzo of 1589.

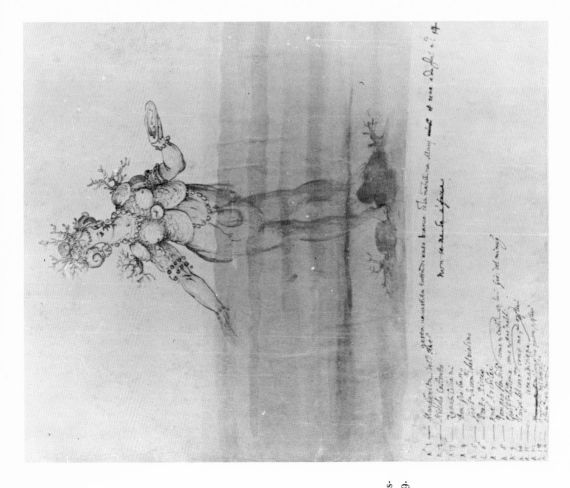

59.   Bernardo Buontalenti's original sketch for the costume of a sea nymph in the fifth intermezzo of 1589.

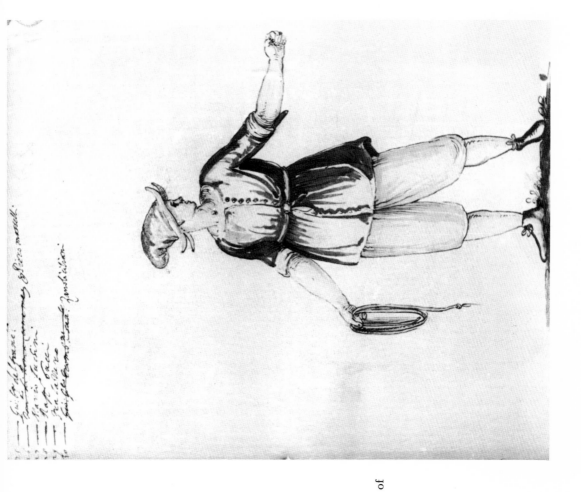

60. Bernardo Buontalenti's sketch for the costume of a sailor in the fifth intermezzo of 1589.

62. Engraving by Epifanio d'Alfano after Buontalenti's set for the sixth intermezzo of 1589.

63. Bernardo Buontalenti's sketch for an Apollo costume, perhaps for the sixth intermezzo of 1589.

64. The cortile of the Pitti Palace, scene of the tournament in 1589.

65. Naumachia in the Pitti cortile (1589). Engraving by Orazio Scarabelli.

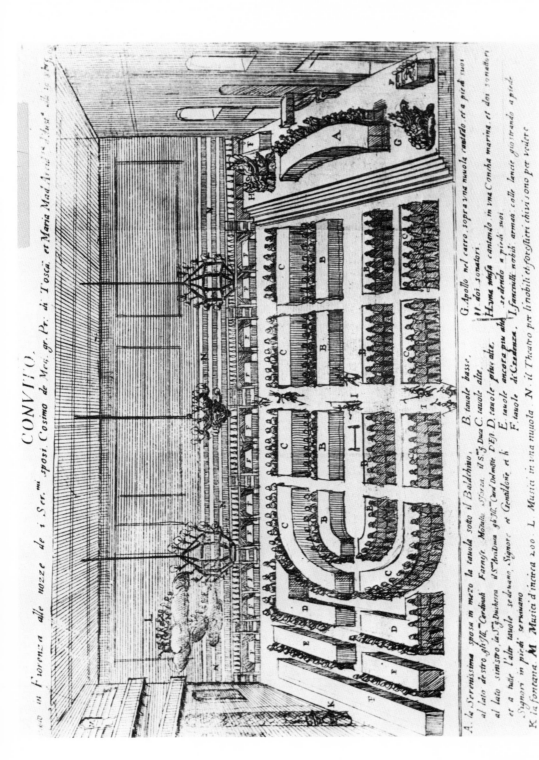

66. Banquet in the Salone dei Cinquecento, Palazzo Vecchio, October 19, 1608. Engraving by Matthias Greuter.

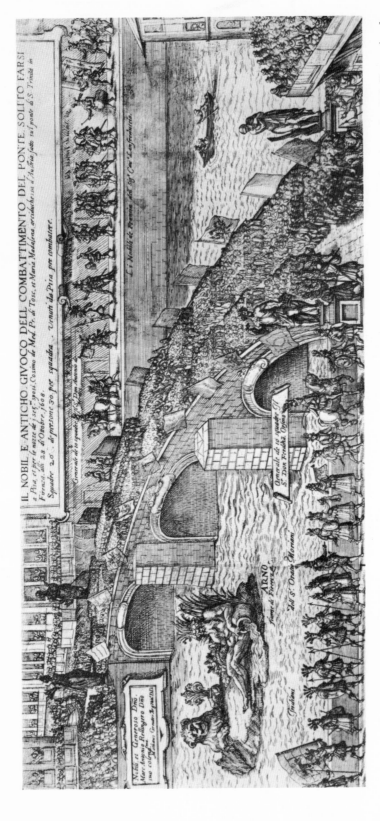

67. Il Giuoco del Ponte, a mock battle fought by noblemen from Pisa on the Santa Trinità Bridge in Florence on October 28, 1608. Engraving by Matthias Greuter.

PALAZZO DELLA FAMA INTERMEDIO PRIMO

Remigio Cantagallina F

Come Seggeri nella valle del Ser.mo Prencipe di
Toscana Cosimo 1608 Giulio Parigi I.

68. The Temple of Fame, designed by Giulio Parigi for the first intermezzo of *Il Giudizio di Paride* (1608). Etching by Remigio Cantagallina.

69. Mount Ida, designed by Giulio Parigi for *Il Giudizio di Paride* (1608). Etching by Remigio Cantagallina.

Astrea Intermedio Secondo

70. The Return of Astraea, designed by Giulio Parigi for the second intermezzo of *Il Giudizio di Paride* (1608). Etching by Remigio Cantagallina.

71. The Garden of Calypso, designed by Giulio Parigi for the third intermezzo of *Il Giudizio di Paride* (1608). Etching by Giulio Parigi.

NAVE DI AMERIGO VESPUCCI INTERMEDIO QVARTO

R.^{migio} Cantta Gallina F.

Conc: reggi nelle valle del S.^{mo}
Prencipe di Toscana l'an 1608:
Giulio parigi I.

72. Tropical sea scene for the appearance of the vessel of Amerigo Vespucci, designed by Giulio Parigi for the fourth intermezzo *Il Giudizio di Paride* (1608). Etching by Remigio Cantagallina.

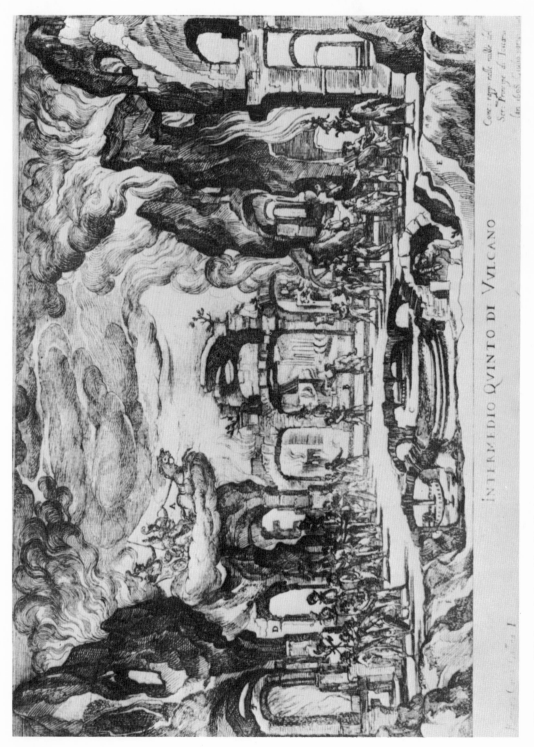

73. The Forge of Vulcan, designed by Giulio Parigi for the fifth intermezzo of *Il Giudizio di Paride* (1608). Etching by Remigio Cantagallina.

74. The Temple of Peace, designed by Giulio Parigi for the sixth intermezzo of *Il Giudizio di Paride* (1608). Etching by Giulio Parigi.

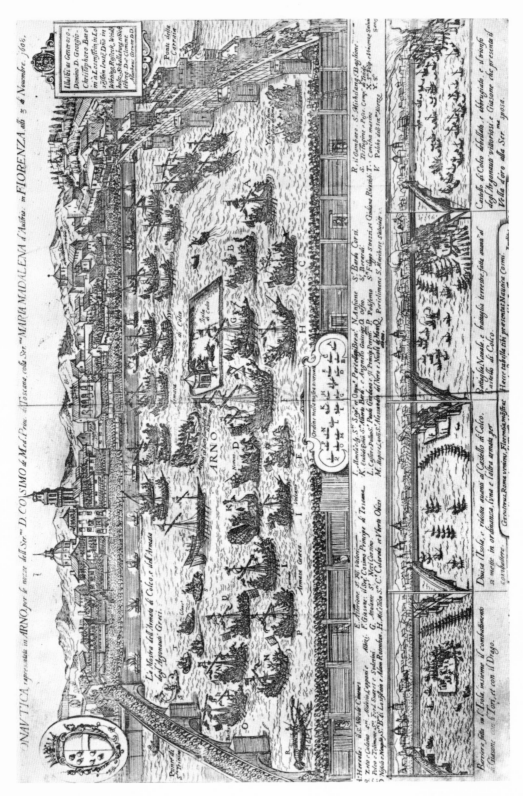

75. View of the Arno River during the Triumph of the Argonauts on November 3, 1608. Engraving by Matthias Greuter.

76. The barge of Hercules, designed by Giulio Parigi for the Triumph of the Argonauts on the Arno River (1608). Engraving by Remigio Cantagallina.

R.^{mgo} Cata Gallina F.

CALAI E ZETI CONDOTTI DA BOREA ET ORITIA

Battaglia Naude rappr: in Arno per le nozze del
Ser.^{mo} Prencipe di Toscana L'Anno 1608 Giulio Parigi I

77. The barge of the twins, Calais and Zetes, designed by Giulio Parigi (1608). Engraving by Remigio Cantagallina.

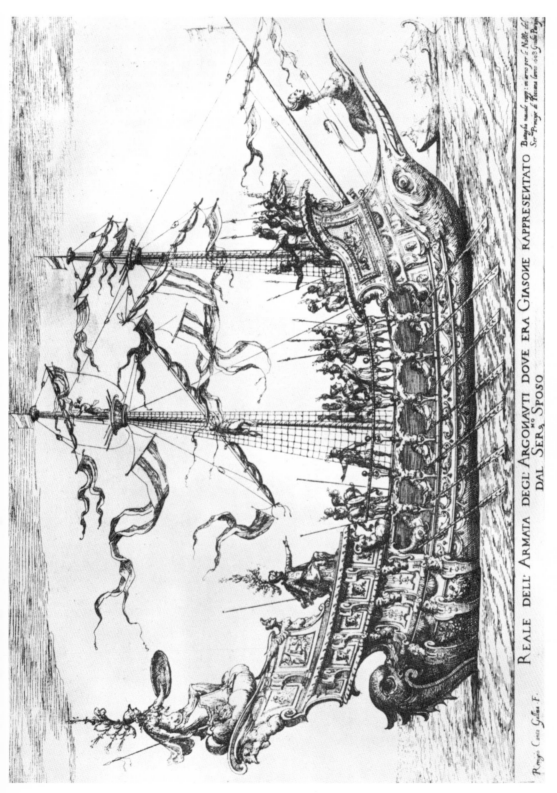

REALE DELL' ARMATA DEGL' ARGONAVTI DOVE ERA GIASONE RAPPRESENTATO DAL SER.^{mo} SPOSO

78. The barge of Jason, designed by Giulio Parigi (1608). Engraving by Remigio Cantagallina.

R. Argo Casa Gallea. F. HICLO E NAVCLEO ARGON: CONDOTTI NEL CARRÓ DI NETTVNNO. Battaglia Nauale Reggi in Arno per i ... Sen Principe di Tosc Arb 6048 Giunio Parigi

79.   The barge of Iphiclus and Nauplius, designed by Giulio Parigi (1608). Engraving by Remigio Cantagallina.

EVRITO ECHIONE E ETALIDE

Condotti da Mercurio fatta dal Sigr Cont Alberto e Sigr Carlo de
Bardi et Agnolo Gucciardini

Battaglia Nauale raffr. Arme per lo mille del
Srmo Princ: di Tosc: del 1608 Iacopo Ligosto I.

80. The floating peacock with Erytus, Echion, and Aethalides, designed by Iacopo Ligozo (or Ligozzi), painter from Verona (1608). Engraving by Remigio Cantagallina.

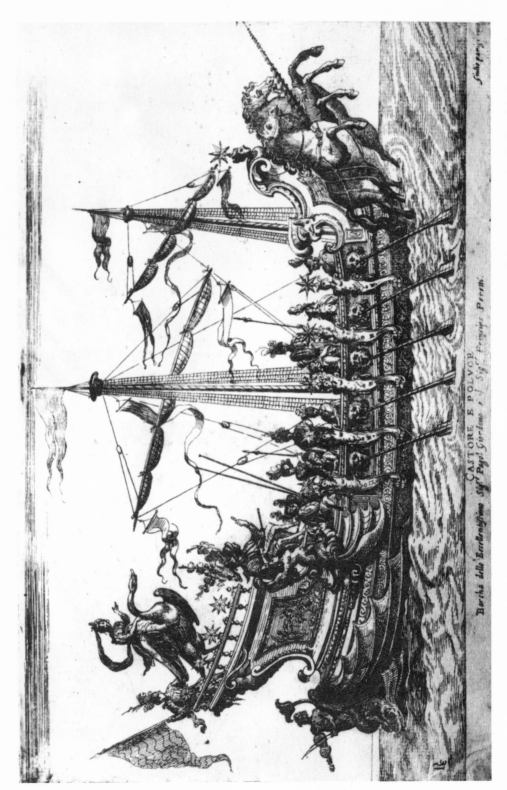

81. The barge of the Dioscuri, designed by Giulio Parigi (1608). Engraving by Remigio Cantagallina.

82. The barge of Agamemnon and Menelaus, designed by Giulio Parigi (1608). Engraving by Remigio Cantagallina.

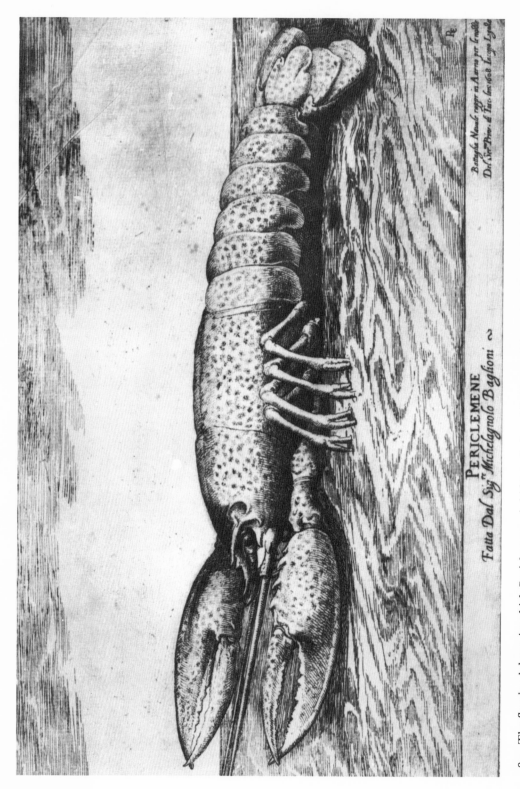

PERICLEMENE
Fatta Dal Sig.r Michelagnolo Baglioni ~

Battaglia Nauale 1599 in Arena per Gusello
Del Ser.mo Prin.e et Duc. Im.1608 Luigi Lippli

83. The floating lobster in which Periclymenus is hidden, designed by Iacopo Ligozo (or Ligozzi) (1608). Engraving by Remigio Cantagallina.

84. The barge of Idmon and Mopsus, designed by Giulio Parigi (1608). Engraving by Remigio Cantagallina.

ANFIONE ARGON: CONDOTTO DA MERCVRIO

85. The barge of Amphion, designed by Giulio Parigi (1608). Engraving by Remigio Cantagallina.

Remigio Cant Gallina F.
ORFEO CONDOTTO DA BACCO
Barca del' Sig: Nicolo Berardi
Battaglia Nauale rapp: in Arno per le nozze del Ser
Principe di Toscana l'anno 1608 Giulio Parigi I.

86. The barge of Orpheus, designed by Giulio Parigi (1607). Engraving by Remigio Cantagallina.

BARCA DI MVSICI RAPPꟲ GLAVCO DIO MARINO EꟲTRITONᵢ

Bacelli Neudi Ragonᵃ etᶜ Arme perlᵉ Nozzeᵈ

Serᵉ Prence di Toscana Anno 608

Franᶜ Cieca Gallee Fᵉ

Giulio Parigi I

87.   The barge of Glaucus with musicians, designed by Giulio Parigi (1608). Engraving by Remigio Cantagallina.

Scoglio d'Arno con quatro fiumi fatto dal Sig.r Filippo Saldin.
Ombrone in Scoglio, con quatro fiumi di Siena fatto da Fra Christofano Ghisi Senese

Battaglia Nauale regg.in Arno per le nolle a
Ser.mo Prencipe di Tosc.[a]n 1608 Giulio Parigi

88. Tuscan river gods on the Arno River (1608). Designed by Giulio Parigi.

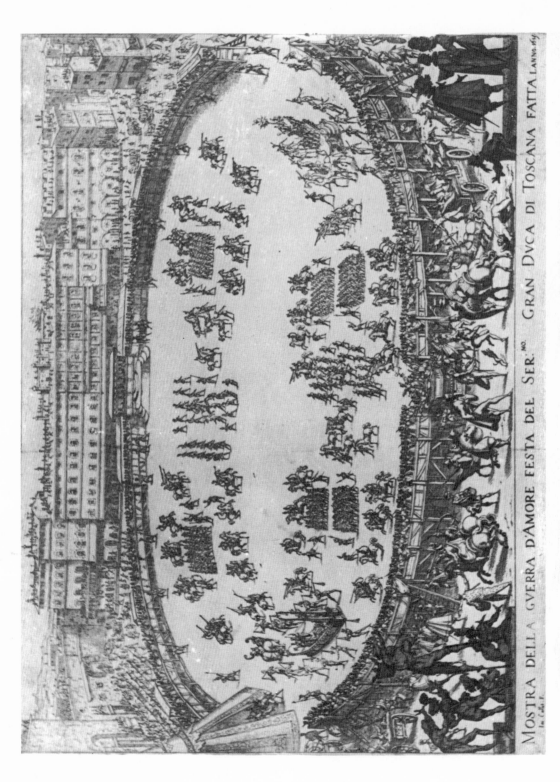

89. The *Mostra* which opened the tournament *Guerra d'Amore* on the Piazza Santa Croce in Florence (1616). Etching by Jacques Callot.

90. Chariots, horsemen, and supernumeraries who participated in *Guerra d'Amore* (1616). Etching by Jacques Callot.

91. Giulio Parigi's sketch for the costume of Aurora in *Guerra d'Amore* (1616).

VNO·DE·GLI·ABBATTIMENTI·DELLA·GVERRA·D·CAMORE
FESTA·DEL·SERENISSIMO·GRAN·DVCA·DI·TOSCANA

Jaq·Callot·F·

92. A battle scene from *Guerra d'Amore* (1616). Etching by Jacques Callot.

98. A scene from *Guerra di Bellezza* on the Piazza Santa Croce (1616). Designed by Giulio Parigi. Etching by Jacques Callot.

Monte di Parnaso fatto in firenze nella festa a Cauallo
per la uenuta del Serenissimo Principe d'Vrbino
Si uedeua nella piu alta parte del Monte Rouere Arme
del Ser.mo Casa d'Vrbino le Muse e Pallade stauano
alla sua Ombra ueniua Coronate delle frondi
dell'istessa Rouere erano sparsi per il Monte tutti
quelli letterati che nomina il Cortigiano con istessa Coroni in
in testa ueniua la fama sul mino= giogo del Monte apiedi la
Seguiuano Cento Semanta de sui minustri. anni 616

Iulius Parigi In. & est delineavit se.

94. Mount Parnassus, a float designed by Giulio Parigi for *Guerra di Bellezza* (1616). Etching by Jacques Callot.

95. Giulio Parigi's sketch for Lady Fame in *Guerra di Bellezza* (1616).

96. The float of the Sun God, designed by Giulio Parigi for *Guerra di Bellezza* (1616). Etching by Jacques Callot.

Carro di Teti fatto in firenze nella festa a Cauallo per la
uenuta del Sereniſſimo Principe d'Vrbino.
Era ſu queſt Carro Teti con le tre Sirene, con le Nereidi,
ei Tritoni, caminauano a pie del Carro Otto Giganti
in forma di tanti Neuunni che figurauano i principali
Mari del Mondo. an. 1616.

97.   The chariot of Thetis, designed by Giulio Parigi for *Guerra di Bellezza* (1616). Etching by Jacques Callot.

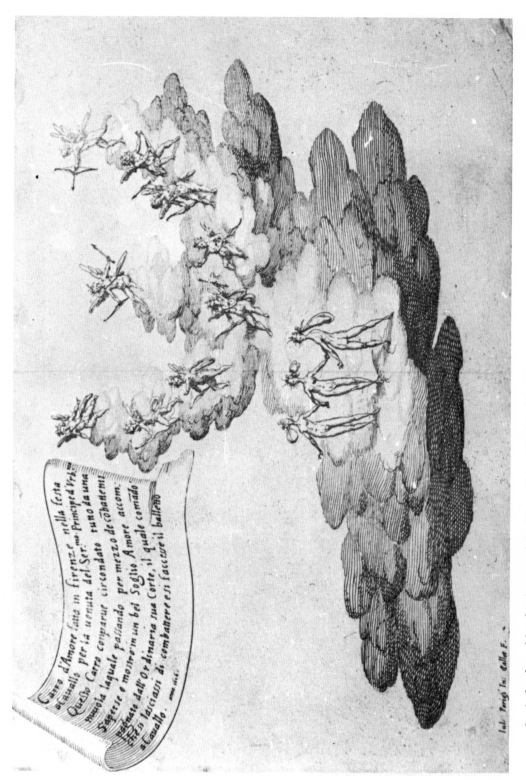

98. A cloud machine for Amor and the Three Graces, designed by Giulio Parigi for *Guerra di Bellezza* (1616). Etching by Jacques Callot.

99. The Inferno for the *veglia La Liberazione di Tirreno e d'Arnea* (1617). Décor by Giulio Parigi. Etching by Jacques Callot.

TERZO INTERMEDIO DOVE SI VIDE VENIRE AMORE CON TVTTA LA SVA CORTE A DIVIDER LA BATTAGLIA.
Giulio Parigi Inu: Iac: Callot delineauit et F:

100.   Courtyard for the Reign of Love designed by Giulio Parigi for the final scene of *La Liberazione di Tirreno e d'Arnea* (1617). Etching by Jacques Callot.

101. Joseph Furttenbach's vague impression of the stage of the Uffizi Theatre. From Furttenbach's *Newes Itinerarium Italiae* (Ulm, 1628).

102. Hell scene from *Regina Sant'Orsola*, designed by Giulio (Alfonso?) Parigi (1624).

Alfonso Parigi I.

BATTAGLIA FRA ROMANI E VNNI
ATTO SECONDO

103. The Huns attacking
Cologne, designed by Giulio
(Alfonso?) Parigi for *Regina
Sant'Orsola* (1624).

LVCIFERO CO I DEMONI FVGATO DA S. MICHELE
ATTO TERZO

Alfonso Parigi. J.

104. St. Michael frightens the devils in *Regina Sant'Orsola* (1624), designed by Alfonso (Giulio?) Parigi.

IREO A PIEDI DEL RE DE GL' VNNI P LA
LIBERATIONE DI S ORSOLA ATTO 4.

Alfonso Parigi I

105. Ireo kneeling before the
King of the Huns in *Regina
Sant'Orsola* (1624), designed
by Giulio (Alfonso?) Parigi.

IL RE DE GL' VNNI FVLMINATO
E ROVINASI, IL TEMPIO DI MART ATTO. V.

Alfonso Parigi I

106. A thunderbolt strikes the pagan temple in *Regina Sant'Orsola* (1624), designed by Giulio (Alfonso?) Parigi.

107. The triumph of the martyr in *Regina Sant'Orsola* (1624). Courtyard by Giulio (Alfonso?) Parigi.

PRIMA SCENA DOVE INTREVIENE NETTVNNO

Alfonso Parigi I. et f.

108. Seascape with Neptune's chariot designed by Giulio (Alfonso?) Parigi for the Prologue of *La Liberazione di Ruggiero* (1625).

ISOLA D'ALCINA. SECONDA MVTA DELLE SCENE

Alfonso Parigi et F.

109. The island of Alcina, designed by Giulio (Alfonso?) Parigi for *La Liberazione di Ruggiero* (1625).

ISOLA D' ALCINA ARDENTE TERZA MUTA DELLE SCENE

Alfonso Parigi I et F

110. Conflagration on the island of Alcina, designed by Giulio (Alfonso?) Parigi for *La Liberazione di Ruggiero* (1625).

111. Horse ballet in the courtyard of the Villa Poggio Imperiale (1625).

QVARTA MVTA DOVE ESCONO DELLE GROTTI CAVALIERI E DAME, DOPO ESCONO I CAVALIERI A CAVALLO   Alfonso Parigi Tav. I

112. Rocky landscape designed by Giulio (Alfonso?) Parigi for *La Liberazione di Ruggiero* (1625).

118. Alfonso Parigi's sketch for the costumes of Fauno, Silvano, and Pan. *La Flora*, 1628.

114. Alfonso Parigi's forest décor for the opening scene of *La Flora* (1628). Etching by the artist.

SBARCO DI VENERE E DELLA SVA CORTE CONDOTTA DA ZEFFIRO NELLE SPIÀGGE TIRRENE

Alfonso Parigius delj: et fecit 1628.

115. The Tyrrhenian shores, designed by Alfonso Parigi for *La Flora* (1628). Etching by the artist.

AMORE CHIEDE LA GELOSIA A PLVTONE

Alfonso Parigi del. et fecit 1628

116. The realm of Pluto, by Alfonso Parigi for *La Flora* (1628). Etching by the artist.

Tempesta commossa da Amore ne Campi Toscani

117. Storm scene for *La Flora* (1628). Designed and etched by Alfonso Parigi.

IL NATAL DE FIORI IRRIGATI DAL FONTE PEGASEO COL BALLO DELL'AVRE

118. Alfonso Parigi's cortile for the final scene of *La Flora* (1628). Etching by the artist.

119. Title page of the libretto for *Le Nozze degli dei* (1637). Designed by Alfonso Parigi, etching by Stefano della Bella.

PRIMA SCENA RAPRESENTANTE FIORENZA

Alfo.ᵛ Parigi Inu.Stefa.ᵛ Della
Bella Deli: e.F.

120. Décor by Alfonso Parigi for the Prologue of *Le Nozze degli dei* (1637). Etching by Stefano della Bella.

SECONDA SCENA SELVA DI DIANA

121.   The grove of Diana. Décor by Alfonso Parigi for *Le Nozze degli dei* (1637). Etching by Stefano della Bella.

TERZA SCENA GIARDINO DI VENERE

122. The garden of Venus, designed by Alfonso Parigi for *Le Nozze degli dei* (1637). Etching by Stefano della Bella.

QARTA SCENA DI MARE.

123. Seascape by Alfonso Parigi for *Le Nozze degli dei* (1637). Etching by Stefano della Bella.

SCENA GROTTA DI VULCANO

124. Vulcan's cave, designed by Alfonso Parigi for *Le Nozze degli dei* (1637). Etching by Stefano della Bella.

SCENA QVINTA D' INFERNO.

Alfo. Parigi Inu. Stefa Della
Bella Delit. e F

125. The realm of Pluto with infernal ballet. Décor by Alfonso Parigi for *Le Nozze degli dei* (1637). Etching by Stefano della Bella.

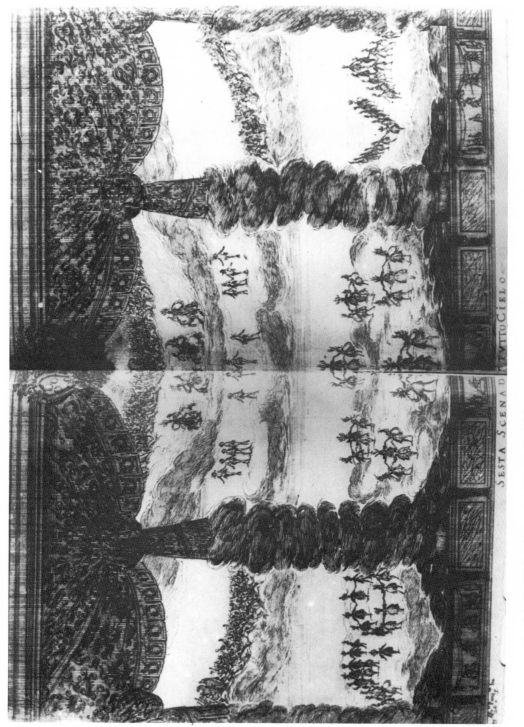

SESTA SCENA DI TVTTO CIELO

126. Celestial Ballet. Décor by Alfonso Parigi for the final scene of *Le Nozze degli dei* (1637). Etching by Stefano della Bella.

127. Horse ballet in the Boboli Garden, Florence, 1637. Choreography by Agniolo Ricci. Technical production by Felice Gamberai. Etching by Stefano della Bella.

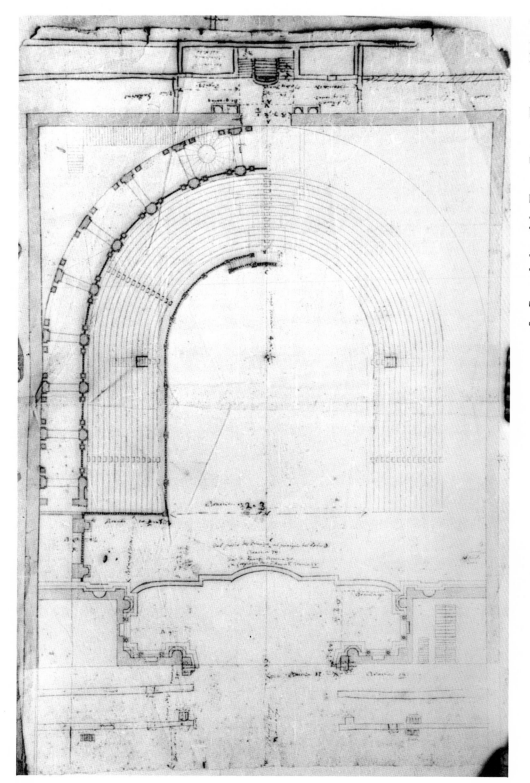

128. Ground plan of the Teatro Farnese (Teatro nel Salone).

129. Title page of the libretto for the tournament-spectacle *Mercurio e Marte* (Parma, 1628).

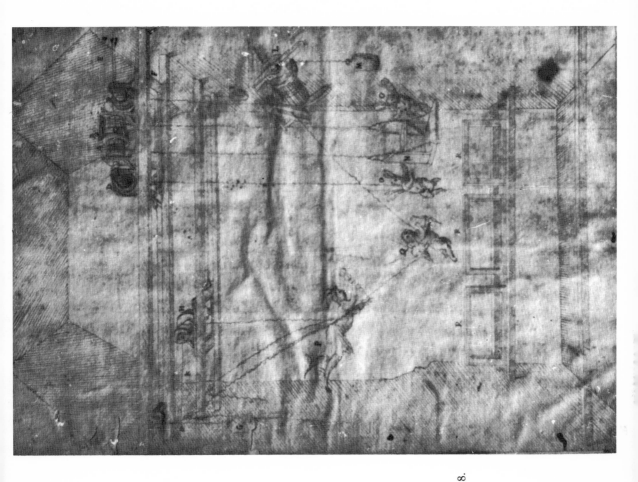

130. Flying apparatus for Mercury. Teatro Farnese 1628.

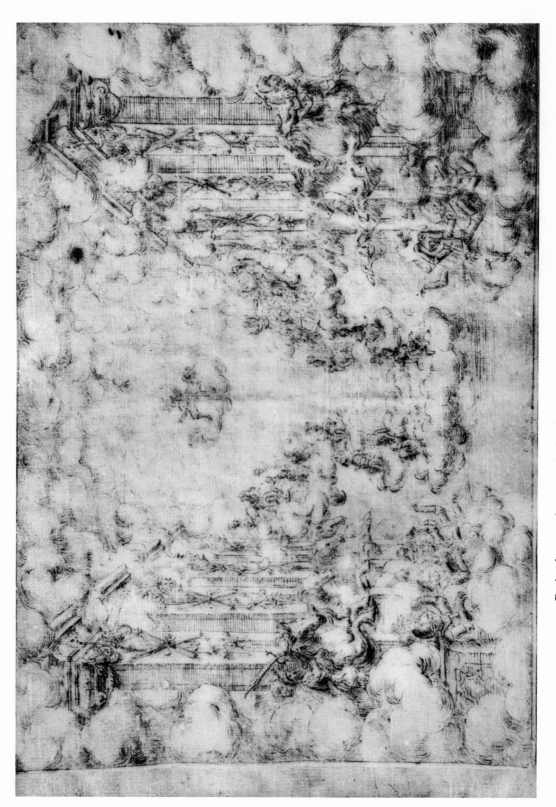

131. Design by an unknown artist for the appearance of Mars, perhaps for *Mercurio e Marte*, Teatro Farnese, 1628.

132. Sketch by an unknown artist for a celestial assembly, perhaps for the final scene of *Mercurio e Marte* (1628), when Discord was thrown into the Tartarus.

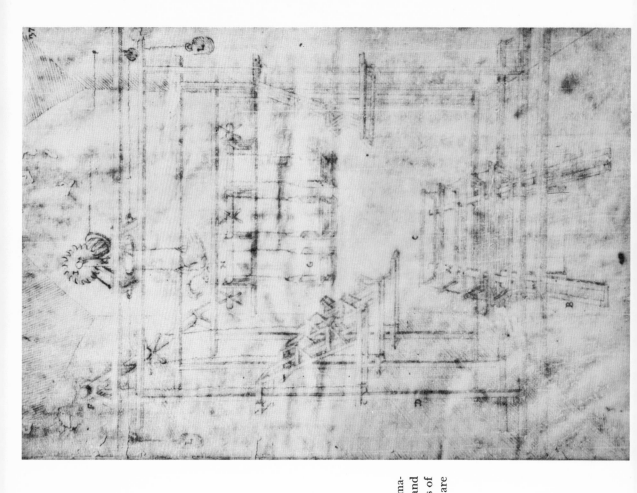

133. Back stage at the Teatro Farnese. View of stage machinery located in the gridiron, with suspended seats and flanking platforms that can be raised or lowered by means of a windlass. The windlass, pulleys, and counterweights are clearly in evidence.

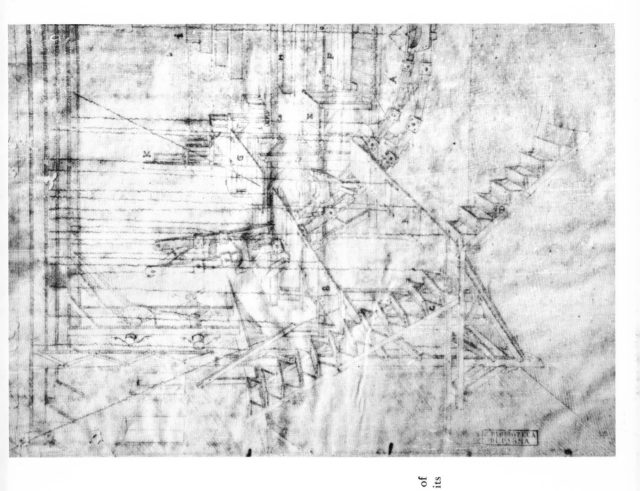

134. Set of stairways and folding platforms on the stage of the Teatro Farnese. The large arc with seats attached to its sides may have been capable of a lateral movement.

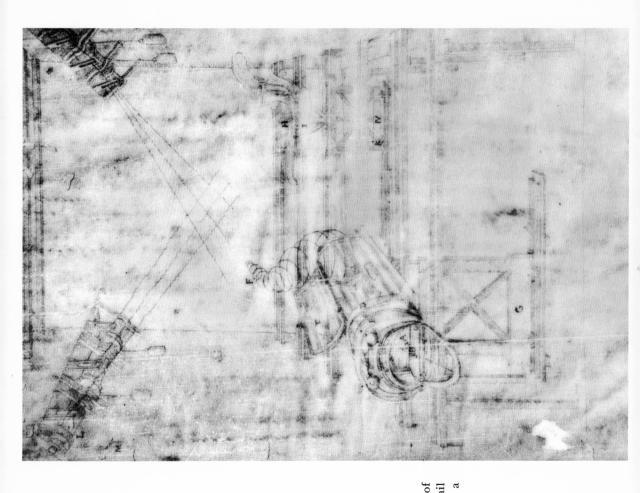

135. Frame for a sea monster with hinged door for entry of operator in the Teatro Farnese. The spring coil assured tail action. At the right upstage a shellshaped chariot for a marine divinity.

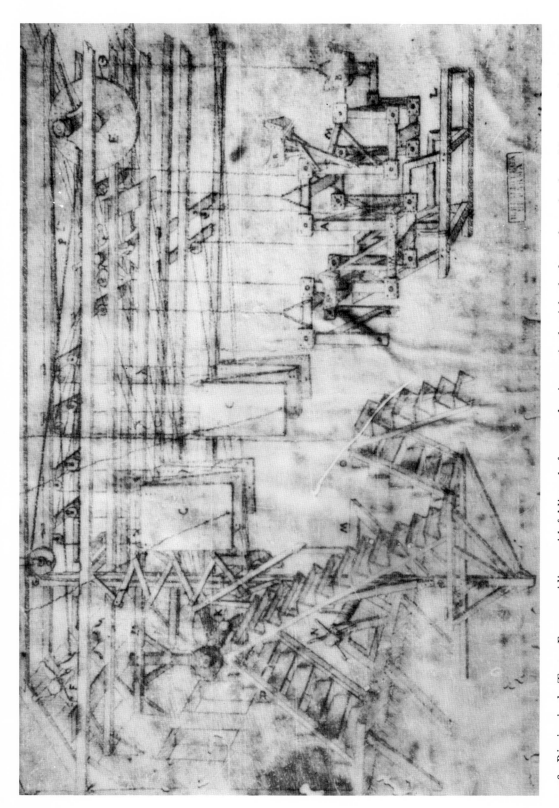

136. Rigging in the Teatro Farnese gridiron, with folding platforms and staircase. At the right the frame for a cloud machine suspended on ropes from pulleys attached to cross beams.